ENI

Be prepared to learn about w ....u in *The Kingdom Unleashed*. Be prep. ....ich the breadth and depth of the vision of Jesus for the kingdom of God. Be prepared to be changed and to be a change agent in your church and community. Be prepared to take part in *The Kingdom Unleashed*. Sunshine and Trousdale's study examines Bible, theology, church history and the lives of ordinary people in all parts of the globe who are living out the kingdom vision. If anything, *The Kingdom Unleashed* will take you out of your world into the wider world of God's work.

—**Scot McKnight,** Julius R. Mantey Professor of New Testament, Northern Seminary; author of many books, including *The King Jesus Gospel*

I could not put *The Kingdom Unleashed* down. This book will open a floodgate that will not be shut—of waves after waves of obedient disciples following Jesus in the Global North. This breakthrough book articulates kingdom movements from countless interviews of ordinary people igniting miraculous movements, and from an unprecedented depth and breadth of research and a historical and theological perspective. *The Kingdom Unleashed* challenges us to re-embrace our calling to follow Jesus at all costs!

—**Mary Ho,** International Executive Leader, All Nations Family

The incredible growth of Christianity in the global south forces us in the global north to re-evaluate ourselves, our message, and our methods. Most importantly, it forces us to examine our hearts and ask, "What is God doing without us?" After analyzing the faltering trajectory of the Western Church, the authors of *The Kingdom Unleashed* give us a template of "Kingdom Movements" taking root so strongly in the south that "Christianity is spreading faster now than at any time in history." From the foundation of the teachings and ministry of Jesus, the book overflows with stories and interviews illustrating the power of God's Word implemented by ordinary people. The book concludes with references to a wealth of resources and practical guidelines to begin replicating the Kingdom values of Jesus in our own communities. This may become *the* book igniting the next phase of revival in the Western Church.

—**Dr. William E Brown,** Senior Fellow for Worldview and Culture, the Colson Center for Christian Worldview

Over the last twenty years, a great role reversal has begun. Rather than Western Christianity educating the non-West, disciples in Acts-like movements have been teaching the established Christian world what the Kingdom of God *really* looks like. Frustration and dissatisfaction over broken ministry models and human-centered agendas have opened our ears to messages that hearken back to something that feels much more like the New Testament. To effect real change, however, *The Kingdom Unleashed* calls us to confront the roots of our broken models. Then the authors take a fresh look at Scriptural solutions, illustrated by testimonies of transformed lives and communities on every continent, to shine a light on a path forward. It's a path any leader, church, or follower of Jesus can take back to God's intended design--at the simple cost of our lives and personal agendas (John 12:24).

—**Steve Smith,** Co-Facilitator, the 2414 Coalition 2414 now.net, Global Movement Catalyst (*Beyond*), Vice President of Multiplication (*East-West*), Author

The Kingdom Unleashed offers a corrective to Western Christians, who have lost sight of the Kingdom of God, true experience of discipleship, hope of revival and awakening, and the power of the illimitable Spirit of God. This comprehensive report reminds us that the Kingdom of God is growing and expanding where men and women take Christ at His Word and devote themselves to simple, radical, daily obedience to Him. Read this book, and let it unsettle your settled soul, so that you hunger and strive to know the kind of faith multiplied millions of believers daily experience in lands and places where the shackles of materialism, narcissism, and status quo living have never taken hold. This book is not a call to revolution. It is an announcement that revolution is underway, as it has been for two millennia, and a call for you to take your rightful place in it.

—**T. M. Moore,** Principal, the Fellowship of Ailbe

A friend recently observed that when you focus on the Kingdom you will get the Church but when you focus on the Church you don't always get the Kingdom. Jerry and Glenn present a Kingdom-oriented model of ministry that has resulted in the expansion of the Church around the globe through ordinary people who have chosen to obey God. As Kingdom people we emulate Jesus, doing what we see the Father doing (John 5:19) and part of what the Father is doing today is the multiplication of disciple-making movements. In *The Kingdom Unleashed*, Jerry and Glenn show you how to join what God is doing today.

—**Mark Fields,** Director of Global and Intercultural Ministry, Vineyard Church USA

This book is a very important book, especially for disciple-making leaders. It describes the spiritual dynamics that must be established in a church or in a network of churches for God to unleash the power of his Holy Spirit for a disciple-making movement. I am asking all my friends who lead churches and all the national discipleship leaders I know to read and pray through this book.

—**Dr. Bobby Harrington,** Executive Director, Discipleship.org

Trousdale, now with co-conspirator Glenn Sunshine, is like the common cold—he just won't go away! Obviously this "Movement" thing has infected him and he is out to infect us. Stay away from this book if you want to continue your comfortable existence, especially if you pastor a western church. You are in for mindset-shifting that will challenge the foundations of your methodology and force you to rethink its connection to your theology. This book should come with a warning label!

—**Roy Moran,** Pastor, Shoal Creek Community Church, Author of *Spent Matches: Igniting a Signal Fire for the Spiritually Dissatisfied*

Books about movements have tended to be either scripture-based, or anecdotal. Finally, Jerry Trousdale and Glenn Sunshine have created an incredible storehouse of knowledge, coupled with actual case studies, that takes disciple-making movements off the page and into reality. In fact, I probably know half the implementers in these case studies personally. Finally we have an instruction manual that provides not only the guidelines, but also extensive history and illustrations for church-multiplication movements.

—**Doug Lucas,** President of Team Expansion, Founder and Editor of *Brigada*

Several times while reading *The Kingdom Unleashed* I found myself praying, "*Thank You, Father—someone has written this!*" Here are needed voices pointing us not only to the Kingdom, but the Gospel of the Kingdom. In my travels with Trousdale, "Hassan" and others mentioned in this book, I have seen the undeniable evidence of the Kingdom invading the darkness. Neither I nor any other person can fully know or describe exactly what God is doing in these regions, but my eyes have seen enough of this glory, from the western tip of Senegal to the eastern shores of Indonesia, to herald the news, "*the Kingdom is being unleashed at a rate hardly imaginable to most in the Global North.*"

—**Nathan J'Diim,** Pastor, Founder of TOAG Internships, SKI Foundation Director

THE KINGDOM UNLEASHED

THE KINGDOM UNLEASHED

THE KINGDOM UNLEASHED

How Jesus' 1st-Century Kingdom Values Are Transforming
Thousands of Cultures and Awakening His Church

JERRY TROUSDALE
GLENN SUNSHINE
WITH GREGORY C. BENDIT

© DMM Library, Murfreesboro, Tennessee.

Page composition by Crosslin Creative.net

ISBN: 978-1-7322399-0-6

TABLE OF CONTENTS

SECTION 1
GREAT NEWS AND BAD NEWS

SECTION 2
FIVE CATEGORIES OF SPIRITUAL MALPRACTICE

SECTION 3
WHAT IN JESUS' NAME IS A CHRISTIAN TO DO?

SECTION 4
KINGDOM VALUES AND THE LIFESTYLES THEY REQUIRE

SECTION 5
THINKING AND ACTING LIKE JESUS DID

FOREWORD
BY HARRY BROWN

Do you feel the ground shaking? Probably not, because the nature of earthquakes is that the farther away you are from the epicenter, the less you will feel the earth tremble. The spiritual plates are shifting but not likely where you live. Right now, spiritual earthquakes are happening in the places where missionaries have **gone to** for the last 200+ years (generally referred to as the Global South). But in the places the missionaries **came from** during that same two centuries (generally referred to as the Global North), hardly a tremor can be felt.

What is causing the spiritual ground to shake? The Kingdom of God is being unleashed! That statement contains two powerful concepts that require us to look below the surface: they are "unleashing" and "the Kingdom."

"Unleashing" describes the release of what is being restrained - in this case, what is being held back is the power of God, and the people of God. Ironically, the power of God is not being held back by the evil one. It lays dormant behind an unlocked door called 'obedience' waiting for the people of God to open the door and let it flow. And the people of God who are being unleashed are the ordinary and unlikely folks in faraway places who, for a very long time, have been told they were not qualified or ready, and so they sat.

The Kingdom is about restoring the rightful reign of the King. In simple summary, "The Fall" damaged man's relationship with God, with his fellow man and with his environment. Authority over all things on earth was transferred to the enemy by man's voluntary act of obedience to Satan and disobedience to God. The concept of the Kingdom is about reversing the curse by destroying the works of the devil and restoring what was broken.

From the very inception of His public ministry, Jesus began declaring the gospel of the Kingdom (Mt. 4:23). What made His message "good news" was the revelation that the damage affecting everyone and everything could be restored. Disobedience had caused man and his world to wobble as he moved away from God. Obedience is the antidote to bring things back into harmonious alignment. Here is the essence: obedience to the will of God ushers in the Kingdom of God.

The Great Commission has a crescendo. Weave the elements together from Matthew, Mark, Luke, and Acts and you will get a progression that says; Wherever you go—be my witnesses—call to repentance—baptize—make disciples and teach them to obey all that I have commanded. This staircase is a required journey for everyone who claims the name of Christ and the top stair is all about making obedient disciples.

And that leads us to the final dimension necessary to set the stage for the unleashing of the Kingdom; the idea of "movements." A movement is about something that maintains its character and spreads widely without depending on the original sources. Individuals in isolation who chose to obey bring change within their lives and that is good as far as it goes, but micro solutions don't solve macro problems and the world is a mess.

The mess will not be completely cleaned up until the Lord returns but things can change on a large scale. The Kingdom is the byproduct of the righteous rule of the King expressed deep and wide. This is what we witnessed in the First and Second Great Awakenings that swept over America and Britain.

Society begins to change specifically because many people from all walks of life align their actions with the will of God in all aspects of their life. When lots of people stop being part of the problem and become part of the solution, you have a revolution in the making!

The Global North has much to be proud of in what it has accomplished in the last two centuries of missionary work. But the cold, hard reality is that we have pretty much found the ceiling on what can be accomplished with the approaches we are using. By contrast, what God is doing through His people in the Global South is creating an upheaval that is tossing the status quo out the window. A timeless truth states, "The humble get better." It is time for all of us on this half of the globe to listen and learn from the folks on the other side.

The worldwide Protestant church recently celebrated the 500th anniversary of one of the true turning points in the history of Christianity: the Reformation. Looking from our vantage point in history now, it is easy to see that the Reformation was a 'game-changer'. But back when it was unfolding, I guarantee you that it was not a clear, smooth transition from one paradigm to another. It didn't happen all at once, it evolved in different ways in different places and often it was downright messy! Some embraced the change, some thought parts were okay, and some rejected it entirely.

I believe that another "Reformation" is underway as the Holy Spirit re-energizes the kind of viral movements that 'turned the world upside down' in the early days of the church. These movements will have lots of different dimensions and expressions but the common denominator in all true movements will be ordinary people multiplying obedient disciples in their natural networks. Saying the same thing a different way, the

Kingdom of God goes viral when the people of God choose to obey and challenge their friends and family to do the same.

As a life-long resident of California, I am quite familiar with the awesome power of the ground shaking. And when I say "awesome" I don't mean the cheap version of the word that some use to describe, a good meal, a nice concert or an exciting football game. No, I am talking about the kind of "awesome" power that is far beyond what man can do or imagine. It is in the realm of God alone.

This is the kind of power being unleashing through Disciple-Making Movements. The spiritual seismographs in the Global South are blinking red and the needles are dancing across the page as ordinary and unlikely people are unleashing the Kingdom of God in their families and communities. Not everyone in the Global North will see it, believe it, or learn from it. But for those who do, the Kingdom of God can be unleashed right here too.

Harry Brown
January 2018
San Jose, CA

FOREWORD
BY YOUNOUSSA DJAO

It is a privilege to write a preface for the book written by two men whom God has used as a blessing in my life. Jerry Trousdale and I know each other and have been working together since 2003. We have gone through some challenges together and have also seen God do amazing things, witnessing alongside other sisters and brothers the unleashing of God's Kingdom by the Lord Himself. My connection with Glenn Sunshine was first through his books. Glenn's sharp theological and historical thinking have been means that God has used to help me deepen my own reflections on cultural issues. They have authored together a key book for anyone who wants to understand the Kingdom movements that God is making happen in the Global South today.

The Kingdom of our God is expanding in unprecedented ways in the last 20 years in the Global South. That part of the world, that used to be the mission field, has become a mission force. In Africa, God is using ordinary people to make breakthroughs in historically very resistant people groups. These disciple makers are taking the Good News they received to places it needs to go. As an African, I am very grateful to be alive and experience this season of church history, and the history of missions.

In 1989, I started my involvement in missions. Very quickly, I realized that not only was it time for the Church in Africa to take its responsibility in missions, but it would have to do it differently. Alongside other mission-minded brothers and sisters,

I started mobilizing and training churches to reach out to unreached or least reached people groups. For years, I tried to find an effective way for the Church in Africa to do missions. The models I had been exposed to were very expensive, took a long time, and were not that relevant to the African context. The Church in Africa cannot do missions the same way the Church in the West does. The contexts are different, as well as the means.

Since 2005, I have been witnessing God powerfully move using ordinary people to expand His Kingdom among nations across Africa. Kingdom movements are bringing salvation and transformation to nations. God is unleashing His Kingdom through the implementation of simple principles by ordinary people.

A new generation of Christians from the Global South are doing missions and expanding the Kingdom everywhere. In Africa, God's Kingdom is sweeping through Islam, African traditional religions, and cults across the continent. The Church in the Global South is not only growing in number and maturity, but it is also taking its responsibility to expand the Kingdom in the rest of the world. The Kingdom of God is being unleashed in so many places in the Global South! But that is just part of the story.

What we see God doing in the Global South would not have come about without the huge investment from the Global North in our part of the world over many decades. You can see that when you travel in Africa. It is all happening in soil that was sown with the sweat, blood, and even the lives of thousands of Global North missionaries. These missionaries, and many more who are still alive, made great sacrifices to expand the Kingdom outside the Western world. The seed they sowed has produced a great harvest in the Global South church.

In many countries in Africa, there are Western missionaries' graves that can be seen. These testify to the price they paid so that the Church in Africa might be birthed. Many missionaries, women and men, have given the prime of their life for missions in Africa.

The Kingdom of God was unleashed in Africa through the sacrifices of these godly, courageous, and committed missionaries from the Church in the Global North. The unleashing of the Kingdom of God through the Church in the Global South today has its roots in the unleashing of the Kingdom of God through the Church in the Global North.

It took a few decades for the churches of the Global South to take on the missionary mantle ourselves. But when we did, it was largely unencumbered by the weight of the humanism and secularism that has seriously wounded the Global North church. We have many ways in which we can improve, but no church can long survive with a bifurcated Kingdom perspective. The Lordship of Jesus, and abundant dependence on prayer, have no substitutes.

We Africans, and I believe also Asians and Latin Americans, are grateful to the church in the Global North, and we are praying passionately for God to restore what has been lost so that the 21st century church can see the Global North church rise again.

God is compressing time in our ages. Spiritual breakthroughs in hard places that took decades to happen 40 years ago are happening in a few years. So, may the Global North Church rise quickly and take its place in the yoke we pull together. May God break the power of worldviews that have diminished the vision of the church in the Global North and sapped its strengths that God still intends to use.

May God protect the Global South church from losing focus.

I do not believe that the story of the church in America, Europe, and the Pacific Ocean will end with closed churches everywhere. I, alongside many Africans, am praying! And if you are jealous of what God is doing in the Global South, then that is a very good jealousy.

We need you, dear brothers and sisters. Your breakthrough will not likely come from schools, seminars, or conferences, but from millions of disciple-makers who rise to the challenge of a restored vision of the Kingdom of God coming on earth as it is in heaven. Education is good, but, the Great Commission will be accomplished only when ordinary disciples take the Good News to their natural social networks and become disciples who make disciples.

This book explains the Kingdom principles and values behind the extraordinary Kingdom expansion that we see today in the Global South. These Kingdom movements that are sweeping across Africa, Asia, and Latin America are acts of God. He is blessing the obedience, commitment to prayer and the implementation of these principles and values. This will happen anywhere the Church decides to do the same.

Younoussa Djao
January 2018
Abidjan, Côte d'Ivoire

ACKNOWLEDGMENTS

Jerry and his wife Gayle learned the lessons of the Kingdom together over almost 50 years, and she was the first to sense God's calling back to the nations, a decision that led directly to the Trousdale family's journey into Kingdom movements.

Writing this book has been a very long process, with many ups and downs along the way. Glenn's wife Lynn supported him throughout the project with unfailing good humor, patience, and encouragement.

Frank Couch, a former Senior VP at Thomas Nelson, resonated with the Kingdom Unleashed theme and in 2014 strongly encouraged us to write this book, giving wise counsel in the process.

Harry Brown, the president of New Generations (formerly Cityteam International), encouraged Jerry to take some time to finish his part of this manuscript, and invested many hours of his time reading and commenting on the emerging text.

David Watson, a good friend and one of the first movement pioneers in the modern era, coached many of the catalysts you will meet in this book, and he provided valuable manuscript advice.

Carolyn Cantwell, who is a disciple maker all the time, and also a New Generations colleague, collected and processed hundreds of DMM narratives and interviews over the last seven years that form part of the core of this book.

John King, a former pastor and now Final Command Ministries' Global DMM Trainer, has helped shape the biblical presentation of the Kingdom of God in this book. And John has given many hours over three years to help us accurately describe Jesus' Kingdom values without which there are no movements.

Younoussa Djao and Shodankeh Johnson have been very close colleagues of Jerry on this 15-year journey, and they sacrificed many hours to help us accurately describe what God is doing in in the world, even as they pray for the church in Europe and North American to rise. Shodankeh was also one of Glenn's inspirations for becoming involved in this project.

Hugh and Nancy Maclellan provided valuable help that facilitated the initial research for this book with many interviews with key pioneers of Kingdom Movements.

We also want to recognize the help of more than 40 movement catalysts from both the Global North and South who have together launched hundreds of Kingdom movements. Their candor and passion have insured that this book is not simply theoretical. These pioneers learned from the Bible and in partnership with Lord what we are sharing explicitly.

We also want to thank Alee Anderson, project manager and editor extraordinaire, for her patience through multiple delays and her hard work to make this book the best it could possibly be. The book would not have been what it is without her help.

Our thanks and love to you all.

TERMS

This book was written by experts in the field and uses insider language. It is important that you familiarize yourself with these terms to help you fully grasp the book's meaning within the context of these incredible movements, bringing hundreds and thousands of unreached people groups to Christ.

Contextualization: presenting the Gospel in culturally relevant terms.

Catalyst: in the context of Movements, a person who trains, coaches, and mentors others to discover Christ in Scripture, learn obedience, and to lead and start Discovery Groups and plant churches, without taking part directly.

Discovery Bible Study (DBS): an inductive approach to discovering God in Scripture and learning to obey Him. It has four basic steps: read/hear the text; restate it accurately from collective memory; decide what must be done in light of the text, in the form of "I will . . ." statements; and consider who needs to hear the lessons from the text and determine when to share it with them.

Discovery Group: a group of unbelievers who meet together to discover God via a Discovery Bible Study using a set of Scriptures appropriate for the group. The leader is coached by a Movement Catalyst with an expectation that the group will become a church over time.

Disciple Making Movement (DMM): a process of disciples making disciples, and churches planting at least 100 churches, with four or more generations of replication

Evangelical: though this word has several definitions, here we will use it to designate groups that are theologically conservative, hold a high view of Scripture, and believe that people need to have a conversion experience in order to become true (as opposed to merely cultural) Christians. Different organizations studying Christianity use different definitions of the term, but these are generally accepted as part of the definition. Especially in the Global South, Pentecostals and Charismatics are a particularly important segment of evangelicalism.

Global North: what used to be called "the developed world," that is, Europe, North America, and Oceania, not including Mexico.

Global South: the rest of the world—Asia, Africa, and Latin America.

Person of Peace: a person in whom God has put a capacity and willingness to introduce the Gospel of the Kingdom into their family or social network.

Prayer Walking: an intentional process of walking or driving through a community, praying for neighborhoods, leaders, and people of peace. The intent is to invite God to prepare the hearts of leaders and ordinary people to welcome the Gospel of the Kingdom.

Unreached People Group: a term used by Evangelicals regarding a social segment of any society in which fewer than two percent of the people are Christ Followers.

Unengaged People Group: a social segment of any society in which the Gospel has either never been introduced or it simply has not thrived. There are no known Christ Followers in this place capable of making disciples.

NOTE TO THE READER

Several of the Kingdom Movement catalysts interviewed for this book requested that their names and locations be anonymized due to security concerns for themselves or for colleagues serving in sensitive areas. The stories of some ministries are also told in this book, and a few of them have also chosen to be anonymized. We will provide links to these catalysts and ministries where security allows on the book's website (www.kingdom unleashed.org) that may add value to your journey into Disciple Making Movements.

GREAT NEWS
AND BAD NEWS

FIFTY THRILLING AND DISTURBING YEARS

He told them another parable: "The kingdom of heaven is like a mustard seed, which a man took and planted in his field. Though it is the smallest of all seeds, yet when it grows, it is the largest of garden plants and becomes a tree, so that the birds come and perch in its branches." (Matt. 13:31–32)

KINGDOM MOVEMENTS:
1st CENTURY ANSWERS TO 21st CENTURY BARRIERS

Over the last 50 years, and especially since the turn of the 21st century, the Spirit of God has been birthing a new concept in the earth. Instead of addition, the Spirit of God is calling forth multiplication. The outcomes of these phenomena are called by names including Disciple Making Movements, Church Planting Movements, T4T, or Four Fields.

Such movements have been seen before in Christian history, but never with such force, across scores of countries, in such difficult places, and in such large numbers. These movements have already begun to alter the spiritual landscape of historic Hindu, Islamic, Buddhist, and Animistic regions of the world. But for many Christians, these movements are still a mystery.

This book is about these movements, which by any name, come under the category of Kingdom Movements. It was Jesus' prayer and His mandate . . . His Kingdom coming on earth as in heaven. We will focus specifically on Jesus' Kingdom values and lifestyles that empower these desperately needed movements. Jesus gave his first century disciples specific instructions for advancing the Kingdom, and those same first century directives are animating the new 21st century movements.

Those of us living in the Global North are observing an ever-increasing cascade of spiritual discouragement and tragedy in our world, while our brothers and sisters in the Global South are experiencing today what Jesus meant when he said that kings and prophets longed to experience the Kingdom coming in such a way.

In this context, let's explore Jesus' 1st century answers to 21st century challenges.

HOW THE KINGDOM COMES IN AFRICA

Hassan is the president of Mission for All[1] in an African nation. He was exposed to the biblical principles of Disciple Making Movements (DMM) while visiting the United States in 2001, and was challenged by the concept of training and equipping indigenous leaders to plant reproducing churches in their own communities. He slowly began to introduce some of the DMM ideas to his organization; then, in 2005, Mission for All invited David Watson to his country to train approximately 50

---

[1] Hassan and Mission for All are pseudonyms.

Christian leaders from six African countries—and the DMM initiative was launched.

From the very first day, this initiative was bathed with intercessory prayer. The ministry had always made prayer a high priority, but this was the point at which intercessors were recruited, trained, and depended upon for every new initiative—recruited and trained by the scores, then by the hundreds, and now by the thousands, and depended upon to uphold all initiatives with constant, behind-the-scenes prayer.

In the last 13 years, the number of churches in one African country has increased from 50 churches to many thousands, with at least one disciple-making church in every corner of the country with an average of 54 members per church. The goal is to establish a church in every village or urban neighborhood. This movement has also planted more than 2,200 new churches among unreached people groups in eight African countries, and more than 400,000 people have become Christ Followers—the great majority from formerly unreached people groups.

Transformation of Muslim Communities

Mission for All reached out to one particularly resistant Muslim community that had martyred six Christian evangelists a few years ago. They found that the biggest need in the area was for a school, so Hassan approached the Muslim leaders and offered to send a qualified teacher (who was also a trained church planter) if the community provided the necessary resources. The good will generated by this act of service gave the church planter the opportunity to gradually begin sharing stories about God, leading to the introduction of Jesus as the Savior. In two years, seven churches were planted.

The work has required heavy sacrifices.

Mission for All's selfless ministry had a profound impact on the Muslim communities, which eventually became receptive to Discovery Bible Groups. As they began to obey what they found in the Bible, entire communities were transformed. For instance, it became far less common for men to abuse their wives or children, ancient clan hostilities ended with reconciliation and cooperation, and families that had never helped others became generous with their resources and time.

The change was most obvious to their neighbors. The risk of persecution is high, yet in a few years, thirty-five separate Muslim communities have initiated contact with Mission for All, asking them to send the "storytellers" who brought the message that produced transformation among their neighboring towns and villages.

Facing Opposition

Jesus told His followers that they would face opposition in building His Kingdom, and Hassan and his brothers and sisters in Mission for All were not exempt. God was doing amazing things within those communities, and many thousands of Muslims were coming to Christ—so the day came when the Muslim clerics banded together and took action against Mission for All, demanding that the ministry shut its doors. The conflict eventually reached the office of the Muslim Governor of the state—including the demand that Hassan be deported. The Governor called a meeting to attempt to bring a peaceful resolution to the situation.

This gave Hassan the opportunity to talk openly with his country's leaders, telling them about the grace and saving work of God in the nation. He outlined some of the many ways that Mission for All and other Christians had ministered to the many communities—the mobile medical clinics, the "barefoot dentists," the safe water programs, seed banks, sports ministries, and simple schools, all for the purpose of serving Muslims. The sheiks and imams who were in attendance at that meeting, somewhat begrudgingly at first, all gradually acknowledged that Hassan was speaking the truth. After a while, Hassan stopped speaking, and there was a brief silence.

The Governor broke the silence. "It would appear," he said, "if Muslims were doing as many good things for our own people as these Christians are doing, we would not have the problem of Muslims becoming Christians. My recommendation is that we Muslims learn how to be better servants from these Christians!" Many of the Muslim clerics who had entered that meeting burning to have Hassan deported walked away with his business card or plans for further conversation with him.

God's power among the twelve movements currently happening in this African nation can be clearly seen in the fact that this small country is now sending DMM missionaries to many other countries with a high success rate. The DMM model is working almost everywhere in the country, and continent, and dramatic transformation is the outcome.

This nation is just one of many countries now bearing witness to the truth of Jesus' imagery: The Kingdom of God is like seed that grows into a great tree, a pearl of great price, and a banquet for ordinary heroes and heroines (Matt. 13:44–46, Luke 14:16–24).

THE KINGDOM UNLEASHED

Christianity is spreading faster now than it has at any time in human history.

If that statement surprises you, it means that you probably live in the Global North where Christianity is—at best—holding its own. But Christianity is exploding in the Global South. Consider:

- There were nine million Christians in Africa in 1900; by 2000, there were 335 million (37 times as many) with most of the growth occurring since the 1960s.[2]

- In Latin America in 1900, there were 50,000 Protestants; today, there are more than 64 million (1,280 times as many), again with most of the growth occurring since the 1960s. A significant majority of these Protestants identify themselves as Charismatic or Pentecostal Evangelicals.[3]

- The number of Christians in Asia grew from 101 million to 351 million between 1970 and 2010.[4]

- In China, it has been estimated that 10,000 people *per day* become Christ Followers, and even by conservative estimates, Christianity has grown 4,300 percent in 50 years. By 2030, China will have more Christians living in it than any other nation on earth.[5]

- There are 3.7 times as many Protestants in Africa as in North America—and the gap grows dramatically every year. This has happened just in recent decades

2 http://www.christianity.com/church/church-history/timeline/2001-now/the-explosion-of-christianity-in-africa-11630859.html

3 https://www.ncronline.org/blogs/all-things-catholic/dramatic-growth-evangelicals-latin-america

4 http://www.virtueonline.org/christianitys-surge-indonesia

5 https://www.ncronline.org/blogs/all-things-catholic/uphill-journey-catholicism-china;http://www.telegraph.co.uk/news/worldnews/asia/china/10776023/China-on-course-to-become-worlds-most-Christian-nation-within-15-years.html

◉ In 1980, sixty-five percent of the world's missionaries were sent out from the Global North; by 2020, that situation will be reversed, as sixty-three percent will be coming from the Global South.[6]

Beyond just the numerical growth, we are now seeing widespread Kingdom Movements led by indigenous Christians that are multiplying rapidly in regions throughout the Global South.

◉ In the Islamic world, there were no movements[7] among Muslims[8] until the nineteenth century. Today, every region of the Muslim world is experiencing replicating movements, even in some of the most extreme areas. The number of movements is summarized here:[9]

YEARS	NUMBER OF MOVEMENTS AMONG MUSLIMS
1800s	2
1960s	1 (influenced more by politics than faith)
1980–2000	11
2000–2017	> 100 new movements

---

6 https://s3-us-west-2.amazonaws.com/missio-graphics/Volume+5/missiographic_percent_christian.pdf

7 As mentioned, there are many names for the Kingdom movements in the world today, including Church Planting Movements, T4T, Four Fields, and others. In this book, we will use names that describe movements in terms of the spiritual process (Disciple Making Movements) or the spiritual outcome (Kingdom Movements).

8 Defined by the researchers as 100 new churches or 1,000 baptisms in a twenty-year period.

9 Confirmed field data from New Generations, Movement Dashboard, and partner ministries.

🌐 In terms of the distribution of Kingdom Movements (Church Planting Movements, Disciple Making Movements, T4T Movements, and others), today there are an astonishing 651 total movements being tracked in scores of countries, but only 8 are in North America, Western Europe, or Oceania.

The Kingdom of God has been unleashed and is advancing forcefully throughout the Global South. How did this happen?

> *The Kingdom of God has been unleashed and is advancing forcefully throughout the Global South.*

Missions to the Global South

In the foreword to this book, Younoussa Djao writes that the Global North played an indispensable role in the explosion of growth in Africa, Asia, and Latin America, all of which is built on work done in the middle of the twentieth century or earlier by missionaries from the Global North. Missionary activity increased significantly following World War Two, especially after the deaths of Jim Elliot, Ed McCully, Roger Youderian, Pete Fleming, and Nate Saint in 1956. These missionaries helped establish Christian communities in many areas where we are seeing rapid growth today.

Along with the work of missionaries, missiologists were developing new principles to aid in cross-cultural evangelism. Donald McGavran contributed two significant ideas. First, he argued that the goal of missions was not to transform society in a Western image, but to bring the people to Christ in the context of their own culture. And this meant that the closer you were to the culture, the more likely you were to be successful in making disciples and planting churches.

Second, he recognized the importance of "bridges of God," people in the target ethnic group or a closely related group who brought access to the community and could present the Gospel in a culturally relevant way. This is an important concept that we will address in depth in a later chapter, but we will be referring throughout the book to "persons of peace,"[10] those people whom God has prepared in advance to open a door into a community.

Ralph Winter built on McGavran's work in an electrifying speech to the Lausanne Congress for World Evangelization (1974). He shifted the focus of missions from reaching nations (understood as political entities) to reaching people groups; unreached people groups could be identified and strategies developed for reaching them. Together with other pioneers, McGavran and Winter's work changed the face of world missions and helped prepare Christians for what God was about to do.

The missionary effort was remarkably successful. The church in the Global South grew so rapidly that, by the 1980s, they were sending missionaries to other countries. These missionaries went primarily to other regions of the Global South, although some went to the Global North, mostly serving the expatriate communities from their own countries.

Movements Begin to Spread throughout the Global South

Then, about 25 years ago, something historic began happening in Asia.

---

[10] Luke 10:6

In some places where few churches had ever been planted, some intrepid Southern Baptist missionaries began to pioneer a radical new strategy based on Jesus' own ministry model. Instead of using traditional missionary practices, they used Jesus' disciple-making instructions in Luke 10 and Matthew 10. They took Jesus' teachings literally when He said that disciple-makers would endure hardships and make big sacrifices. They decided to trust that Jesus' model of ministry was just as relevant today as it was for the Twelve and the seventy-two.

Disciple-makers would endure hardships and make big sacrifices.

Eventually, they and those whom they trained saw hard sacrifices yield surprising successes inside totalitarian regimes, in the strongholds of Hinduism, among the same people groups that brought Islam to Africa, and in some of the most brazen shrines to Satan in the world. Places and peoples that had never yielded to Jesus' love or His lordship were being transformed into His image—in staggering numbers.

As noted before, researchers are counting more than 650 Kingdom movements like these in scores of countries. For example, New Generations (formerly CityTeam International) is in partnership with more than 700 ministries and churches engaging 480 people groups or urban communities in Africa and Asia. Most of those were previously unreached or unengaged, and 110 are now considered movements (defined as at least 100 churches with four or more generations).

Other organizations are also having remarkable results. And as more and more ministries are sharing their research with one another, it is becoming apparent that what God is doing is dramatic, widespread, and accelerating.

The Other Side of the Story

Yet despite this unprecedented growth, two things stand out: first, the growth is almost entirely in the Global South (primarily Africa and Asia); second, growth there is largely offset by the decline of Christianity in the Global North. In Europe, church attendance has declined,[11] and in the United States, it is, in part, being maintained because of legal and illegal immigration from the Global South, where Christianity is thriving. It is clear, as Philip Jenkins says, that the center of gravity of global Christianity has shifted definitively to the Global South.[12]

This shift raises lots of questions. What happened? Not long ago, the church of the Global North was the center of world Christianity and provided its leadership. How did it decline so rapidly? And more importantly, why did the church in the Global South take off, and what does the church in the Global North need to learn from it?

The rest of this book explores these questions. Chapters Two through six examine some of the reasons for the weakness of the church in the Global North. We look at historical dynamics, worldview issues, and institutional challenges, which together have combined to lead the church away from the biblical values at the heart of movements. Chapter seven outlines Jesus' approach to disciple making, and chapters eight through

---

[11] http://www.economist.com/news/international/21684679-march-christianity-future-worlds-most-popular-religion-african

[12] *The Next Christendom* (New York: Oxford University Press, 2011), 1.

eighteen explore ways in which that approach has been adopted in the Global South and how the same strategies can be appropriated in the Global North.

Throughout the book, we will examine the biblical assumptions that underlie the movements in the Global South, how those are translated into action, and the outcomes we see from following these strategies.

A word of caution: much of what you read here may seem too critical of the church in the Global North, and you may find the principles we outline self-evident.

Concerning the first of these, if we are going to address the problems of the church in the Global North, we need to be clear about what those problems actually are. The authors are firmly committed to the church, and want to see the Gospel flourish in the Global North as it is in the Global South.

Concerning the second, we would ask you to consider not just your theory but your practice: what you do reflects your beliefs and your priorities, so if this does seem self-evident to you, is it evident in your practice or just your beliefs? Keep in mind, the approach we outline here is like a recipe: it doesn't work without all the ingredients in place.

Let's begin by diagnosing some of the ailments of the Global North church and start looking at the solutions through the lens of Disciple Making Movements.

FIVE CATEGORIES OF SPIRITUAL MALPRACTICE

REDUCING JESUS' KINGDOM TO A METAPHOR

[The New Testament] celebrates the sovereignty of Jesus from first page to last. But of course neither Matthew nor Paul nor Revelation supposed for a minute that this meant that utopia had already arrived, that the vision of Isaiah 11 was already fully in place. Christians were being persecuted, facing violent opposition, celebrating the lordship of Jesus in a world where Caesar and his type of power still seemed to be solid and unshaken.

—N. T. Wright, *How God Became King*

A DMM PASTOR REFLECTS ON THE KINGDOM OF GOD

Francis is from a country in West Africa, where he is both a church planter and a regional director serving hundreds of disciple makers. Five years ago, he launched a Discovery Bible Study in his backyard in the growing edge of a large city. That one Discovery Bible Study became many Bible studies, which in turn became a thriving church of 300 people with a vision of being a center to equip and serve hundreds of smaller churches. They are almost finished building a space that will accommodate 1,000 people.

We asked him this question: in your church, what signs tell you that the Kingdom of God is being established? What things make you say: "That's the Kingdom of God; we are moving in the right direction"? He replied,

> For me, the Kingdom of God has to be, first and foremost: people, families, communities, receiving Jesus as Lord because He is the King of the Kingdom. We can't talk about a Kingdom when the King is not acknowledged, so when I see families and communities and people acknowledging Jesus as King and Lord and Master over their lives, for me it is a pointer to show that the Kingdom of God has come, because He is the King. At the moment when you accept Him as Lord, you are part of His Kingdom, and you can't be part of the Kingdom of God when you do not acknowledge Him as King.
>
> Beyond that, I believe that obedience is also a sign; it should be a pointer that indeed, the Kingdom of God is reigning in this person's life, in this family, the Kingdom of God is reigning in this community. It's when people submit to His lordship and obey His commands. Jesus says to His disciples, "How will you say that I am Lord and Master over you, when you do not obey the things that I tell you to do?"
>
> So obedience to what He says, obedience to Scripture, is indeed a pointer that I use to know that the Kingdom of God is reigning, and these are things that I look for. It is not about excitement, it's about seeing disciples who are ready, who are willing to obey the Holy Scriptures. It's a key pointer.

When Francis was asked about the practical effects of his ministry, he further elaborated on the nature of the Kingdom,

> We are beginning to learn that the Lord's desire is to restore us back to where we were before we fell, in the case of Adam

and Eve. We are looking at DMM at this point, thinking that it has to be holistic, which means that we want to see lives transformed fully. We want to see Scripture transformation in the lives of people.

We also want to see physical transformations happening in the lives of people. We also want to see social transformations; we also want to see mental transformations—so that it is a holistic one.

So we are not only concentrating on getting people saved, having them to be praying, having them come to disciple and Bible studies, all of which is good; but we are also focusing on other aspects of the human being, which has to deal with the social well-being, the spiritual and physical and mental well-being.

That's why we try to establish schools, we also have clinics, because we are human beings, so we also have to make sure that we help communities with wells and, in doing that, we are bringing transformation into the lives of the people, working alongside them. So we have some projects that have to do with agriculture, helping communities with seed and all of that, just to empower them. As the Lord is interested in the whole man, so we tend to get our communities where we are working, where we are entering, to be going in that direction. We've seen a lot of communities, their kids have to be going several miles to school, so we've worked with those communities, and today they have schools. We have instances where people have to walk to the stream to get water to drink, and sometimes the kids are going to the stream, and in the process, they drown because there are no people around there! So we work with those communities and bring transformation to them.

For this pastor and church planter, the Kingdom of God is concrete and tangible, and expressed in transformed lives, families, and communities through obedience to Christ the King. It is not a lofty concept, a distant ideal, or a metaphor; it is a lived reality among real people, and it brings wholeness and healing to all dimensions of life. But how does this align with what the Bible says the Kingdom is?

THE GOSPEL OF THE KINGDOM

The coming of the Kingdom of God was at the heart of Jesus' message, and that "Kingdom" theme has been at the root of the Gospel throughout most of church history. Yet the idea of the Kingdom is strangely absent from much of evangelical thinking today.

> *The coming of the Kingdom of God was at the heart of Jesus' message.*

Let's start with a definition of the word *kingdom*. In Greek, the word is *basileia*, and it does not refer to a king's geographical territory but to the recognition of his royal authority. In other words, you have a *kingdom* any place where the king's *authority* is recognized and obeyed. So a Roman legionary who left Roman territory on imperial business carried the kingdom with him, since he acknowledged Caesar's authority over him and was obeying him. When we talk about the Kingdom of God, then, we are referring to people who acknowledge the Lordship of Christ and who are striving to obey Him at all times in all places. Jesus came to proclaim that, in Himself, the rule of God was breaking into the world that is in rebellion against Him.

The Kingdom of God in the Old Testament

The Kingdom concept is implicit throughout the Scriptures and is central to what it means to be human. In Genesis 1:26–27, we are told that human beings were created in the image of God. In the ancient Near East, a person who was called "the image of a god" was believed to be the official representative and regent of that god, and thus to have the right to rule under that god's authority. So when God makes man in His image, He immediately gives him dominion over the earth. We are to rule here, but we are to do so as God's stewards, under His authority.

In Genesis 3, Adam chooses to misuse his authority in this world by acting out of his own interests rather than God's. The effect of this is that all humanity became subject to sin and death, and human cultures fell under the influence of Satan.

When Satan tempted Jesus, he "showed him all the kingdoms of the world in a moment of time, and said to him, 'To you I will give all this authority and their glory, *for it has been delivered to me, and I give it to whom I will.* If you, then, will worship me, it will all be yours'" (Luke 4:5–7, emphasis added). Jesus did not dispute Satan's authority over the kingdoms of the world, at least in this age. We know from Scripture that the earth is the Lord's, but this passage suggests that human kingdoms have been delivered to Satan.

Despite this, however, human beings retain the image of God and, by God's grace, even the most depraved cultures retain some knowledge of God and His ways (Acts 14:17; Rom. 1:18–2:16). God promised that redemption from sin and death would come through the seed of the woman, who would crush the serpent's head and be wounded in the process (Gen. 3:15).

God's call to Abraham established his descendants as a holy nation through whom the whole world would be blessed, and the seed of the woman became more clearly identified as the seed of Abraham. From there, it was narrowed further to the seed of Isaac, Jacob, and Judah.

The Messianic line was narrowed further with the coming of David. David was far from perfect, but he was a man after God's own heart, humble and with a tender conscience. God promised that his line would rule Israel forever, and more, that the Messiah would sit on David's throne and would rule over all earthly kingdoms, bringing blessings to those who submit to Him and judgment on those who persist in rebellion against Him. His kingdom would extend over the whole world and bring righteousness and peace in its wake.

The Kingdom of God in the New Testament

The core message of John the Baptist was, "Repent, for the Kingdom of Heaven[1] is at hand," which was the very same message that Jesus preached when John was put into prison. John described what repentance and Kingdom living looked like: "Whoever has two tunics is to share with him who has none, and whoever has food is to do likewise" (Luke 3:11). In other words, repentance and living in light of the Kingdom means identifying the needs of those around us and doing what we can to meet those needs, rather than insisting on our own rights, privileges, and possessions.

---

[1] Matthew uses the phrase "Kingdom of Heaven," where other New Testament writers use the phrase "Kingdom of God" to avoid unnecessarily offending the Jews by using the term "God" more than was absolutely necessary. A comparison of the Gospels shows that the two phrases are interchangeable, contrary to some theologians who argue that they refer to different things.

Jesus' teaching centered on the Kingdom. The Sermon on the Mount is a description of life in the Kingdom, and a significant percentage of His parables teach about the Kingdom. He explained that His Kingdom is not of this world; in other words, it is not like earthly kingdoms that are under the dominion of Satan. Rather, the Kingdom is built on repenting of our sin and rebellion against God and restoring our relationships with God and with our neighbor, resuming our role as regents acting under God, with authority to establish and advance God's reign on earth as it is in heaven.

When the Kingdom (*basileia*) is properly understood as acknowledging and obeying the authority of God, it is also revealed to be the center of the Great Commission: "All authority in heaven and on earth has been given to me. Therefore, go[2] and make disciples of all nations, baptizing them in the name of the Father and of the Son and of the Holy Spirit, teaching them to observe all I have commanded you" (Matt. 28:18–20). The Greek word for "disciple," *mathetes*, refers to a student or an apprentice learning something under the direction of a master. In this case, we are told what disciples are to be learning: we are to teach them to observe everything that Jesus commanded— in other words, to acknowledge and obey Jesus, to whom all authority has been given.

We should note that there is a difference between the Kingdom and the church. God's purpose is to build His Kingdom; the church exists to promote and advance the Kingdom. The church is to prepare and equip Christians to bring Christ's authority (i.e., the Kingdom) to bear in all areas of life. Like a

---

[2] "Go" is not a command in Greek; it is a present active participle, meaning "as you go" or "wherever you go."

Roman soldier outside of the Empire, Christians bring the Kingdom with them wherever they go as long as they acknowledge
Jesus as Lord and act in obedience to Him. The Kingdom is thus
much broader than the church. To put it differently, the church
is not an end in itself, but the means to build the Kingdom.

The Lordship of Christ

The Kingdom is another way of talking about the Lordship of
Christ. The most ancient confession of the Christian faith is
"Jesus is Lord," meaning that He is Lord of all. And "all" means
all, not just personal salvation or personal morality, but our families, our work, our recreation, our relationships, our health, our
resources, our politics, our communities, our neighbors—*all*.
And that means that we are to obey Him in all areas of life.

The Lordship of Christ is the central reality in all of creation, and it is the central fact of the Christian life. It should
shape how we see ourselves and how we understand the world
and our place in it—in other words, it is to be the center of our
worldview. At its core, having a biblical worldview means understanding what the Lordship of Christ means in every area of
life. Growing as a Christian means progressively living out the
Lordship of Christ more and more faithfully in more and more
areas of life.

This means that Christians are not to be concerned only
with people's souls; they are also to be concerned with their
wellbeing in this world. Christians have always tended to
the sick and built hospitals; they have always fed the hungry;
they began the first charitable institutions in human history.
Why? Because Christians have always believed that the body
is important. Christians have always opened schools; in fact,
most of the major universities in the world, historically, were

founded by Christians. Why? Because Christianity is concerned with the mind.

Christians were the first to develop technologies that make the laborer's work better, easier, and more productive. Why? Because work is a positive good, given to us before the Fall. The Fall brought with it drudgery and painful toil, but Christ came to redeem us from the effects of the Fall, and so we are to restore dignity to work. As Christians, we are to bring joy back to the work we do. Christians invented the idea of universal human rights. Why? Because the Bible tells us about human dignity founded on the image of God and on the Incarnation of Christ.

All of these are examples of living out the Lordship of Christ as citizens of the Kingdom of God—a concept that William Carey understood.

WILLIAM CAREY: A MODEL OF KINGDOM MINISTRY

William Carey was born in 1761, the son of a weaver. He was apprenticed to a cobbler and eventually inherited his shoemaking business. Most people with this background would have been locked into the working class for the rest of their lives, but Carey had other ideas. Early on, for example, he took an interest in languages. While an apprentice, he taught himself Latin and Greek with the help of a local vicar. As a shoemaker, he learned Hebrew, Italian, French, and Dutch.

A fellow apprentice convinced Carey to become a dissenter from the Church of England. He eventually became a Particular Baptist; but he was also influenced by the writings of Jonathan Edwards, who imbued him with a passion for missions. In 1789, he became a full-time pastor and worked hard to overcome the hyper-Calvinism of the Particular Baptists, who argued that God alone brought about people's salvation—and therefore there was no room in their thinking for missions or evangelism. At one point, he proposed that the Northampton Association of Baptist Pastors should discuss the Great Commission—to which his own spiritual advisor responded, "Sit down, young man. When God wants to convert the heathen, he will do it without consulting you or me!"

When God wants to convert the heathen, he will do it without consulting you or me!

But Carey had a passion for missions, so he spent years studying the Bible and the history of missions and, by 1792, he had won allies in the Northampton Association of Baptist Pastors. In that same year, he formed the Particular Baptist Society for the Propagation of the Gospel amongst the Heathen (later called the Baptist Missionary Society); he left for India the following year.

Carey and his companions engaged in an almost unbelievable range of ministries in India. They were involved in extensive evangelistic work, of course, and many Hindus came to Christ as a result of their ministry. But he also believed in promoting the welfare of the Indian people. He wanted to build a solid economic base for that nation, so he brought the first steam engine to India and encouraged local blacksmiths to copy it. He also established the first banking system in India, and he taught up-to-date methods of agriculture and forestry, also making important contributions to botanical knowledge in the process. Along with economic development, he fought for human rights and social development, including moral reforms, an end to child sacrifice, for *sati*, medical treatment for lepers, and the abolition of the caste system among converts to Christianity.

Impressive as this is, it is nearly insignificant compared to Carey's multifaceted work in education. He studied and mastered several Indian languages and translated classical Indian literature into English for the first time. He eventually became a professor of Bengali, Sanskrit, and Marathi at Fort William College in Calcutta. His studies enabled him to produce the first Sanskrit dictionary, opening the language to European scholars. He also taught astronomy in an effort to move India beyond the fatalism found in astrology. And his work was not simply scholarly, either. He brought the first printing press to India and developed typefaces for Indian languages. He also established the first newspaper in Asia and the first lending libraries in India, using books imported from England.

With his companions, Carey began learning the hundreds of dialects spoken in India and reducing them to 73 written languages, complete with grammars and dictionaries. His work enabled Bengali to emerge as the major literary language of India. As a result, Indian philosopher Vishal Mangalwadi considers Carey the father of the Indian Renaissance in the nineteenth and twentieth centuries, as well as the father of modern India.[3]

Carey set up schools for all castes, breaking the Brahman monopoly on learning, and he was instrumental in founding

---

[3] Many nationalists in India reject this idea and resent Carey and the other missionaries for both religious and political reasons. They see them as bringing in a foreign religion (ignoring the presence of Thomas Christians in India for the previous 1,700 years or so) and as tools of British colonialism. Yet this misunderstands the goals that the missionaries had for India; all of their educational and development work was intended to make India into a modern nation that could stand as an equal among the other nations, free from colonial domination. The objection thus misses the mark; in fact, without Carey, it is hard to envision how India could have been unified.

the first college in Asia at Serampore. The language of the college was Bengali; Indian families wanted their children to learn enough English to get jobs, but Carey was more interested in producing educated Indians than English-speaking workers for the British East India Company.

In the midst of all this, however, several significant tragedies occurred. His wife had a nervous breakdown and he was urged to put her in an asylum. He insisted on caring for her himself at home, but she eventually died of a fever. Then a fire destroyed his print shop and with it his research and notes, though the press and the typefaces survived. He started his work over again and, by his death in 1834 at age 72, he had supervised the translation of the Bible into 44 different Indian languages.

The goal of Carey and the other missionaries was to comprehensively improve the lives of the Indian people. They worked to end social practices that destroyed lives; they brought science, technology, economic development, and education— the supplying of which they saw as flowing out of their Christian faith. And they knew that, over time, this would transform India, preparing it to emerge as an independent modern nation. Carey had a vision—not just for the Gospel of Salvation, but for the Gospel of the Kingdom.

HOW DID WE GET FROM A KINGDOM WORLDVIEW TO WHERE WE ARE NOW?

This is not how Christians in the Global North tend to understand the Gospel today. We have replaced it with a truncated version of the Gospel that thinks of Christianity either in terms of personal salvation and perhaps personal morality, or in terms of social action. But this is nothing new, nor did it emerge out of thin air. The problem began long ago.

The Fact-Value Distinction

In the wake of the Reformations of the sixteenth century, religious and intellectual forces put increasing emphasis on human reason in all areas of life. Culturally, this developed into the Enlightenment in the seventeenth and eighteenth centuries; in religion, the more extreme versions were Unitarian rationalism and Deism, though even orthodox theologians tended to emphasize reason in their approaches to theology.

One critical thinker during this period was Scottish skeptic David Hume (1711–76). Many eighteenth-century Deists had argued that the world is exactly as it should be, that "whatever is, is right" in the words of Alexander Pope. Hume argued otherwise, saying that you cannot derive an "ought" from an "is." In other words, values, ethics, and religion cannot be extrapolated from the physical world.

This was the foundation for an idea now known as the fact-value distinction: "facts," meaning things that are empirically verifiable, are distinct from "values," things that cannot be demonstrated empirically. Knowledge is connected to facts, and anything that is not factual (empirically verifiable) is a matter of conjecture, opinion, or faith—and thus not objectively true or knowable. Francis Schaeffer called this "upper and lower story thinking," and it is foundational to the way that people in the modern West see the world. It even affects the way that we see religion.

By the turn of the nineteenth century, the intellectual world, once dominated by Christians, was increasingly framed in terms of the fact-value distinction; and thus, religion was dismissed as irrelevant to anything in this world—the world of fact.

To carve out a place for religion, Friedrich Schleiermacher, the father of liberal theology, argued that science is the only reliable source for knowledge of the physical world, while religion provides a different kind of knowledge, based on experience and emotion, which science cannot provide. Prior to this, most theologians—and most scientists—believed it possible to have an integrated view of the world that incorporated both science and God. In fact, the leading figures of the scientific revolution thought of their work as a form of theology, since coming to understand the creation reveals the mind of the Creator.

Schleiermacher was the first major theologian to surrender the physical world to science and to limit religion to things that cannot be demonstrated scientifically. The effect of this was to relegate religion to the realm of opinion, not fact, and therefore to dismiss its significance within intellectual life.

FACT-VALUE DISTINCTION	
Global North Culture's Worldview	Biblical Worldview
• The physical world is all that's real	• The physical and non-physical worlds are both real
• All facts deal with the physical world; anything that isn't physical (ethics, morality, religion, aesthetics, etc.) is a matter of opinion ("values"), not fact	• There are facts (i.e., truth) about both the physical and non-physical worlds
• All physical events have purely physical causes	• The non-physical world influences the physical world; there can be non-physical causes of physical events
• There is a sharp separation between the world of fact and the world of values; facts can shape values, but values cannot be used to explain facts	• The physical and non-physical worlds are integrated into a single reality

The Bifurcated Gospel

In the nineteenth century, liberal religious leaders began to look for something more than Schleiermacher's experiential apologetic to defend their relevance within society. From the beginning of the church, Christians had pursued a holistic ministry that combined evangelism with social welfare—in short, to deal with every human need that they found. In the early nineteenth century, this was one of the hallmarks of the British evangelicals who spearheaded the battle to abolish slavery in the British Empire, among a great many other philanthropic activities.

Liberal theologians had surrendered the understanding of the physical world to atheist scientists, so they were forced to find a justification for the church's existence—and they found it in the realm of social action. They began to argue for what we now call "the social Gospel," the idea that true Christianity is about helping the poor, the weak, the powerless, and the afflicted, while dismissing evangelism as unimportant to the Gospel.

A Tragic Overreaction Makes Things Worse

Conservative Christians absolutely rejected this reduction of Christianity to social action. Their response, however, inadvertently exacerbated the problem: they began to argue that Christianity is about saving people so that they can go to Heaven, and thus—unintentionally but in effect—that it has no relevance to this world. It might be worthwhile to engage in philanthropy— we are to love our neighbors after all—but this has nothing to do with the Gospel. Any suggestion that it did amounted, in their minds, to an endorsement of the social Gospel, which they viewed as an affront to true Christianity.

This even affected missionaries. In the first era of modern missions, the so-called "coastal missions" preached a holistic Gospel; in the second era, following the rise of the Social Gospel, the inland missions focused on evangelism nearly to the exclusion of dealing with social problems.

This combination of the fact-value distinction and the bifurcation of the Gospel has left much of the evangelical world with a vision of religion that is fundamentally other-worldly. Christianity is reduced to personal salvation and personal morality, and nothing more. Many have even followed Schleiermacher into a religion that is focused on emotional experience and lacking intellectual content.

Ironically, in seeking to preserve the spiritual elements of the Gospel, evangelicals have secularized it. Secularization sees religion as a purely private matter that should play no role in public life. By reducing the Gospel to the personal, many evangelicals have confined the faith inside the walls of the church, focusing on programs and making worship comfortable by mimicking the culture.

> *In seeking to preserve the spiritual elements of the Gospel, evangelicals have secularized it.*

In other words, we have ceded the culture to the forces of secularism.

This drastically reduced Gospel has neither the power nor the desire to advance the Kingdom. Its message may fill the pews, but it denies Jesus' authority over the world, whatever our words or our hymns may say.

KINGDOM VISION		
Historic Christianity	**Liberal Christianity**	**Evangelicalism**
• Rejects Fact-Value Distinction	• Accepts Fact-Value Distinction	• Influenced by Fact-Value Distinction
• The Gospel as a source of truth	• Christianity as a source of non-rational religious experience	• Christianity as a source of non-rational religious experience
• Holistic Gospel: Evangelism and Compassion	• Bifurcated Gospel: Compassion without evangelism	• Bifurcated Gospel: Evangelism with limited compassion

Lights in the Darkness

Not all theologically conservative Christians have followed this track, of course. Evangelicals have joined with Catholics in opposing abortion, starting pregnancy support centers, supporting low-income women in pregnancy, providing adoption services, and so on.

Organizations such as Prison Fellowship have not only evangelized prisoners but have provided training in life skills and organized aftercare, as well as being involved in criminal justice reform. Rescue missions and homeless shelters run by Christians have done much good work in helping the poor, the mentally ill, the addicted, and the indigent. All of these ministries and more are engaging in Kingdom work.

The Kingdom and Movements

The Global North's loss of a full-orbed vision of the Kingdom is a major barrier to the launch or growth of movements. Movements flourish where a holistic Gospel is proclaimed and lived, and not just by a few individuals or small ministries. Only when we see churches adopt a Kingdom vision as part of their fundamental ethos will we see movements begin and spread in the Global North.

Steve Smith is a prominent catalyst of movements in Asia and the US, and the co-author of *T4T: A Discipleship Re-Revolution*. He had this to say:

> For years as a church planter in Los Angeles, I really longed to get committed disciples. Sometimes I was successful, and sometimes I wasn't. But finally I realized that I had everything reversed, I was going about it the wrong way.
>
> It was the parable of the treasure hidden in a field that made me see it—the man found it and covered it up, but what caught me was the next phrase: "in his *joy* he goes and sells all that he has" to buy the field. What I realized was that I'd been asking people to be committed to the King—without showing them the amazing treasure of Who He is and the life we have in Him! Once I began to unfold His majesty and glory, then we began to see people joyfully giving up all to have Him.
>
> So now, wherever I go, it is to help brothers and sisters unveil the majesty of the King and what His plans are.

CHAPTER
3

PRAYING SMALL PRAYERS TO AN ALMIGHTY GOD

We don't see prayer as a program; we see prayer as a lifestyle. We begin by prayer. They see us praying; we pray together and they know that, when we come together, we pray. And everything we do starts with prayer.

And so we don't teach them prayers for them to start learning how to pray. They see us begin with prayers. Even when somebody is a new believer, we take them with us on a prayer walk. And sometimes they don't even understand why we do this. Finally, they learn that it is something they have to do.

I had a new Muslim-background disciple going for prayers with me and he asked me, "Why are we walking and talking? And who are you talking *to*?" I said, "I am talking to God." They learn by doing rather than by sitting in a class. Our philosophy when it comes to prayer is that you learn prayers by praying. You don't learn prayers in a class.

If somebody is not praying, we also ask them why they are not praying, because we really want to depend on God and that is all about prayers. Otherwise, you just use a lot of human effort to try to solve problems. So it becomes a *lifestyle* of prayer rather than a *program* of prayer.

—Dr. Aila Tasse, Disciple Maker, *Engage! Africa* Video series

THE MORAVIAN PRAYER MOVEMENT

In 1415, Bohemian reformer Jan Hus had challenged the wealth and political power of the Catholic Church and the immorality of the clergy, and thus he had to be eliminated. It wasn't long before, at a church council meeting at Constance, he was labeled a heretic and was executed. The people of Bohemia supported Hus and protested his execution. Referred to as Hussites by their detractors, they rose up in revolt when threats were made against them. Pope Martin V called crusades to put down the rebellion, but the Bohemian Hussites defeated every army sent against them. Finally, the Pope gave in; he allowed them several reforms that they had demanded, and a *de facto* national church in Bohemia was established.

In 1457, a group broke off from the main body of Hussites, calling themselves the Unity of Brethren. With the Protestant Reformation, many of the Hussites became followers of Luther or Calvin; in fact, the Hussites are considered the first Protestants in the Czech Republic. By this point, about ninety percent of the population were Protestants or Hussites. When the Thirty Years' War broke out in 1618, Catholic armies destroyed the Bohemian army at the Battle of White Mountain (1620), and the kingdom was forcibly re-Catholicized. Protestant schools were closed,

Protestant noblemen were executed or exiled, and Bohemia lost nearly three quarters of its population in the course of the war.

The Unity of Brethren did not go away, however. Many went into exile throughout northern Europe, but some stayed underground in the borderlands between Moravia and Silesia. This group continued to be persecuted, so they contacted Count Nicholas Ludwig von Zinzendorf in 1720, a Pietist known for helping those in need, and he gave them permission to settle on his estates. The Unity of Brethren moved to Germany and established the town of Herrnhut on Zinzendorf's property.

Unfortunately, the town was soon divided into factions over theological differences that threatened to tear the settlement apart. Zinzendorf intervened and helped restore unity to the believers through the "Brotherly Agreement" adopted by the Moravians on May 12, 1727. Then on August 13, the group experienced a renewal that they compared to Pentecost in which they "learned to love one another."[1] This marked the beginning of the Renewed Unity of the Brethren, also known as the Moravian Brethren or the Moravian Church.

On August 27, 1727, two weeks after that renewal, 24 men and 24 women agreed to spend an hour each day in scheduled prayer, covering all 24 hours in the day, seven days a week. The idea soon grew, and the practice of continual prayer went on non-stop for more than one hundred years.

Out of this prayer meeting, the Moravians felt called to engage in foreign missions. This was the first major Protestant missionary movement not associated with colonization; it even

---

[1] J. E. Hutton, History of the Moravian Church, second edition revised and enlarged (1909), Project Gutenberg ebook 2099, https://www.gutenberg.org/files/2099/2099-h/2099-h.htm.

predates what is usually considered the beginning of the modern mission movement with William Carey. Starting from a population of 300 in 1727, within 65 years they had sent 300 missionaries around the world, including to North and South America, Africa, Asia, the Caribbean, and the Arctic. They were the first to evangelize slaves; some even sold themselves into slavery to gain access to slave communities. The Moravians were also the first to send laymen into the mission field rather than just ordained ministers.

John Wesley traveled to Georgia before he was a Christian on a ship that also carried some Moravian missionaries. In the middle of the Atlantic, a storm came upon them suddenly, catching the crew unprepared. In a scene of chaos, the mast snapped in half and the passengers went into panic—all except the Moravians, who were calmly praying and singing together on deck. This made a deep impression on Wesley, and he eventually became a follower of Christ at one of their meetings back in England. The Moravians thus played a critical role in the Wesleyan Revival, the start of Methodism, and the beginnings of British evangelicalism, which led to abolitionism and American evangelicalism, among other things. All of this grew out of repentance and a 100-yearlong prayer meeting!

Two Important Lessons on Prayer

There are two lessons that we have learned from our fellow believers in the Global South. First, the church in the Global North does not pray enough. Second, when we do pray, our priorities tend to not be the same as God's priorities. Let's consider both of those lessons in this chapter.

Prayer was central to Jesus' life and ministry. As a rabbi, Jesus prayed at least three times per day using standard liturgical prayers. But the Gospels frequently tell of Him also withdrawing into the wilderness for prayer, often spending the entire night praying, such as when He needed to make decisions about the direction of His ministry (e.g., Mark 1:35–39) or before appointing the Twelve. This raises the immediate observation that, if Jesus needed to spend extended times in prayer—He who was in full and unhindered communion with the Father—how much more do we need to do the same if we are going to have the Spirit's guidance and power?

> *Jesus needed to spend extended times in prayer. He who was in full and unhindered communion with the Father.*

The Amidah

Observant Jews in Jesus' day prayed the Amidah (also known as the Eighteen Benedictions) three times per day. They understood this to be a sacred obligation, and failure to do so was a sin. These prayers took a good amount of time, however. Rabbis and other "professionals" could be counted on to recite them regularly, but praying the entire Amidah three times per day could be a burden for the average person with a job and a family. Students thus asked rabbis for a more concise version of the prayers that would be more practical for them to say to fulfill their religious obligations.

This context helps explain what was happening in Luke 11 when Jesus' disciples came to Him and asked Him to teach them to pray, the way that John the Baptist taught his disciples to pray:

the disciples wanted to find the core of the Amidah that they could recite three times daily. Jesus' answer was to give them the Lord's Prayer, which is remarkably similar to some of the shortened versions of the Amidah that survive from the period.[2]

For Jesus, then, the Lord's Prayer was the distilled essence of what prayer should be. He intended it to be recited, but it also reflects His priorities for prayer, making it a model for how we should pray all the time. It is also a summary of His entire ministry and message.

Many Christians often repeat the words of the Lord's Prayer and yet, when we pray in our own words, we generally miss the prayer's key themes. This is both remarkable and lamentable—yet a closer look at what Jesus said will help us see what He was focused on. Let's look more closely at the Lord's prayer in order to discover Jesus' top three priorities concerning prayer:

- That the Father's name would be glorified in the world around us

- That His Kingdom would be ushered in with power

- That the people of the world—and particularly His followers—would obey the Word and will of the Father.

Our Father in heaven, Hallowed be Your name

Jesus' first priority is God's glory. His intent in this petition is something like: *May the holiness and glory of God in heaven be manifested where I live!*

---

2   If there is any doubt that this was the context for the prayer, consider that the Didache, the earliest surviving extra-biblical Christian literature, instructs believers to recite the Lord's Prayer three times per day (Didache 8, http://www.newadvent.org/fathers/0714.htm).

Your Kingdom come

The second thing that Jesus asks us to pray for is that the Kingdom of God will advance on earth. *May the reign of God in heaven be established where I live!*

Your will be done on earth as it is in heaven

It is likely that the phrase "as it is in heaven" actually applies, not just to "your will be done," but to all three of the preceding petitions: "Hallowed be your name, as hallowed on earth as it is in heaven. Your Kingdom come on earth as it is in heaven. And may the perfect will of God be established in me as fully as it is established in heaven—and among all the peoples of the world!"

Do you see a common theme in the first three petitions? Out of a heart of gratitude they are a plea that:

- *God's glory* may be revealed to people where I live
- *God's Kingdom reign* and authority may advance where I live
- *God's will* may be established in perfect obedience where I live

Before moving to the next petitions, it is worth asking how closely our top three prayer priorities align with Jesus'. Are they God's glory, God's Kingdom, and God's will, or are they more about us than about God?

Give us this day our daily bread.

May the resources of God's Kingdom sustain our needs day by day.

And forgive us our debts, as we forgive our debtors

May the Lord be merciful to me, a sinner, and may I generously extend that same forgiveness to others.

And do not lead us into temptation,

May God's Spirit keep my heart, my feet, my eyes, and my ears from places of temptation.

But deliver us from the evil one.

May the Holy Spirit enable me to resist Satan's temptations, and empower me to be effective in redeeming people unto God from the kingdom of darkness. May the power of evil be voided where I live.

For Yours is the Kingdom and the power and the glory forever. Amen.

This passage is almost certainly not a part of Jesus' original prayer, but it is in keeping with the prayer's spirit. It provides the entire reason for this prayer, and indeed all prayers. Prayer is intended to bring God glory. In modern English, this closing sentence might mean something like this: "We are asking these things because it is Your Kingdom that is being built as You answer these prayers, and it is Your power—and Your power only—which will accomplish these things, and Your answer to our prayer will bring You glory forever."

Jesus taught more about prayer than about any other subject except the Kingdom of God.

Jesus had much more to say about prayer, of course. In fact, He taught more about prayer than about any other subject except the Kingdom of God. We also know that both He and the early church prayed the Psalms, and the great prayers that we find recorded throughout the centuries are saturated with the words of the psalter. We find profound and powerful prayers recorded elsewhere in Scripture, such as in Paul's epistles, but in all cases they reflect the petitions and priorities of the Lord's Prayer.

THE IMPORTANCE OF PRAYER

Prayer was thus central to Jesus' life and the lives of believers in the early church. In monasteries, life was structured around regular times of prayer. Monasticism has a generally negative reputation among evangelicals, but it is worth noting that every major reform in the church, up to and including the Reformation, started in monasteries.

We can also say unequivocally that every major revival and every movement of the Spirit was preceded by long, intense prayer. The question, then, is why do Christians in the Global North spend so little time and attention on prayer? The answer is found in a significant shift in culture that took place between the eighteenth and nineteenth centuries.

From Deism to Materialism

As early as the seventeenth century, thinkers in Europe were becoming increasingly rationalistic. Some began moving toward deism, the idea that God created the universe and then stepped back and let it run on its own without ever intervening in it. This was done in a misguided notion of protecting the glory of God; if God *did* intervene in the world, they reasoned, it would suggest that He did not make it right in the first place. Deists thus had no place for revelation, for miracles, for the Incarnation—or for prayer.

Deism is a fundamentally unstable worldview. It suggests that God acts only as the Creator of the universe, not as its

Sustainer. Therefore, it becomes very easy to drop God out of the system altogether if you can find another explanation for the universe that does not require a Creator. By the early nineteenth century, the scientific establishment began to argue that the universe was eternal, and therefore God was unnecessary. They thus became materialists; that is, they argued that the only things that exist are matter and energy. Given these assumptions, a materialist must conclude that all physical events have purely physical causes, and empirical observation and science are the only things that qualify as true knowledge.

Christians have never adopted a materialistic viewpoint, for obvious reasons, yet elements of materialism have so shaped the cultural mindset in the Global North that they have also shaped the *de facto* worldview of the church. When combined with the fact/value distinction, which we discussed in the last chapter, materialism has had a devastating effect on prayer and on reliance on the Holy Spirit in the life of the church. We acknowledge (at least in theory) that God can act in the physical world—but we tend not to expect Him to. When praying for the sick, for instance, we tend to assume that God will work through the mind and skill of the physician or through medicines or through the normal healing processes of the body, or even by miracles, and so we pray that way. We tend not to pray specific prayers asking for divine intervention in the physical world. Why? Because we have erred in our *thinking*, unconsciously believing that physical events have only physical causes; and because we have erred in our *practice*, relegating God primarily to the realm of values—intangible things—rather than giving Him Lordship over the world of facts that can be measured and studied by science.

The Problem of Affluence

The affluence of the Global North has also had a negative impact on prayer because we unconsciously believe that we do not need to rely on prayer for most things in our daily lives. The Global North is so wealthy that most of us do not have to worry about having our basic needs met. The things that we think we *need* are better described as things that we *want*, and our problems are mostly "first world problems," and our "prayers" are more like selfish wishes. Scripture often warns us of the dangers of affluence, including presuming on the future (Luke 12:16–21) and forgetting the Lord (Deut. 8:17–18) because we assume that we got where we are by our own power or abilities. Jesus' instructions to pray for our daily bread seem irrelevant when we have a refrigerator full of food.

This abundance of resources also seduces the church away from relying on prayer. Consider how decisions are typically made in churches: there is a short prayer followed by a long discussion about the issues; a proposal is made and voted on; and a short prayer is said asking God to bless the decision that was made. We would be far better off spending more, if not most, of our time seeking God's wisdom through prayer rather than relying on our own ideas. Yet we are so used to making our own decisions and relying on our own resources that it seems natural to do that in the church, as well. We pay marketing, media, and management consultants to tell us how to grow the church, how to run stewardship campaigns, how to raise money for a building fund—all examples of relying on our own resources rather than on prayer and the Holy Spirit.

The simple truth is this: secular methods will never produce spiritual results. There are no consultants in the places where the church is growing the quickest. Those brothers and sisters have to depend on prayer and on obeying the instructions given in Scripture for spreading the Gospel.

Lifestyle and Mindset Issues

Another barrier to prayer is lifestyle: we are simply too busy. Churches are built around programs that keep us doing things, and individually we have so much going on that we do not have time to pray. Or so we think. Martin Luther reportedly said that he was so busy that he could not possibly get everything done without taking at least two hours a day to pray. He knew something that we have forgotten.

Our busyness is connected to a cultural bias toward acting to make things happen. Our culture loves slogans and aphorisms such as "God helps those who help themselves" or "if it's going to be, it's up to me." We know in our minds that these notions are not scriptural, yet too often our actions don't line up with that thinking. Our cultural ideal is to be strong, independent, and self-reliant. Yet the Bible tells us that we are strong when we are weak, that we are dependent on God and on one another, that we can do nothing apart from Jesus. Churches hold classes and seminars on personal evangelism, they encourage people to invite their friends to church, but they rarely hold prayer meetings focused on disciple-making and growth of the Kingdom. Yet Jesus tells the disciples not to try to spread the Gospel without waiting first for the Holy Spirit, and every major endeavor in the Gospels and Acts is preceded by deep and intense prayer. In other words, if we want to move the church forward, the critical action that we must take is prayer.

Yet another barrier is a lack of mental discipline. Our fast-paced culture and the constant availability of the internet, often in our pockets, have so affected our minds that our attention span has shrunken from 12 seconds in 2000 to 8.25 seconds in 2015—and the average attention span of a goldfish is nine seconds![3] We can, of course, focus longer on things that truly captivate our attention, but unfortunately, it seems prayer is not one of them.[4] It is thus difficult for us to manage anything beyond short prayers—unlike our brothers and sisters in the Global South who often spend all night in prayer.

Another area where we lack discipline is in the practice of fasting. Fasting is closely associated with prayer, biblically, historically, and currently in the Global South, yet it is rare to find Christians in the Global North who fast. The fact/value distinction discussed in chapter two is again at work here; we do not understand what fasting is supposed to accomplish since we do not see a close connection between body and spirit. And in a consumerist culture like ours, self-denial seems strange, alarming, and unhealthy.

The core element behind these barriers to prayer is this: we recognize *in principle* that God can answer prayer, but we do not believe *in practice* that He does so regularly, if at all. If we did believe in prayer, we would do it more.

Part of the reason for this is, once again, the fact/value distinction, along with the materialistic mindset. The physical world of fact is separate and distinct from the world of the spirit according to this false worldview, and consequently, it is hard for us to see how praying can produce change in the physical

---

[3] http://www.statisticbrain.com/attention-span-statistics/

[4] There are several ways we can use to improve our prayer life. We can use specific times in our routine—driving to or from work, for example—or set prayer reminders on our phone, for example.

realm.[5] We know intellectually that God can make things happen in the physical world, but we do not expect Him to.

Psychologically, we also have to deal with the problem of unanswered prayer (or, more precisely, prayer that God answers with a "no" or a "wait"). People fear to pray specific prayers because too often God has not granted us what we asked for. We provide ourselves with cover in these situations by making sure that we pray "if it be Your will," but we do not believe or trust that God will give us what we ask. Our prayers seem ineffective, which reinforces the fact/value distinction in our minds and makes us less inclined to pray, preferring instead to act.

Prayer is the lifeblood of movements.

The effect of all this is that, even in our discipleship programs, we tend to discount prayer. We offer regular classes on the Bible and train people to lead small group Bible studies, yet most churches have little if any teaching on how to pray. When we do pray, our prayers tend to be so vague that we cannot really say with certainty whether God actually answered them, or whether things would have worked out the same way even without prayer or divine intervention. Often this vagueness is put in spiritual language—bless so-and-so—without any concrete idea of what blessing would look like.

Prayer is the lifeblood of movements. The church in the Global North does not rely on prayer, and if behavior is any

---

[5] This is also the reason why so many evangelicals reject the idea of sacraments: they cannot understand how physical objects can be a means of grace.

indication, it does not believe in it, either. If we are going to see movements in the Global North, we will need to see a new, ongoing commitment to serious, intense, persistent prayer for God to open heaven, to raise up disciple makers and church planters, to guide us to His people of peace, and to empower our work. Without that, there will be no movements and the church will continue its slow, inexorable decline into irrelevance in Global North culture.

Mission for All's Prayer Disciplines

We have covered a broad array of material in this chapter, and it might be good to close with a story that illustrates the practical application of some of what we've been considering. For that story, we'll turn again to Hassan, Mission for All's director, as he helps us understand both the disciplines and the expectation of prayer in the movements taking place in their region.

Prayer and fasting is a high-profile centerpiece of Mission for All, but we did not start that way. We gradually came to embrace the idea—in fact, even before we embraced it, we had started doing a lot of prayer and fasting. We went to seek the face of God. We were convicted that the right path was to bring prayer and fasting into every aspect and area of the ministry.

And so, gradually, as we continued to pray, we saw the success stories, we saw the testimonies. We heard the testimonies, we touched them, we felt them. We lived with the people in whom God performed miracles—ordinary and common people, as well as people who are highly placed. We saw the hand of God and the moving of God, and we were convinced in our heart that this is what needs to be a major priority. And so eventually we were able to become a Disciple Making Ministry.

So I encourage you that this is something that will work. It is not something that is extraordinary. It is not rocket science. It is something that can work because prayer is a key theme in Scripture, critical in being followers of Jesus. Fasting is just part of Scripture. So we can begin, one step at a time—in other words, starting slow to end strong with victory.

That is what we did, and today we want to thank God that we obeyed the Lord and we did it. I want to encourage you: you can obey the Lord and do it, too. Start small, and one day you will be sharing the same testimony I am sharing and you will end strong.

Mission for All's prayer mobilization effort may have started small, but it expanded into a major part of the ministry's life for every member. The regular prayer calendar for all 8,000 Mission for All churches, their partner ministries, and churches being coached in Kingdom movements includes the following:

Annually: 21 days of fasting (two meals) and prayer in all churches starting on January 10.

Monthly: One Friday each month for a half (or whole) night of prayer.

Weekly: Every Wednesday or Thursday, fasting (two meals) and breaking fast with the church gathered for a Discovery Bible Group, and intercessory prayer. Corporate intercession is typically guided by the pastor with a key theme and then a minute or two of spontaneous prayer with every person praying out loud, until the next prayer point is engaged. The experience is of a unified chorus of passionate intercession, with a clear sense of worship and petition, even while learning how to pray for major Kingdom outcomes. It ends with prayers for the gathered disciples' unique needs. These nights have the feel of a celebration of God's faithfulness and provision more than anything else.

Daily: Ninety-minute prayer meetings at forty prayer centers in five countries.

Week Days: All ministry offices and schools stop at noon for thirty minutes of mid-day intercession.

Last day of the month: All Christ Followers are encouraged to come out of their house and engage their neighbors with prayer for God to meet their felt needs.

Last three days of December: Thanksgiving prayers and fasting.

In addition to these regular times of prayer, there are also dedicated prayer events, including the following:

Daniel Prayer Meetings for whatever needs to be restored.

Victory Weekend Retreats for people who are struggling with persistent life challenges. This includes prayers for ministry partners around the world who are facing very difficult personal challenges.

Prayer Mobilizations every quarter, praying for an "open heaven" so that God's blessings would pour down on disciple-making efforts.

Upper Room Prayers every quarter which are prayer gatherings for all senior leaders.

In addition to these organized events, a few thousand intercessors are on call to fast and pray for urgent matters.

What do they pray about? The following are consistent themes for intercession:

- Apostolic teams of disciple-makers and church planters

- Open doors in restricted regions

- Persons of peace to be discovered

- That God would look with favor on partner ministries and their churches

- Key disciple-making pioneers and leaders around the world

- Prayers for Movements in the Global North

- Special prayer needs distributed to all the churches and prayer centers

- Prayers for financial partners.

WHAT MUST JESUS THINK?

Matthew 17:17–20 gives us an account of a time when Jesus was especially angry with his disciples. A man brought his son to the disciples to pray but they could not heal him. Given a 21st century worldview, Jesus' language just might seem extreme to us:

> You unbelieving and perverse generation," Jesus replied, "how long shall I stay with you? How long shall I put up with you? Bring the boy here to me." Jesus rebuked the demon, and it came out of the boy, and he was healed at that moment.

Then the disciples came to Jesus in private and asked, "Why couldn't we drive it out?"

> He replied, "Because you have so little faith. Truly I tell you, if you have faith as small as a mustard seed, you can say to

this mountain, 'Move from here to there,' and it will move. Nothing will be impossible for you."

In Jesus' Kingdom economy there are some things that churches are created to do, and praying down Kingdom authority over Satan is on that list. At least the apostles tried!

In light of that, what might Jesus want to say about our churches' capacities to pray for people in desperate need, including those without Jesus in 21st-century America? What might Jesus say about our excuses for why our churches can't crack the code of millennials?

In light of what we know about the Moravian prayer chain that unleashing a spiritual earthquake in Christian history, and the birthing of the global missionary enterprise—300 people and 100 years that changed our world through prayer—what might Jesus say about our commitment to prayer?

And in light of what *you* know about Mission for All, that from a very small beginning has become a massive prayer mobilization that has already harvested hundreds of thousands of lost people among unreached people groups, what might Jesus say about how we prioritize our time and our activities?

What might Jesus say about our faith that He still answers prayers:

- That the glory of God may be revealed among all the peoples on earth;
- That the Kingdom of God may advance where we live; and
- For God's will to be obeyed on earth as it is in heaven?

We will come back to this theme in a few chapters.

KEEPING ORDINARY PEOPLE ORDINARY

Brothers and sisters, think of what you were when you were called. Not many of you were wise by human standards; not many were influential; not many were of noble birth. But God chose the foolish things of the world to shame the wise; God chose the weak things of the world to shame the strong. God chose the lowly things of this world and the despised things—and the things that are not—to nullify the things that are, so that no one may boast before him.

—1 Cor. 1:26–29

A KINGDOM MOVEMENT CATALYST REGARDING EVERYDAY PEOPLE

We sometimes fail to realize that God uses ordinary people, as opposed to those who have seminary or doctoral degrees. We need to realize that's exactly what God does. God is down there at the very grassroots level, empowering people who are willing to be obedient and follow Him—and it has virtually nothing to do with their knowledge or level of formal training. That surprised me, because I came through a training and seminary process that says, the effective ministers are the well-trained ones.

And I don't discount that value, but it misses what God is really doing in terms of releasing His power. I think God is releasing His power with those ordinary people who are just willing to walk one step at a time in obedience. And it is in a greater way than with those who may have great learning, and great knowledge, and even ministerial experience.

I believed for too long that we seminary-trained ministers were the class that had to do it for them and on behalf of them, instead of recognizing that, in the Kingdom of God, it's *about* them. It's about them being the ministers that God has called them to be—and they will be, if we just let them.

—Dave Hunt

Simply put, we are impressed by people. We all have people that we think of as stars, as celebrities, as heroes, even in the Christian world. They are the preachers, the apologists, the leaders of great organizations, best-selling authors. We look at them and think, "I wish I could be like them" or "I could never be like them", and we admire their skills, abilities, talents, knowledge, whatever it is that we see as the keys to their effectiveness in ministry.

But God does not need great men and women to achieve His purposes; He just needs people simple enough to imagine that He can use anybody to do anything. Consider the story of Geert Groote.

GEERT GROOTE:
SISTERS AND BROTHERS OF THE COMMON LIFE

In 1348, an eight-year-old boy lost his parents to the plague, a disease that was on a rampage throughout Europe, leaving devastation in its wake. Nearly half the population of the continent died within a span of three years.

Unlike many of the orphans left by the disease, this boy was not left destitute. His name was Geert Groote, and his parents had been among the small group of patricians who ran the city of Deventer in the Netherlands. Young Geert thus led a comfortable life under the care of guardians.

He was remarkably intellectually gifted and soon left home to pursue his education at Aachen and the University of Paris. He completed his degree at age 18 and returned home, eventually teaching in Deventer. He was so well respected that he was given a position teaching philosophy and theology at the University of Cologne, where he enjoyed a sumptuous lifestyle.

All of this changed in 1374, when Groote contracted a life-threatening illness that forced him into some serious soul-searching. He resigned his positions and spent three years at a monastery working to figure his life out.

Groote left the monastery a changed man. He converted his house in Deventer into a center to care for poor women and organized them into a lay religious community known as the Sisters of the Common Life. Later, he also founded a male counterpart to the Sisters, the better-known Brethren of the Common Life.

Unlike nuns or monks, the Sisters and Brethren of the Common Life were regular people who took no permanent vows and who could leave the group at any time. They followed a group of spiritual disciplines developed by Groote called the *Devotio Moderna*, or "Renewed Devotion."

The practice was built around four themes. First, they placed a great deal of emphasis on reading, studying, and meditating on the Bible. Second, they believed that faith must come from the heart, which is the wellspring of human action. They therefore developed practices designed to root out the vices from the heart and replace them with virtues.

Third, they worked to develop a strong emotional connection to Jesus at key points in His life, particularly His passion; this was called the "imitation of Christ." Fourth, they wanted to return to the model of the early church and reject the corruption of the late middle ages.

The Sisters and Brethren of the Common Life recognized that they could not practice the *Devotio Moderna* alone; it could only be done in community. They lived together in single-sex households where they could have times of private and corporate prayer and meditation, confession, and mutual correction, as well as attending Mass together.

Unlike monks or nuns, the Sisters and Brethren also had to support themselves with secular jobs. The Sisters of the Common Life supported themselves mostly by making and selling lace, a socially acceptable trade for women. The Brethren had more options than the women. They were literate, given the emphasis on the Bible and early Christian writers in the *Devotio Moderna*, and so many of them earned a living by copying manuscripts and by starting schools. Their goal was to promote church renewal by enabling more people to read the sources of the Christian life and to discover for themselves what the Scriptures had to say about faith and obedience.

Along with starting the Sisters and the Brethren of the Common Life, Groote was ordained as a deacon and appointed as a preacher by the reform-minded bishop of Utrecht. With the bishop's support, he began preaching against the full range of clerical abuses in the church, including drunkenness, using offices in the church to get wealthy, and supposedly celibate clergy who had concubines and were otherwise sexually loose. Groote's sermons were very popular with the laity but, not surprisingly, they angered the clergy. To silence him, the clergy pressured the bishop to ban all preaching by anyone other than a fully ordained priest. Groote appealed the ban to the Pope, but died ministering to plague victims before his appeal could be heard.

The printing press had enormous repercussions throughout the culture and in many ways made the modern world possible.

His work continued, however. The schools established by the Brethren of the Common Life spread literacy throughout northern and central Germany. This led to a growing demand for books, especially the Bible, and this in turn was an important motivation for Gutenberg's invention of the printing press. The printing press had enormous repercussions throughout the culture and in many ways made the modern world possible. The Brethren were among the first to adopt this new technology, installing a press in Deventer around 1477.

By this date, nearly everyone in this part of Europe who received a primary education went to a school operated by the Brethren of the Common Life, including the great Christian humanist Desiderius Erasmus, who attended the Deventer school, and Martin Luther, who went to the school in Magdeburg. Their schools were thus the cradle of the Reformations of the sixteenth century.

And all of this was accomplished by a group of normal laymen and laywomen who sought to live a more faithful life in Christ—nearly all of whose names have been lost to history.

God Loves and Uses Ordinary People

The Brethren of the Common Life were very unusual for their focus on church reform and for their role in education, which previously had been the responsibility of the church. Historically, the church had largely been understood to be a clerical organization, and so most church reform and ministry had been led by the clergy. The main exception to this occurred when kings or nobles decided to correct abuses in the church, usually for political reasons, and so "interfered" with church affairs. But in the Brethren and the Sisters, we find a grassroots group quietly growing their own spiritual lives and giving others the tools to do the same, all the while operating with minimal clerical involvement and making a living through secular means.

We see this over and over again throughout the Bible. God delights in working through ordinary people who are willing to act in faith. Moses was a murderer. Few if any of the Judges were obvious leaders, and many had serious character flaws. When it came time for a king, God first gave Israel a king after the peoples' hearts. Saul was a tall, impressive man, exactly the kind of leader that the people of Israel were looking for (1 Sam. 10:23–24). Judging by outward standards, he should have been an excellent king. And yet he failed because his ego got in the way and his heart was not given over to God.

David, on the other hand, was a man of God. He was also the last and least of his brothers. Samuel came to Bethlehem and asked David's father, Jesse, to bring his sons to a feast—and David was considered so insignificant that he wasn't even invited. His brothers were all much more impressive, but as Samuel was reminded, God looks at the heart (1 Sam. 16:7). Yet David loved God and had a powerful faith—and consequently he became Israel's greatest king.

We see this pattern in the New Testament, as well. We don't know the professions of all the apostles, but we do know that they included four fishermen, a tax-collecting Roman collaborator, and a zealot rebel against Rome—not the kind of people that a rabbi would have taken for disciples, and not who most of us would pick to start a movement to change the world. Then there were the seventy-two whom Jesus sent out in Luke 10. We don't even know any of their names.

These were all ordinary people who did extraordinary things because they were called and empowered by an extraordinary God. In the Kingdom, it is not necessarily the best and brightest who achieve great things for God. Rather, God regularly chooses unlikely, ordinary people to do impossible things to reveal, unequivocally, that His power is the source of all good things.

This raises several questions: How much should the work of the church be in the hands of the laity? How should clergy and laity relate to each other? What should their responsibilities be?

The Role of Church Leadership

The clearest answer to these questions is found in Ephesians 4:11–16:

So Christ himself gave the apostles, the prophets, the evangelists, the pastors and teachers, to equip his people for works of service, so that the body of Christ may be built up until we all reach unity in the faith and in the knowledge of the Son of God and become mature, attaining to the whole measure of the fullness of Christ.

Then we will no longer be infants, tossed back and forth by the waves, and blown here and there by every wind of teaching and by the cunning and craftiness of people in their deceitful scheming. Instead, speaking the truth in love, we will grow to become in every respect the mature body of him who is the head, that is, Christ. From him the whole body, joined and held together by every supporting ligament, grows and builds itself up in love, as each part does its work.

In these verses, Paul discusses the fundamental purpose that God has for the people to whom He has given word-gifts and special functions in the church. These are:

Apostles: This could refer to the original twelve, but Paul's usage elsewhere suggests that he has in mind people who act as pioneers, bringing the Gospel into a new area. This may be cross-cultural, but is not necessarily; Peter was the apostle to the Jews, for example.

Prophets: There are various interpretations of what prophets were and are, but most would agree that they were people who spoke the Word of God into the specific situation around them. In the New Testament era, this typically involved divine revelation; whether or not it still does, or even if it still occurs, is one of the main disputes in the church today concerning the term.

Evangelists: Those who proclaim the Gospel. This may be to people who have never heard it, or it might be to those who are already Christ Followers in order to deepen their understanding of the Gospel.

Pastors: This is simply the Latin word for shepherds. Shepherds are responsible for leading, feeding, and protecting the sheep. Shepherds exist for the sheep, not the other way around. The sheep produce everything valuable—wool, milk, lambs—and it is the shepherd's job to do what he can to support them. Furthermore, the shepherd does not make new sheep, the sheep do.

Pastors are thus responsible for leading the congregation, feeding the people through preaching and teaching, and protecting them from attacks or from straying. As we will see, however, pastors are *not* responsible for carrying out the larger ministry of the church; the sheep are to produce goods and reproduce, not the shepherd.

Teachers: Teachers are closely related to pastors— in fact, it is possible to translate the Greek as a single office, the pastor-teacher. Teachers are responsible for passing on biblical and doctrinal truth in an understandable way, and for coaching and mentoring people in the Faith.

Whether you consider these things to be gifts, ministries, or offices, they would all be included under our idea of *clergy*. And all of them have a common purpose: they are to *"equip his people* [literally, "the saints"] *for the work of ministry."*

Two points are critical here. First, the clergy are not the ones who are doing ministry; ordinary laypeople are. Second, the clergy's job is to equip the laity to carry out their ministries. In the economy of the Kingdom of God the church has no bystander-observers. Every Christ Follower is given giftings by Jesus to serve and build up the body of Christ.

The biblical model for apostles, prophets, evangelists, pastors, and teachers is a coaching model. A team's coach does not win games but instead enables the players to win, giving them the training, conditioning, skills, strategy, and tactics necessary for the team's success. Ultimately, though, the players have to apply what the coach gives them if they are going to win.

It is the same with the church. Pastors and teachers are to coach and mentor members to identify their ministries and to carry them out. Each person's ministry is unique and vital, since the body cannot function properly without each member doing his part (vs. 16).

A team's coach does not win games but instead enables the players to win . . .

The beauty of God's design for ministry is that it empowers the laity and multiplies the people doing the church's work; it is no longer just the pastors, but everyone working for the Kingdom. This unlocks the church and opens the door to the kind of explosive growth that is impossible when it is only the professional staff doing the bulk of the ministry. It removes the confining boundaries between "us" and "them" when it comes to Kingdom expansion.

The goal of the members' ministry is "*that the body of Christ may be built up.*" Building up the body includes bringing new people into the Kingdom (remember, the sheep reproduce, not the shepherd) plus supporting and serving each other in whatever capacity God has assigned to each person.

Coaching and training is an on-going process, as the church's ministry is to continue, "until we all reach unity in the faith and in the knowledge of the Son of God and become mature, attaining to the whole measure of the fullness of Christ." The first goal that Paul lists is "unity," a major theme in the letter to the Ephesians. If we exalt our own role, denomination, organization, or theological school at the expense of another, we are sowing disunity. But if the body works together properly and humbly, unity follows. Unity leads to knowledge of and intimacy with Christ (John 17:20–26), from which flows maturity and, in the end, the whole measure of the fullness of Christ.

Paul's teaching here presents an incredibly dynamic and exciting vision of the church, which exalts the humble—the common, ordinary person—and makes the visible leaders of the church into support staff for the congregants. The question is: why don't we see it more often in the Global North? Where did we lose this vision of the church?

Clericalization and Institutionalization

The church's overall vision of ministry shifted fairly early in church history. Paul's vision was of pastors and teachers equipping ordinary believers to carry out the ministry. On their first missionary journey, Paul and Barnabas established a number of churches and then returned to appoint elders (Acts 14:23); this indicates that churches can function without elders, at least on the initial founding. However, as shown by examples in Acts and by the pastoral epistles, having elders was the preferred model.

In the pastorals, the term elder (Greek *presbyteros*) is interchangeable with the term bishop (Greek *episcopos*; Titus 1:5, 7).

By the end of the first century, the terminology had changed and the title *episcopos* was given to the senior elder in an urban church.

This changed further under Constantine. Rodney Stark explains:

> The first three centuries of Christian growth is entirely consistent with conversions having occurred as a *network phenomenon*, the faith's having spread through ties of family and friendship. The movement began with perhaps no more than a thousand converts in the year 40; three centuries later more than half of the population of the empire (perhaps as many as 33 million people) had become Christians.
>
> *This result can be attributed to the work of missionaries only if we recognize a universal mission on the part of all believers* . . . soon after the conversion of Constantine there came more than a millennium during which Christians no longer sustained missions.
>
> For far too long, historians have accepted the claim that the conversion of Emperor Constantine caused the triumph of Christianity. . . . To the contrary . . . in doing his best to serve Christianity, Constantine destroyed its most vital aspect: its *dependence on mass volunteerism*.[1]

In other words, prior to Constantine, the church grew through the efforts of ordinary believers; after Constantine, "the ministry" became professionalized. The elders developed into priests, even though the two words are different in both Greek and Latin. The priests did the work of the church through preaching and administering the sacraments. Deacons had originally been an independent office, but now they shifted, as well, to become primarily a stepping stone on the way to the

---

[1] *One True God* (Princeton, NJ: Princeton University Press, 2003), 59–60, emphases added.

priesthood.[2] The laity became the *recipients* of the ministry performed by the priests, rather than being the ones *performing* the ministry themselves.

Early on, we also see the development of monasticism, where men and women left the secular world to live in closed, single-sex communities focused on prayer and work (*ora et labora*). Medieval people saw this as the highpoint of spirituality, to the point where calling someone "a religious" meant that he or she was in a monastic order. From the monasteries, celibacy spread into the broader church so that, by the thirteenth century, it was mandatory for all priests in the Catholic Church.[3]

By this time, the church was essentially understood to mean the clergy, not the laity. Laymen could participate in it (and they were legally required to in most places); they could obtain benefits from it; but the heart of the church was made up of priests, and, aside from financial support, they could get along quite well doing the work of the church even without the laity.

But there was pushback against this trend, even in the medieval church. In the thirteenth century, Franciscans and other groups of friars and sisters lived according to a rule of life following the example of the monasteries, but they were not confined to monasteries; they did their work in the secular community. From the other direction, lay religious organizations also developed what were known as "confraternities." These tended to focus on a particular charitable or religious activity, such as

---

[2] Different denominations have different understandings of the diaconate. In the early church, deacons were responsible for distributing alms, a job which required some women to be deacons. Later, the office was limited to men and was responsible for church finances. Later still, it became a step to priesthood.

[3] In the Orthodox Churches, priests can marry, though monks and nuns cannot; bishops are always drawn from monks, so they are celibate.

providing dowries to poor girls so that they could marry. Sometimes, members of confraternities were permitted to preach. The Sisters and Brethren of the Common Life had much in common with confraternities, though they were structured more like monasteries than normal confraternities.

This began to change with the Protestant Reformation. One of Luther's most cherished ideas was the priesthood of all believers, which in theory broke down the distinction between clergy and laity. Protestants sought to break down the divide between sacred and secular by insisting that all non-sinful and non-criminal work was sacred and should be done to the glory of God. Being a pastor was no more a sacred calling than being a farmer or a baker; all were ordained by God and were essential to the life of the community. Luther and other Protestant leaders argued that the father was to be the first pastor to the family. They also insisted that liturgies and the Bible be in the local language so that everyone could understand them. In these and a host of other ways, Protestantism elevated the spiritual status of the laity.

But there were other trends that resisted this. Luther, for example, initially argued for the "perspicuity of Scripture;" that is, the Bible is sufficiently clear that its core message can be understood by anyone. This is why he translated the Bible into German: he believed that, once people read it for themselves, they would find out that he was right. Then he discovered that people did not interpret it the way that he did, with the result that the Protestant movement fragmented. Zwingli understood the Lord's Supper differently than Luther, a major issue in the period. Then there were Anabaptists and Spiritualists and all kinds of people with ideas that Luther did not find acceptable. He thus changed his view, arguing that laymen should be able to read the Bible, but they also needed trained experts (i.e., theologians and well-educated pastors) to guide their interpretation so that they did not go off-track. Different branches of Protestantism produced study Bibles to guide people to the "correct" interpretation of Scripture. This produced the desired effect of solidifying theological positions, but it brought the undesired side effect of elevating the theologians who developed them into positions of *de facto* authority as interpreters of Scripture.

Protestantism lessened the distance between pastors and laity, but it did not eliminate it. For a variety of reasons, pastors were still seen as the religious professionals; they were the ones who preached, taught, celebrated the sacraments, married people, buried people, and visited the sick. The pastors still did the work, assisted by a small number of people in the congregation.

Protestantism lessened the distance between pastors and laity, but it did not eliminate it.

A similar trend occurred in churches during the twentieth century, with the growth in specialization and professionalization in the business world. Staffs of churches increased in size, and specialists were hired for specific jobs: youth ministry, women's ministry, men's ministry, music ministry, family ministry, caring ministry, counseling, and on and on. Professionalization and specialization has come to dominate the ministry model, particularly in megachurches.

The trend toward specialization is also seen in a misunderstanding of the observation of missiologist Donald McGavran that it is much easier for the Gospel to penetrate a culture (or subculture) through people in or near that culture. A few church-growth people grabbed onto this fact to argue that churches should find a particular demographic niche and market to that specific segment of the population to get the best results; there should also be programs targeted to each demographic within the congregation.[4] The tendency, however, has consistently been to target an affluent suburban demographic rather than to reach out to the last, the least, and the lost.[5]

Among the laity, the dominant consumerist worldview in the culture affects how people view the church. We have a range of options for churches, and we go to the one that best meets our perceived needs. We ask, "Do I get anything out of the preaching?" "How is the children's program?" "What is the youth program focused on?" "Do I like the music and worship style?" This, in turn, feeds back into our culture's preference for specialization and expertise, as we rely, for example, on the Sunday School to provide our children's spiritual education, in effect sub-contracting our responsibility as parents to church volunteers. The consumerist mentality also leads pastors to tailor their preaching to appeal to the "felt needs" of the congregation, often drawing more from pop psychology and self-help books than from the Scriptures, and eventually moving toward Prosperity Gospel, "health and wealth" preaching.

---

[4] This is another example of attempting to do spiritual ministry through secular means, as discussed in chapter three.

[5] Jerry was Donald McGavran's pastor toward the end of his life. McGavran had largely lost his sight and had an assistant who read him mission correspondence and journals every morning, and he would respond to them by making notes or writing memos or articles. He also asked Jerry for updates on the country where he served and, when Jerry was insufficiently informed, McGavran would rebuke him for not paying enough attention to his people.

THE CHANGING ROLES OF LEADERS AND LAITY

	Early Church	Post-Constantine	Protestantism	DMM
Leaders	**Qualifications:** • Spiritual maturity • Character • Giftedness **Role:** • Equipping • Sacraments	**Qualifications:** • Training (sometimes) • Ordination **Role:** • Sacraments • Preaching (sometimes)	**Qualifications:** • Education (often) • Call to Church **Role:** • Preaching • Administer Communion • Teaching (sometimes)	**Qualifications:** • Character • Giftedness **Role:** • Facilitator • Catalyst • Coaching • Mentoring • Training
Laity	**Role:** • Compassion • Evangelism	**Role:** • Receive the Sacraments • Give money • Obey the Church	**Role:** • Fathers as family pastors • Learn Bible • Receive Communion • Give money • Do work "as to the Lord"	**Role:** • Compassion • Making Disciples • Church Planting • Communion

This focus on clergy and other professionals is not the vision for ministry that Jesus had when He sent out the seventy-two (as we will see in chapter six), and it is not what Paul had in mind in his teaching about the church. Pastors and teachers are important as trainers and mentors, but the work of ministry is to be carried out by the church as a whole; "every-member ministry" is the New Testament model of the church as we can see here in the life of Lori Baldwin.

LORI BALDWIN'S STORY

Lori Baldwin was a graduate of the Perspectives on the World Christian Movement course. As a graduate, she was invited to attend a twelve-week class on how to facilitate the kind of disciple making needed to bring about great movements of God in North America. That invitation got her attention.

Lori was a single mom with two teenage daughters, and the logistics of participating in the class were daunting: a two-hour round trip drive, a three-hour class, plus outside readings and homework. This would stretch her limits of stress and endurance. However, she had attended a one-day seminar about this ministry model, which left her intrigued about the concept of Discovery Bible Studies, one of the key tools being used throughout the Global South in Disciple Making Movements. Despite the strain that it would put on her personal life, Lori decided to take this class.

Each week, she found herself discovering biblical principles of engaging lost people, with Jesus Himself as the template for a disciple-maker. Obedience-based discipleship—as contrasted with knowledge-based discipleship—was a powerful concept. Throughout the class, she felt that she was discovering things that had been hiding in plain sight in the Bible.

Lori's favorite part of the course was a weekly Discovery Bible Study with five of her colleagues. This provided a new circle of friends, as well as answers to the missing paradigms of learning and obedience to God's Word. Each week, the group read from the Bible, then answered several questions:

What did I discover about God in this passage?

What did I discover about people in this passage?

How will I commit to obey this passage this week?

With whom will I share what I have learned from this passage?

She was being challenged by God every week and held herself accountable to keep her promises to Him.

By the time the twelve weeks were completed, Lori had become convinced that consistent discovery of the Bible and obedience-based discipleship could transform any person and empower her home church to be much more successful at making disciples in the community. She was also surprised that anyone could lead others in the process, without stress or pressure to be a Bible expert. This gave her feelings of confidence and hope that she could do more work for the Kingdom than she ever imagined.

The church Lori attended was a growing, multi-campus congregation in Tennessee, and the leaders announced the new five-year goals one Sunday morning, hours before her final class on disciple-making would conclude. As she listened to the presentation, she felt that the goals for engaging lost people and making disciples were very low. She had become convinced that God could do so much more through the thousands of members in her church. So, in the final Discovery Bible Study of the

Engage! sessions, Lori committed to obeying the passage for that night by introducing this bold disciple-making strategy to Mike, her missions pastor.

Mike was new to his position, and he had recently been given a daunting assignment to shape a missions program that would raise the bar of disciple-making in the church. Unfortunately, all the discipleship plans that he found were variations on a single theme, and none had proven effective at his church. He finally stopped ordering materials, and he and his wife started praying together for God's wisdom on how to make disciples. They found a classroom in the church and it became their prayer chapel.

So when Mike and Lori met, he was deeply intrigued by the Discovery Bible Study. During every Bible study, each participant is encouraged to answer an "I will obey God" statement, each person reports on how he has done in living out the prior week's commitments. That really spoke to Mike, because it was so simple to facilitate and allowed the Word of God to do what it promised: radically change people's lives.

Mike soon had the opportunity to experience a Discovery Bible Study. He immediately understood its powerful potential. So he quickly worked with Final Command Ministries to launch this new Disciple-Making class. He was excited, but on the first night, out of thousands of church members, only fifteen people showed up—and they were pretty much the usual "missions junkies."

But his discouragement was short-lived. Within the first week there was a dramatic surprise. Those fifteen people had started several new Discovery Bible Studies. And they kept going and began to multiply. By the end of twelve weeks, more than 100 new groups had sprung up inside the church! Mike was so thankful to Lori—he could hardly believe how well this method worked.

It should be noted that the stated goal of the course is to equip people to launch Discovery Bible Studies *outside* the church among lost people—not people from the inside. Though it could have been assumed these fifteen were only discipling people who were already Christians, this was not the case. The multiplication was also among the unreached in Tennessee.

The leadership of the church knew that biblical equipping of the lost was exactly what was taking place. Bible studies were doing a great job of getting large numbers of their people into the Word of God and, as it were, letting the Bible disciple them to new levels of Christian responsibility and maturity.

And at that point, participants naturally began inviting lost people into the process. The organic nature of this type of disciple-making was unlike anything that this church had ever seen. And soon people started taking Discovery Bible Studies to their workplaces and schools and Starbucks, and this ministry model began to reshape disciple-making both inside the church and outside. Some of the results of this process include:

- Ordinary people who previously wouldn't have considered teaching a Sunday school class were now facilitating Bible studies outside the church.

- Discovery Bible Studies were happening thirty times a week among victims of human trafficking.

- One member of the church began helping 160 people in China to do a weekly Discovery Bible Study via the internet.

❧ The church's ministry in Haiti adopted disciple-making movements that facilitate multiplication. This has led to the training of 1,500 new leaders as of this writing.

The executive pastor of the church summarized the impact on his church with these words:

> Today, some of the most passionate leaders in our church have emerged from this Disciple-Making class."

Since that evaluation several years have passed, during which time the senior pastor tragically passed away. Eventually, the new pastor decided to replace the church's disciple-making movement approach with a more traditional model; one with which he was familiar.

But the impact of Lori's obedience to a simple "I will" statement, and this one church's experiment with obedience-based disciple-making has had a remarkable Kingdom impact. Other churches and ministries have adopted Disciple Making Movements. Scores of churches were planted in Latin America. And of the original fifteen *Engage!* participants, several have found God's vision for their lives as full-time, disciple-making catalysts.

CHOOSING KNOWLEDGE OVER OBEDIENCE

Dallas Willard and the Gospel of Sin Management

A leading American pastor laments, "Why is today's church so weak? Why are we able to claim many conversions and enroll many church members but have less and less impact on our culture? Why are Christians indistinguishable from the world?"

Should we not at least consider the possibility that this poor result is not in spite of what we teach and how we teach, but precisely because of it? . . . History has brought us to the point where the Christian message is thought to be essentially concerned *only* with how to deal with sin: with wrongdoing or wrong-being and its effects. Life, our actual existence, is not included in what is now presented as the heart of the Christian message, or it is included only marginally. That is where we find ourselves today.

Once we understand the disconnect between the current message and ordinary life, the failures just noted at least make a bit of sense. They should be expected. When we examine the broad spectrum of Christian proclamation and practice, we see that the only thing made essential on the right wing of theology is forgiveness of the individual's sins. On the left it is removal of social or structural evils. The current gospel then becomes a "gospel of sin management." Transformation of life and character is *no* part of the redemptive message. Moment-to-moment human reality in its depths is not the arena of faith and eternal living.

—Dallas Willard, *The Divine Conspiracy*

THE CLAPHAM CHRISTIANS

Late-eighteenth-century Britain was a mess. Drunkenness was rampant, with the lower classes drinking gin and the upper classes Bordeaux. It was so bad that members of Parliament often showed up drunk at Westminster. Animal cruelty was commonplace, with bear-baiting and bull-baiting popular "sports," and public executions were popular entertainment—often carried out for petty crimes. Bodies of executed criminals were often publicly dissected before being burned. Children were put to work in factories in horrendous and dangerous conditions and were frequently chained to the machines where they worked. Twenty-five percent of the women in London were prostitutes, with an average age of sixteen. Most girls entered the trade at fourteen, though there were some brothels that specialized in girls under that age.

Where was the church in all this? After the numerous wars in sixteenth- and seventeenth-century Europe, many people across the continent were worried that being too engaged with religion would lead to more war. Nowhere was this fear more pronounced than in England, where King Charles I had been beheaded during the English Civil War (1649). When Charles II came to the throne in the Restoration (1660), religious dissent was quashed and religious practice was reduced to formalities: attending church on Sundays and holidays, having babies baptized, church weddings, etc. Anything more than that was condemned as "enthusiasm," roughly the equivalent of calling someone a fanatic or "holy roller." And so the Christians in England refused to speak out or even to recognize the problems in their country.

However, some people were not content with this kind of formal religion. The Wesleys, for example, formed the "Holy Club" at Oxford even prior to their conversion, where they practiced spiritual disciplines and lived an ordered way of life, which led to being labeled "Methodists." With the conversion of the Wesleys, the Methodists entered a broader movement that included the Great Awakening in the Americas and the Evangelical Revival in Britain. The Methodists were pressured out of the Church of England to form their own associations, but other Evangelicals stayed and worked for reform within the Anglican Church.

John Newton is the former slave trader turned pastor who is best known for writing the hymn "Amazing Grace." He was also a major inspiration for an influential group of British evangelicals in the village of Clapham (now part of London) which has been labeled "the Clapham Sect" by historians. This group's most famous member was William Wilberforce, the parliamentarian who led the effort to end the Atlantic slave trade. The Clapham Sect is best known for leading a decades-long effort to end the slave trade and ultimately to abolish slavery itself in the British Empire. Members were also involved in a wide range of philanthropic activities including:

- Prison reform
- Improving working conditions in factories
- Establishing the RSPCA and ending bullfighting, bear-baiting, and other kinds of animal cruelty
- Promoting Sunday Schools (which gave a basic education to children who could not go to school during the week)
- Founding Freetown in Sierra Leone as a haven for free slaves and a beachhead for the Gospel in Africa
- Facilitating foreign missions, including founding the Church Missionary Society and the Society for Missions to Africa and the East
- Encouragement of thrift to help the poor
- Founding of the Religious Tract Society and the British and Foreign Bible Society

Why were the Clapham Christians involved in so many things? Partially because, like their younger contemporary William Carey (see chapter two), they had a full-orbed Kingdom vision and believed in a holistic Gospel. To the Clapham Sect, evangelism and social action were both demands of the Gospel.

They also understood that disciples *obey*. Wilberforce and the rest of his circle believed that being a Christian involved more than a profession of faith or even a conversion experience; it involved obeying Jesus' commands in every area of life, especially the Law of Love. In an environment as depraved as England's at the time, that meant working to change the attitude of society as a whole toward the poor and weak—the last, the least, and the lost. This progressive attitude lay behind the drive to abolish the slave trade, as well as the Clapham sect's philanthropic work. Wilberforce linked them in his diary: "God has set before me two great objectives, the abolition of the slave trade and the reformation of manners," by which he meant changing the way that people treated one another.

All of this work was built around obedience to Jesus' command to love, whether missions and evangelism or working to improve society. And the Clapham Sect transformed English society through persistence, integrity, and a great deal of creative effort. They and the Methodists almost certainly helped to prevent England from following France into bloody revolution. Wilberforce was said to have "made goodness fashionable."

This is the kind of change that can occur when people adopt a Kingdom mindset, a holistic Gospel, and give themselves over to obedience to the commands of Christ in every area of life.

THE KINGDOM, OBEDIENCE, AND DISCIPLESHIP

As we saw in chapter two, Jesus' central message was that the Kingdom of God—recognizing and obeying God's authority in every area of life—was breaking into the world, and we need to change the fundamental orientation of our lives in response to its presence. Similarly, the Great Commission tells us to make disciples, that is, to make apprentices to God who are being taught to obey everything that He has commanded.

Obedience is the essence of discipleship and is central to the Gospel that Jesus taught. If we aren't teaching people to obey everything that Jesus commanded, we aren't preaching the same Gospel that He preached. And since we proclaim that Jesus is Lord, that is our central problem.

Faith and Works in the Bible

The immediate objection that Evangelicals will raise to this understanding of the Gospel is that we are saved by grace through faith, not by works (Eph. 2:8–9). The relationship between faith and works is one of the most fundamental issues that we need to deal with and has been the source of endless arguments in the church, from Pelagians on the one hand saying that we are saved by works, to antinomians on the other saying that once we are saved, nothing that we do matters.

This argument shows up in biblical theology in the alleged "contradiction" between Paul, who taught salvation entirely by grace, and James, who tells us that faith without works is dead (James 2:26). Many prominent scholars have suggested that this so-called contradiction represents a serious split in the theology of the apostolic and post-apostolic church.

However, there is, in reality, no significant difference between the two. James never says that we are saved by works; he says that our works demonstrate our faith (James 2:18). Similarly, Paul tells us that we are not saved *by* works, we are saved *for* works (Eph. 2:10). Our faith may save us, but if this faith isn't accompanied by a changed life and good works, it isn't true faith. This is why Paul always follows his discussion of salvation with a "therefore," teaching on how we are to live in light of the Gospel. Paul and James are simply describing two sides of the same coin.

Further, this objection that obedience-based discipleship contradicts the doctrine of justification by faith indicates a misunderstanding of the nature of faith. True faith involves three things: *notitia*, or knowledge; *assensus*, or assent; and *fiducia*, or trust. *Notitia* deals with content; we must know what it is that we believe. *Assensus* points to the fact that we have to agree that it is true. For example, it is possible for an atheist to understand Christian theology but not to believe that it is true. That atheist has *notitia* but not *assensus*. But even that is not enough; demons have both *notitia* and *assensus* but they tremble in fear of the truth (James 2:19). What is missing is *fiducia*, which is personal trust and reliance on what is believed. There is no true faith where that kind of trust is missing.

SALVATION FORMULAE			
Traditional Catholicism	**Traditional Protestantism**	**The Gospel of the Self**	**Antinomian Evangelicalism**
Faith + Works = Salvation	Faith = Salvation + Works	Faith = Salvation + Personal Desires (Wealth, Health, Happiness, etc.)	Faith = Salvation

So now we need to expand our understanding of the word *faith* to include not just "believe" but "trust," and for that, we need to turn to the Old Testament. In the Septuagint, the Greek translation of the Old Testament, the same word that is used for "believe" in the New Testament is typically translated as "trust" in the Old Testament. For example, Proverbs 3:5 tells us, "Trust in the Lord with all your heart, and do not lean on your own understanding; in all your ways acknowledge him and he will make your paths straight."

What this tells us is that, if we trust God, if we truly believe Him, we will also accept that what He tells us to do is genuinely what is best for our lives. When our opinion differs from His Word, we are the ones who are wrong—not God. We need to submit to Him, acknowledge Him, and follow His ways even when our reason or our emotions tell us to do something else. To put it differently, faith involves trusting that God loves us enough to tell us the truth about ourselves and the world, and that His instructions on how we are to live are given to us for our own good. If we truly believe that and place our trust in God, we will respond by obeying Him, even when it goes against our desires or what we think makes sense.

This means that every time we fail to obey what God tells us, we proclaim that we don't believe Him or trust Him. We are saying either that He doesn't love us and want what's best, or that we know better than He does about what we should do and how we should live. Just as our faith is demonstrated by our works, so is our unbelief demonstrated by our disobedience.

The Law of Love

These same principles apply to love, as well. A Pharisee asked Jesus which commandment is the greatest, and He replied quoting Deut. 6:4–5: "Hear o Israel, the LORD our God, the LORD is one. You shall love the LORD your God with all your heart and with all your soul and with all your might." The point of this verse is easy to misunderstand today, since we live in a very different historical and cultural context than that of the Israelites. In the ancient Near East, loving one of the pagan gods meant obeying that god. If you did not obey the god, you did not love the god. This is why the passage that Jesus quoted is bracketed in Deuteronomy by commands to obey God and to remember what He has done for the people.

But we do not need to look at Old Testament culture to understand this. All we need to do is look to Jesus' teaching on loving Him:

- "If you love me, you will keep my commandments." (John 14:15)

- "Whoever has my commandments and keeps them, he it is who loves me. (John 14:21)

- And he who loves me will be loved by my Father, and I will love him and manifest myself to him." (John 14:23)

- "If anyone loves me, he will keep my word." (cf. 1 John 5:1–5)

So loving Jesus means obeying Him, whereas not obeying Him means the opposite. It is as simple as that.

> *If you did not obey the god,*
> *you did not love the god.*

In our focus on the greatest commandment, however, we must remember that Jesus' answer is the one that every observant Jew would have recognized. After all, they were supposed to recite that verse several times every day. The real punchline in Jesus' response was what He said about the second commandment. He cited Leviticus 19:18: "Love your neighbor as yourself." Jesus was the first person to highlight this verse; no Jewish commentator before Him focused on it. It is hard to escape the conclusion that this was the point that He really wanted to emphasize, since the greatest commandment was so well known and widely recognized by His audience.

Jesus further emphasized the necessity to love our neighbor in the commandment that He gave His disciples at the Last Supper: "This is my commandment, that you love one another as I have loved you" (John 15:12). Since loving Jesus means obeying His commandments, we are obligated to love our neighbor if we love Jesus. As John reminds us, "If anyone says, 'I love God,' and hates[1] his brother, he is a liar; for he who does not love his brother whom he has seen cannot love God whom he has not seen" (1 John 4:20).

But what does it mean to love our neighbor? Jesus answers this in the parable of the good Samaritan (Luke 10:25–37). In essence, loving our neighbor means taking concrete actions to meet his needs. This is echoed in 1 John 3:17: "But if anyone has the world's goods and sees his brother in need, yet closes his heart against him, how does God's love abide in him?" This parallels the description of true faith in James 2:15–17: "If a brother or sister is poorly clothed and lacking in daily food, and one of you says to them, 'Go in peace, be warmed and filled,' without giving them the things needed for the body, what good is that? So also faith by itself, if it does not have works, is dead."

So love is action more than simply feelings, just as faith means action, not simply intellectual beliefs or emotional experiences. Living in love means living a life of obedience to Jesus and doing good works.

It doesn't matter where we look—in the Old Testament, in the Gospels, in Paul, in James, in John—all point to the centrality of repentance, transformation of life, and obedience as essential to the life of faith.

---

[1] In 1 John, we are not given any middle ground: we either love our brother or we hate him. There are no alternatives.

THE PROTESTANT REFORMATION

These truths of Scripture were recognized by the Protestant Reformers. There were many streams of Protestant thought during the sixteenth century, but nearly all of them agreed on three key ideas which are summarized by three Latin phrases: *sola fide*, we are saved by faith alone; *sola gratia*, we are saved by grace alone; and *sola scriptura*, scripture alone is the final authority on theological matters.[2] Protestants disagreed on pretty much everything else, but if there is a core to Protestant thought, it is found in these three *soli*.

Evangelical and Reformed Christians today quite properly see themselves as the theological heirs of the Reformation; in fact, their thought has more in common with the Reformers than many of the churches that are the institutional descendants of the Reformation. And not surprisingly, evangelical and Reformed Christians today claim to adhere to these three *soli*.

The problem is, though, that too many American Christians do not understand what these three critical doctrines mean. In fact, a lot of evangelicalism misunderstands all three. For present purposes, we need to look briefly at the first two.

Sola fide

Sola fide (by faith alone) is a restatement of a core concept from the Apostle Paul: that we are saved by faith, not works. This is the key argument in several of Paul's epistles, and it is, perhaps, best summed up by Ephesians 2:8–9, "For by grace you have

---

[2] These were articulated in the sixteenth century but not brought together until the early twentieth century. Later in the twentieth century, two other solas were added to the list: *solus Christus*, Christ alone, and *soli Deo Gloria*, glory to God alone.

been saved through faith. And this is not your own doing; it is the gift of God, not a result of works, so that no one may boast."

The Reformers saw this and many other passages in Paul as saying that our sins disqualify us from making any contribution to our own salvation. We are guilty before God, and there is nothing that we can do to atone for that guilt. So what we were powerless to do for ourselves, God did for us by sending Jesus to pay our debt through the Crucifixion and to give us new life through the Resurrection.

Sola gratia

This brings us to the second great *sola* of the Reformation: *sola gratia*, or "by grace alone," we are saved entirely by God's grace. The Greek word for grace (*charis*) refers to gifts from God that we do not deserve. With respect to salvation, it is the "great exchange" whereby our sins are transferred to Christ and his righteousness is transferred to us; He dies for us and we die with Him, and His resurrection confers new life onto us. All of this is accomplished within our hearts by the work of the Holy Spirit.

The major Protestant reformers—Luther, Zwingli, and Calvin—saw grace as not simply providing forgiveness of sins but transforming us to become more and more like Christ. Both of these effects were activated in our life by faith. Grace operating through faith secures our justification and leads to our sanctification, though the Reformers sometimes noted a difference between our passive role in justification and our more active role in doing the "hard work" involved in sanctification.

The essential point here is that the grace that saves is also the grace that leads to inward transformation and holiness of life (Titus 2:11–12). *Sola gratia* properly understood thus covers the whole of salvation, which includes both justification and sanctification, not justification alone. Similarly, sola fide says that we are saved by faith alone, but true faith leads to obedience. In other words, faith results in both justification and good works. This is essentially what James 2:14–25 is saying: our works demonstrate our faith, and if our faith does not result in works, it isn't genuine faith. (Note vs. 18.)

According to the Reformers, then, grace operating through faith was the solution to humanity's ills. It is the answer to the guilt incurred by our sin and the just judgment that we deserve. It is the way back to the life that we were meant to have in our creation: a life of holiness, love, and obedience to God. Grace is the vehicle through which God's holiness, justice, and wrath are reconciled with His love, compassion, and mercy.

And it comes to us at the terrible price of the sacrifice of His own Son.

GETTING IT WRONG

American evangelicals claim *sola fide* and *sola gratia* as part of their theological heritage, but they typically miss the point of it on several levels.

First, the doctrines are anchored in a profound understanding of the absolute, blazing holiness of God and of the depths of human sin. If we even begin to get a grasp of God's absolute holiness, and if we recognize how far short of it we are, then we realize that we have nothing we can offer to God—all that we can do is to trust that Christ's righteousness is credited to us and our sins are placed upon Him in accordance with God's promise. Without understanding this, the full impact of *sola fide* and *sola gratia* is lost.

Unfortunately, the holiness of God is not something that evangelicals tend to emphasize. We like to talk about God's love, grace, even mercy, but not His holiness. Talking about God's unyielding demands sounds so *Old Testament*, and certainly not as if it is closely tied to the Gospel. No, we too often think, God loves us and accepts us as we are, as long as we aren't committing any of the more spectacular sins. No need to deal with my minor peccadilloes (literally, little sins)—God doesn't really care about those!

And then there are the many things our culture accepts that God's Word says are wrong. We often act as if we know so much better than the biblical authors and, since our culture has changed so much, those sins don't really matter, either. Besides, we wouldn't want to be judgmental and tell people what God says about their behavior. That wouldn't be loving! After all, God loves them just the way they are. The common assumption is that culture trumps Scripture.

In truth, *all* sins matter to God. They are offenses to His holiness, and they ruin lives. Not warning people of the damage that their sins cause to themselves and to others is the exact opposite of being truly loving to people. Until we understand our desperate need for forgiveness, until we understand the true moral guilt that we have incurred by our lives, we will never understand what Jesus did for us. We will never understand grace, and we will never understand why *sola fide* is so vitally important.

Second, we delight in the verse that tells us that we aren't under law but under grace (Rom. 6:14). Since we are saved by faith, not works, we think that what we do doesn't really matter much. It is common to think, "I don't need to focus on obedience because, even if I fail, Christ will fill the lack. Given how busy I am, how many responsibilities I have, God will understand if I don't do all the stuff that He tells me to do. After all,

I'm under grace, and doing stuff is all part of the works that I have been set free from in Jesus."

And yet the Reformers understood obedience as an evidence of faith. Even Romans 6:14 is in the context of obedience—avoiding sin and living righteously. As James tells us, faith without works is the kind of faith that the demons have (James 2:19). It won't save you because, if your faith is real, it will inevitably result in a changed life.

Further, Scripture consistently tells us that we are going to be judged on the basis of our works, which include not simply avoiding sin but also taking positive action on behalf of others (Matt. 25:31–46). And that judgment includes believers (1 Cor. 3:12–15). We will be saved, but only as one escaping a fire. We will suffer great loss at the judgment seat of Christ if we are not building our lives right.

Jesus' own warning about the judgment is even sterner. Many who think that they are saved because of the great visible things they did in Jesus' name will be rejected as lawless ones whom Jesus never knew (Matt. 7:21–23).

Sola gratia and *sola fide* should lead us to delight in God's law, to obey all that Jesus commanded, and to live a life full of love and good works. True faith implies nothing less. And that is precisely what too many churches are not teaching.

Where does this leave Evangelicals today?

Many evangelical and Pentecostal churches fall into the trap of preaching a version of the Prosperity Gospel, which says that God wants to bless us in every way, particularly by improving our lives in this world through making us healthy and wealthy. This is a heresy, which sometimes leads to gross abuse of the poor,[3] and it completely ignores Jesus' teachings about taking up our cross and the inevitability of persecution. If the Prosperity Gospel were true, why did the martyrs of the Church Universal—including the Apostles—end up being tortured and killed if they could have "spoken health and prosperity into their lives?" What does the Prosperity Gospel say about our persecuted brethren in the Middle East, or North Korea, or Nigeria?

Another popular American heresy is the Therapeutic Gospel. This is predicated on the idea that Christianity is there to make you feel better about yourself and even about your actions. Sermons are reduced to feel-good homilies or pop self-help advice. Its focus is on affirming people and accepting them where they are. Uncomfortable topics, such as abortion and other types of sin, are avoided because we don't want to turn people off or make them feel uncomfortable or unwelcome. After all, we assume, people have enough stress and negativity in their lives without encountering it in church.

However, this merges easily into Moralistic Therapeutic Deism, the *de facto* religion of a significant percentage of Millennials. Moralistic Therapeutic Deism holds that the purpose of life is to be happy and to feel good about ourselves. Having fun is a core value for many Millennials. God created and watches over the world, but He is uninvolved in our lives—except when He is needed to solve problems.

In reality, Moralistic Therapeutic Deism, the Prosperity Gospel, and the Therapeutic Gospel are all variations of the

---

3   Through the "law of sowing and reaping," they argue that to become wealthy you have to "sow" money into a worthwhile cause, which generally means their ministry. Thus, you find people flying private jets to impoverished areas to preach their message and to encourage the poor to give to them.

same heresy, which can best be described as the Gospel of the Self. Ultimately, this sees Christianity as fundamentally being about "me, me, me." The Gospel is a means to get what *I* want—whether better health, more money, or self-esteem—not to be transformed by Christ into what *He* wants me to be.

This is no different from H. Richard Niebuhr's description of liberal theology: "A God without wrath brought people without sin into a kingdom without judgment through the ministrations of a Christ without a cross." We offer what Dietrich Bonhoeffer called cheap grace by preaching an undemanding Gospel, with no emphasis on the necessity for repentance and change in the fundamental principles by which we govern our lives:

> Cheap grace means the justification of sin without the justification of the sinner. Grace alone does everything they say, and so everything can remain as it was before. "All for sin could not atone." Well, then, let the Christian live like the rest of the world, let him model himself on the world's standards in every sphere of life, and not presumptuously aspire to live a different life under grace from his old life under sin . . . .
>
> Cheap grace is the grace we bestow on ourselves. Cheap grace is the preaching of forgiveness without requiring repentance, baptism without church discipline, Communion without confession. . . . Cheap grace is grace without discipleship, grace without the cross, grace without Jesus Christ, living and incarnate.

Cheap grace isn't real grace. It isn't the grace of the Reformers, of the historic church, or of the Bible. It isn't the Gospel that Jesus taught, which included warnings to count the cost of following Him. Jesus told us that we would have trouble and be persecuted, and He demanded that we lay down our lives for Him.

This "grace" won't save you and won't bring about the Kingdom because it isn't the Gospel.

ONE MISSIONARY AGENCY PRESIDENT'S JOURNEY

When you meet Doug Lucas, you might not realize that he is the president of Team Expansion, a mission agency of approximately 300 missionaries around the globe. Jerry was asked to speak at a Team Expansion meeting some time back, and he thought that Doug was simply the guy who played piano with the worship team—he definitely does not push himself center stage.

About five years ago, Doug invited all of Team Expansion's missionaries to take training for a new ministry model, which we know as Disciple Making Movements.

Doug sought information and help from several streams of movements, from other leaders whose stories you will read in this book. And in record time, Team Expansion has begun to see some remarkable breakthroughs and momentum in surprising places. And without pressuring existing missionaries who were trained to do traditional ministry, about 80% of Team Expansion's missionaries have now transitioned to Disciple Making Movement ministry models.

We asked Doug if he could identify the reasons that Team Expansion has been able to relatively quickly see so much success in transitioning from traditional missions to Disciple Making Movements.

I would say, one of the really helpful factors down through the years for Team Expansion is that we have never been a very top-down, dictatorial kind of organization. We've always extended a tone of freedom to each team. But that's not the core of the reason, I don't think.

First: A Lot of Prayer

We have indeed bathed this with a lot of prayer, and so that's got to be a factor. If someone says, "Okay, our team wants to try this out," we don't even let them get started unless they commit to praying an hour a day each morning before they hit the road. We also invest in prayer at headquarters, 30 minutes every morning in prayer, and then a day each month in fasting and prayer.

Second: Patience with People

We've never said: "Look, If you don't want to convert to this approach, then I'm sorry, there's no place for you in the organization." We've been extremely patient. And there are leaders of our teams who are still kind of dragging their feet, and we don't make them feel like they're disenfranchised. We just keep on organizing trainings, we keep on sharing the case studies and the stories, with the anticipation that sooner or later, they will come along and want to embrace this.

Ghana Case Study: Our team of Terry and Amy in Ghana, has really helped us. They decided to adopt this in 2013 after nine years in Ghana. They were trained in July 2014, and were hooked and immediately started implementing this. So, we kept up on their outcomes, and basically just made those statistics known. By the time they got to February of 2016, they were at 324 baptisms.

They had been there for nine years and had around thirty baptisms. Now we are at twenty-eight months into their experience and now they have 650 baptisms with 187 groups with an average attendance of more than 2,000 people. They are working with eleven different, unreached people groups, 10 of which are unreached Muslim people groups.

Everybody knew Terry and Amy and when they heard how this lovely couple was having this success they started saying: "Well, could the same thing happen to us in our area?" Then our leaders would gather together and talk about what was happening with Terry and Amy, a winsome and friendly couple, and that just created more encouragement.

Taiwan and North Africa are other areas where new momentum observed has created even more momentum.

Third, Leadership Accountability to Make Disciples

There's been a profound change in the way that our team leads. For twenty-five years, we sort of led vicariously. We thought that, as a group of leaders, we could lead by coaching and holding others accountable, by giving feedback to our field workers. Vicariously we were involved in the Great Commission because we worked in a missionary institute.

And that's the way we were living our lives for those first 25 years. I think what Disciple Making Movement principles have done to us, as a leadership, is that they've helped us to understand that none of us is exempt. We all have to be involved in doing this.

And so, I had to self-analyze in my life and ask myself, "How will this impact me?" So I started doing prayer walking in my home area of Louisville, searching for Afghan refugees that I could start working with. I started working with the guys I was playing soccer with on Wednesdays, and trying to figure out, "How do I invite those guys to a group?"

How do I get this Somali guy to come and tell his story so that, in turn, we can tell him our story? How do I start viewing myself as a personal trainer in this, not just a president of an organization?

I had to start grappling with these things myself as a leader, because I was not doing it before. I was just acting as an organizational administrator. I had to start finding ways that I could personally be involved in all of this, because if I didn't, it didn't make sense to the people we were training. It didn't have credibility. "Why does he opt out just because he's an administrator?" Everybody has to be involved in it.

I had to construct models for what all this would look like, so I went to the Bible college I attended. I asked the college, "Would you want us to come in and train a small group of your students to operate in the background as disciple-makers who would have a plan for disciple making the rest of the students of the college?" And they said, "We would *love* for this to happen, because we think it might help us emphasize missions."

So, we did. They got us twelve students, and we went in and trained those twelve students. About six of them have fallen by the wayside, because they say they're too busy, which is about what we encounter in any situation. The other six have just finished multiplying into their second generation, and soon they will start their third generation of groups.

I just went over for a second-level training with them, and will keep on going, kind of re-encouraging them, and by the year's end, with reproducing and multiplication, they could easily have 500 students involved, and it's a college of about 600. So it could have a profound impact on making obedient disciples at that college.

DEPENDING ON CHRISTIAN INSTITUTIONS THAT CAN'T MULTIPLY

I Just Want to See Your Kingdom, No Matter What!

INTERVIEW WITH DAVID PARISH

David Parish was the senior pastor at a large church, the director of a Christian school, and the president of a mission agency. In 2003, his mission agency was planting between twenty and thirty churches a year, but David was worried that "one and done" was less than satisfactory. His church was very large, but it seemed to have plateaued. It was time to seriously seek God's counsel. On February 19, 2004, he took a walk in a park where he liked to walk and pray.

I was walking on the trail, praying, just crying out to God. And in that encounter with God, there was a Kingdom of God moment when I said to God: I'm tired of just pressing our church and our agenda and trying to build our organization. I want to see your Kingdom. No matter what. It doesn't have to be our group. I just want to be a part of advancing your Kingdom.

Lord, you can have your church—you can have it back. Because, up to that point, it was kind of my church, and I was focused on my own plans for it. So I prayed, "Lord you can have it. Let it work for the advancement of the Kingdom."

It was a defining moment and, instantly, I knew that something was going to change—though I didn't know exactly what. As time went on, over the next year, I kept praying "Lord, what is it? What's got to change?" I knew He wanted to show me something, but I still didn't get it! I did a lot of praying. It seemed like the Holy Spirit said to me, over and over, "Wait for the open door." For months, I tried all kinds of prayers and He would keep saying, "Wait for the open door!"

I knew that the Lord had asked me to finish a number of things. In preparation, I finished all of the things that I needed to complete: in the church, in my own life, in a graduate degree, and it was all done. I completed everything. I had no more vision for the church. Once I had been a visionary leader, but now all I knew to do was just bring messages from the Word, not knowing what else to do.

Then, in June of 2005, my wife and daughter went out one day and I had the house to myself. So I went to my study and I started praying—it was an unusually strong prayer. No one could hear me, so I was free to pray my heart. I began to cry out to God and all of a sudden, I thought about the "open door." Then I prayed, "God, I don't care the cost, if I have to give up everything, my life, whatever, show me what the door is."

And when I said those words, as clear as I know how to listen to the Holy Spirit, I got the oddest thought: *Go turn on your computer and find a Perspectives on the World Christian Movement.* I had heard of it but never taken the course. I had a copy of the book but had not read it. So I googled "Perspectives Tennessee" and discovered a three-week intensive class that started the next week in Nashville. I made the phone call and registered.

Over the next weeks, I drove hours to Nashville every day to take a three-hour class and drive home. On the fourth day Jerry Trousdale was teaching the class and talking about what God was beginning to do in Africa, through movements. I realized that Jerry knew these movements firsthand—he was the first person who had given me answers to my questions about Kingdom multiplication. I had actually heard an answer to my yearlong prayer. God was finally giving me some clear direction.

This began a cascade of activity for David, as he began researching what God was doing in Africa, seeking out training courses in disciple-making, and so on. He had already spent many months in intensive, persistent prayer, and now he was called upon to make some significant time sacrifices, as well. He and one of his missionaries named Randy Travis attended a Disciple-Making training with David Watson. They travelled to Africa to see the movements that were beginning to multiply there, and David asked Hassan (from chapter one) to come to his church and teach them about prayer and disciple-making.

Meanwhile, Randy and his son Keith returned to Honduras to introduce Disciple-Making Movements to the existing churches that they had previously planted. He contacted his church plants and asked them to try a new approach to making disciples. Thirteen leaders agreed to give one year to see what God might do. They developed compassion ministries to demonstrate God's love, and they also launched Discovery Bible Studies.

In six months at the end of 2008, there were twenty-five new Bible studies—but nothing was multiplying. And they remained stuck. Eventually David Watson and Paul Watson went to Honduras to see how Randy and Keith were doing. He quickly saw that most of those thirteen leaders were teaching the Bible studies themselves, instead of facilitating a discovery Bible process. They didn't trust that lost people could discover the Bible and obey it without some mature Christian oversight. So they imparted their knowledge, but the groups did not get the excitement of discovering truth and choosing to obey it personally. There was no transformation—and, therefore, no replication.

Only three of the thirteen disciple makers were willing to stop teaching and see how discovery might work. And it turned out that those three pastors were enough—with God's help. Disciples made disciples, and churches planted churches. And suddenly the door was thrown wide open!

David's years of waiting have been redeemed with wonderful fruit. In March 2014, there were 545 churches and groups in Honduras, but as this book goes to press in early 2018 the movements are spreading with a total of 7,595 churches and groups to eighteen generations. And every day an average of seven new groups form, and twenty-two people are baptized into Christ. As you would expect David notes in all his reports that these outcomes cannot be explained as the work of anyone, except God's Holy Spirit.

In that same spirit David also urges every one of his team members to freely give away everything God has taught them about Kingdom movements. This includes everything that they have learned about mentoring and disciple-making. Thus far, they have trained, coached, and mentored fifty other ministries and denominations, and together they are forming a network that is planting churches in Honduras and now spreading into other countries in Central America, the Caribbean, and South America.

"When I prayed that prayer those years ago for the open door," David reflects, "I could not even have dreamed about this. Nothing we have done can account for this level of harvest. That's what tells me that God is doing this. I think I'm more in awe of God now than I have ever been. And we want to see more! We don't want to see just 7,500 groups and churches, we want to see 100,000. We don't want to just see Honduras; we want to see all of Latin America. We want to see God bring closure on the Great Commission in Latin America."

THE CONTINUUM OF MOVEMENTS TO INSTITUTIONS

David Parish's story gives us a window to begin to understand the structural barriers, which typically hinder movements in the Global North: an institutionalized approach to the church that makes it difficult for movements to start.

Institutions are not in themselves bad. They provide a framework for training leaders, organizing activities, planning and strategizing, developing resources, and a host of other functions to support movements. However, institutions sometimes develop in such a way that they become ends in themselves and lose the essential elements needed to sustain growth.

Timothy Keller in his book *Serving a Movement* discusses the challenges:

> I am not suggesting simplistically that movements are good and institutions are bad—rather, that organizations should have both institutional characteristics and movement dynamics, though there are some tensions and trade-offs in the balance.

Citing the work of Hugh Heclo, Keller suggests four key characteristics of a movement:[1]

1. **Movements are marked by a compelling vision.** The key to the success of the vision is its simplicity and availability, often in the form of content that transmits, expounds, and applies the vision. Institutions, on the other hand, are defined by a statement of purpose and are held together through rules and procedures.

2. **The unifying vision in a movement is so compelling that it leads to a culture of sacrificial commitment and intrinsic rewards.** Individuals put the vision ahead of their own interests and comfort. In institutions, individuals have carefully defined rights, responsibilities, and compensation, with external, measurable standards for determining success and failure.

3. **Movements are characterized by a stance of generous flexibility toward other organizations and people outside their own membership rolls.** The vision encourages sacrifice, and members of a movement are willing to make allies, cooperating with anyone who shares an interest in the vision. Institutionalized organizations on the other hand, are more committed to the importance of inherited practices, right procedures, and accredited persons.

4. **Movements spontaneously produce new ideas and leaders and grow from within.** Institutions by their nature are structured for long-term durability and stability and are prone to resist risky new ideas.

---

[1] Tim Keller, *Serving a Movement* (Grand Rapids, Mich.: Zondervan, 2016), 195–199.

Of course, some institutional functions will always be critical in a viral movement. But when the institutional functions begin to take over, movements can die. Characteristics of institutionalization in the context of movements include such things as non-reproducible and non-scalable practices, professionalization, and more concern about doctrinal correctness than practical obedience. We will explore these further in later chapters. Whenever institutions are allowed to dominate the dynamics there will never be a "critical mass" for even a small movement.

If, however, institutional functions serve the movement rather than serving themselves, the problems of institutionalization can be avoided.

Some missions strategists have attempted to define the lifecycle of movements, though in practice they have identified less the stages of movements as the stages in institutionalizing of churches planted among unreached peoples. They define four phases in this process:[2]

1. Unreached Phase. Outsiders enter an area and lead people to faith. There are relatively few Christians, liturgical structures are informal, and churches meet in homes, under trees, in storefronts, etc. If this work is to grow into a movement, the concept of the priesthood of all believers must be stressed, so that the people understand that they can go directly to God and can engage in the priestly work of evangelism and ministering to others. Leadership is developed informally, mainly through mentoring.

2. Movement Phase. In this stage, outside missionaries are replaced by empowered indigenous believers, resulting in dramatic growth. Liturgical structures remain simple. Networks

---

2   Steve Smith, Neill Mims, and Mark Steves, "Four Stages of a Movement," *Mission Frontiers* (Nov/Dec 2015): 38–40.

of local leaders develop, and those leaders with more responsibility get further on-site training. This is the period of fastest growth.

3. Formalizing (or Established) Phase. The churches begin to standardize some elements of the movement. Brick-and-mortar churches are built, though informal churches also continue. Leadership training also becomes more formalized and more systematic. Credentialing develops, and gifted leaders begin to stand out. Professional leadership gradually replaces lay pastoral leadership. At the same time, the laity is increasingly intimidated by the professional leaders and, since the laity do not have the credentials, they begin to step away from ministry, leaving it in the hands of the professionals. The clergy/laity divide had been negligible up to this point, but now it becomes sharper.

4. Institutional Phase. Formalizing reaches its logical conclusion. There are lots of churches, mostly purpose-built, and Christians are accepted in society. Leadership training is done in institutions—seminaries and Bible schools—and most leaders are full- or part-time. There is minimal lay leadership, and it is difficult to motivate the laity for ministry. For example, lay people bring unsaved friends to church rather than evangelizing them themselves. Growth typically plateaus.

Problems occur when missionaries from Institutional Phase churches attempt evangelism in an unreached environment; they want to reproduce what they are familiar with, resulting in very slow growth. One missionary in sub-Saharan Africa found that it took an average of twenty-two years to plant one Institutional Phase church in an Unreached Phase environment. Leadership development is also envisioned along institutional lines; there is no one with the "right" credentials among the indigenous people, despite there being leaders who fit the biblical criteria.

	Evangelism	Liturgical Structures	Meeting Place	Leaders	Laity
Unreached Phase	Outsiders	Informal	Informal	Developed through mentoring	Emphasize priesthood of all believers
Movement Phase	Indigenous people	Informal	Informal	Leadership networks develop; training done on the ground	Emphasize priesthood of all believers
Formalizing Phase	Indigenous people	Becoming formalized	Some purpose-built churches	Credentialing Professionals replace lay leaders	Begin to step away from ministry; divide with clergy grows
Institutional Phase	In churches	Fully Institutional	Purpose-built churches	Institutionalized training full- or part-time professionals	Minimal lay leadership Difficult to motivate for ministry

Similarly, when Institutional Phase leaders go to Movement Phase areas, they may respond in one of several different ways. They may dismiss what is happening. They assume that house churches aren't "real" churches; they dismiss their leaders because they lack qualifications; they don't understand the concept of every believer being a disciple-maker and potential church planter, etc.

Alternately, they may get excited about it and offer to invest resources into the movement. They may consolidate simple churches into a single large church, or provide salaries for leaders, or build church buildings. Any of these actions will prove fatal to the movement, however, as shown by experience in Africa. For the movement to continue, it needs to be scalable and replicable by indigenous believers; outside investment is neither, and as a result, these well intentioned efforts end up killing the movement's momentum.

Elephant churches are large and reproduce slowly. Rabbit churches are small, agile and reproduce very quickly.

A parallel problem can occur when Movement Phase believers encounter Institutional Phase churches: they are often awed and inspired by the buildings, institutions, and gifted leaders, and they want the same for themselves. When they try to transplant these things, however, they kill the progress of the movement because this type of institution is not organic, nor is it easily reproducible in their local context.

However, there has proven to be a surprisingly successful model in Africa, one where a denomination develops a two-track ministry: they can continue their work while at the same time allowing the movement churches to keep growing on their own in loose affiliation with the denomination. This process can also occur in reverse. When an Institutional Phase church wants to shift toward movements, the best strategy may well be developing a parallel track or even a separate ministry altogether.

Whether movement churches will sustain momentum as well over the long term as they would have if they had remained completely independent remains to be seen, but overall, this a viable approach for Institutional Phase organizations to engage with movements in the Global South.

NEW HYBRID STRUCTURES IN THE GLOBAL SOUTH THAT ARE EMERGING TO SUPPORT MOVEMENTS

In the DMM world, churches are described as either "elephant churches" or "rabbit churches." Elephant churches are large and reproduce slowly. Rabbit churches are small, agile and reproduce very quickly. Most DMM churches are rabbit churches, but some have grown to the point that they look like elephant churches, though they continue to have rabbit DNA.

We are now seeing some Kingdom Movements that are more than twenty years old, and even more that are more than thirteen years old. Each has created its own organic structure to facilitate all phases of Kingdom-centric ministry values and outcomes, with institutional support systems. They are recognizable as churches or ministries, often both, but they all have a very distinct Kingdom DNA and exist to launch and support Kingdom movements. The functions of sending, sowing, accessing, disciple-making, leadership training, research, and apostolic sending exist within the same structure.

THE CHALLENGE FOR THE GLOBAL NORTH IS VERY REAL

The reality of the rapid spread of Kingdom Movements creates both excitement and stress for Global North ministries and churches. When Global North Christian leaders experience Kingdom Movements personally, within a few days we realize that we will probably have to figure out how to be part of what God is doing, or just abandon the idea because the whole reality is so very different from our worldview assumptions, our paradigms, and our expected outcomes.

Some leaders changed direction years ago because they were hungry for something they had never experienced.

David Parish's story is one example of this. He led a very successful Institutional Phase ministry with a successful church, school, and mission agency, but he found that needed to completely retool before movements could begin. Producing more Institutional Phase churches could not generate a movement since they simply do not multiply naturally. David had to pay the price of letting go of his church and his school in order to make the transition to a replicating, reproducing ministry.

David remembers, "I felt it was time to say to the church, I'm going in this direction of disciple-making ministries, so I think you need different leadership. We took a year to transition, to make it as easy on everyone as possible. I had seen transitions happen where people were hurt, so I wanted to avoid that, transitioning in honor."

It took several years to see any results, but he is now seeing a harvest beyond his imagination.

DAVID BROODRYK'S STORY

David Broodryk planted a church in South Africa in 2004. Over the next seven years, the church grew to about 100 members, but David realized that the church he planted wasn't advancing the Kingdom the way that he thought it should. He began to transition away from traditional ministry to a DMM model. He tried to take his church along with him over a one-year transition but lost sixty percent of his members. David reflects,

> I went to the whole church, I went to at least all the big givers in the church, and I said to them, "I want to change our contract." And they said, "What do you mean—we don't have a contract." And I said, "Yes we do. The contract is, I serve you and you pay my salary. I want to change that contract. I want to write a new contract: I serve others—not just you, but others too—and you still pay my salary. Are you prepared to do it?" So I had to make that very clear, moving from traditional ministry to where we were going, was a significant shift. That I was asking them to finance something that they would not see a return on.

Fortunately, enough members agreed to support him that he could begin a major transition in his ministry. Without any clear models, he came to believe that his job needed to change. If movements were going to start, they could not depend just on him, since he was only one person who could only be in one place at one time. Instead, he needed to think of himself more as a catalyst than as a pastor and teacher.

This was difficult for him on a variety of levels. His friends in seminary thought he was crazy and rejected him. His ministry reputation was shot. And then there was the even more personal stress that the change caused.

I would say that the biggest issue for us was identity. I'll never forget the lesson that the Lord taught us on identity through that journey. We took a year to close that church, and we closed it, and my wife went into a deep depression and I completely lost my way. I would sit and stare at my computer for hours looking for a solution—actually, we were both very depressed for nine months. I lost all energy, all zeal. I started complaining, I said, "God, we are doing what you told us to, and it is worse than it ever was!" It was a very dark, dark, time—dark night of the soul, I suppose you can call it.

I will never forget, nine months after we did that, Michelle and I were sitting on the veranda having tea, and we started talking about this, kind of complaining, "things are worse than they ever have been, we don't have money and we don't have the people"—and it was like something happened in our conversation, both of us came to the instant realization that our whole identity had been ripped out from under us—and, more significantly, we suddenly recognized that our identity was falsely placed. Our identity had been that we were a pastor and his wife, and it wasn't just what we did—it was who we *were*. And we had literally given that up, God had ripped it out from under us.

It was actually very remarkable, because within five minutes of realizing this, the Lord shifted us and we realized that our identity needed to be in Him, not in the work we do, not in the ministry. It was an instant lifting of Michelle's depression. I woke up the next morning and started booking airline tickets to go and plant new churches where for nine months I hadn't been able to.

Since then, David has been a catalyst for movements in Africa, Russia, Europe, and North and South America, influencing more than 100,000 people and over 200 organizations. He has been responsible for developing DMM strategies and training material for urban areas and has been a DMM trainer and mentor around the world.

THE FORMULA FOR CHANGE

What would motivate our two Davids to take such enormous risks to their ministries? They both moved to a radically different paradigm for ministry, one that violated everything that they had been taught and had ever experienced, replacing them with strategies that were seen as unproven, controversial— maybe even fraudulent (according to skeptics, at least). Students of organizational behavior use a *Formula for Change* that was developed by David Gleicher and refined by Kathie Dannemiller to look at the factors that lead to successful organizational change. The Formula is:

D x V x F > R

D refers to *dissatisfaction* with the status quo; *V* refers to *vision* of what is possible; and *F* refers to the *first concrete steps* that can be taken toward the vision. These multiplied together must be greater than *R*, the *resistance to change*.

To these, we should add another element: courageous leadership. All change comes through committed leadership, and it always takes courage, especially change in the context of ministry. History, tradition, established practice, priorities, doctrinal specifics, polity, and a host of other factors can create opposition to change within an organization, and that doesn't even touch on external resistance and spiritual warfare. As we continue through the book, pay attention to the stories and note the courage that it took for these leaders to catalyze movements.

With both David Parish and David Broodryk, there was strong dissatisfaction with the state of their ministry (the *D* in the formula). The dissatisfaction in both cases related to a vision of the Kingdom advancing with power in the world, something that they saw in Scripture but did not see enough within their ministries.

Parish sees three common responses to God:

First: My Needs

A lot of people just live at the level of their own needs and desires. God meets my needs—I can be healed by God—and I am saved. Indeed, God invites us to let Him meet our needs—but many Christians never get beyond that.

Second: My Ministry

Some Christians settle for a mentality of "this is my ministry," my church, my organization. And that is where some church growth theories end. There are certainly some good things about finding our gifts and developing ourselves to serve better, and they can be used for the Kingdom of God—but the key is that we must rise to the level of a Kingdom mentality. Our focus must be on building the *Kingdom*, not building our *ministry*.

Third: It's About the Kingdom of God

This is the place where Christians ask the question: What is it going to take to see God's Kingdom come into this place? When we start asking that question—and are willing to go wherever the answer leads—that is when we will see Kingdom fruitfulness. Then we can start using the principles and strategies that we are learning because, in God's Kingdom, we constantly recognize and acknowledge the sovereignty of God. We remember that it is *God's* Kingdom, not *our* kingdom, and we understand that He is the One who will make the growth happen. In the Global North and especially in America, our admiration for strong leadership, competitive spirit, and hands-on attitude makes this extraordinarily difficult: we want to build our brand,

and we want to run things our way. But if we try to do this in a movement, we choke off the growth.

Along with their *dissatisfaction* and *vision*, both Davids also found concrete *first steps* that they could take (the F in the formula), which then led them into a totally new direction that eventually bore fruit.

The *resistance* that they had to overcome (R in the formula) came from several sources, most of which were connected to expectations and assumptions that are common within Stage 4 ministries. Denominational structures, ecclesiastical and theological traditions, habits, models of ministry, and a host of other institutional elements *resist* change, especially when it is as radical as those required by movements. And there are also the kinds of worldview issues that form a barrier against movements—*resistance* in our thinking—that have been discussed in the previous chapters. And on a personal level, their friends from seminary, colleagues, denominations—even their own churches—*resisted* the new direction. DMM violated everything that they had been taught about ministry.

Further, as David Broodryk points out, it also violated their identity as pastors, since they would no longer be the people *doing* the ministry, but catalysts for *others to do it*. He puts it this way:

I really do think that entry into DMM is a death experience: unless the seed falls to the ground and dies, it can bear no fruit. It's a death experience, a complete shift to change to the DMM approach. But the problem is, you can't risk failure without that; risking failure in itself is a sort of death experience.

If who you are is dependent on whether this thing works or fails, then you will never take a risk, you'll never do it. But if your identity is in Christ, then you say, "I'm going to try this; if it works, great, He gets the glory; and if it doesn't work—well, it didn't work, but I am still secure in who I am in Him."

Most leaders haven't done that, they are not secure in who they are in Him. Their security is based on the success or failure of what they do. And then that thinking makes you unwilling to take any risks. You also become afraid to give everything away without expecting anything in return. You become trapped by protecting your reputation—but DMM demands all those things. You are no longer building your reputation, you're not building your income, your business, you aren't building fame, not any of those things. You might plant 100,000 churches, but still nobody knows your name.

This is not going to work, it's not going to fly if your identity is in the *ministry*, if your identity is not firmly rooted in *Christ*. But when you root your identity in Him, then you can plant a million churches and no one knows your name and no one cares—and it's not a problem. This is an extremely core issue. It is very significant for us.

Jesus tells us that unless a grain of wheat falls into the ground and dies, it can bear no fruit (John 12:24). The resistance to DMM is found in this verse, because it is very difficult to let your identity, your reputation, even your own ministry, die. But if you have a Kingdom vision, if you know that it isn't *your* ministry but God's, it becomes possible to let go of your goals to receive His.

INSTITUTIONAL PHASE MINISTRIES AND MOVEMENTS

The institutional church has been beaten up quite a bit over the last few decades for being too rigid, out of touch, and ineffective.

While some of the criticisms have validity, it is important to recognize that Institutional Phase ministries contribute a great deal to the Kingdom. For example, without these institutions, we do not get substantial biblical scholarship, theological development, apologetics, worldview training, and the like. Institutional Phase churches also frequently help stock food banks, run soup kitchens, collect clothing for the needy, supply volunteers to homeless shelters, and perform other services to their communities.

The truth is, though, they are **not** good incubators for movements. However, this does not mean that an Institutional Phase ministry cannot change. Francis, whom we met in chapter 2, started a Discovery group about eight years ago that emerged as a church. As of this writing, that church is constructing a 1,000-seat sanctuary, funded entirely by the African community. It is a fully indigenous church that is now clearly in the Formalizing Phase or perhaps even the Institutional Phase. Yet it does not operate like churches in the Global North. Instead, it sees itself as an equipping center, preparing its people to pray, to engage in spiritual warfare, to start Discovery Groups, and to plant churches. Francis says the growing church is becoming an elephant church but with the DNA of a rabbit church. It will be a training center and a sending center while it also becomes a significant center of prayer, healing, and restoration for the local urban community. In this way, this large church will continue to catalyze momentum in both Unreached and Movement Phases even as it has some elements of the Formalizing Phase. However, it is unlikely that Francis's growing church will ever become an Institutional Phase church as described in the chart above.

The church in the Global South is much closer to the Unreached and Movement Phases chronologically than the churches of the Global North, most of which have been in the Institutional Phase for centuries. It is thus simpler for Francis to build movement DNA into his church than it is for Global North churches. In other words, those Christians continue to operate in the Movement Phase simply because it is still their experience and their DNA. They may have some complex structures but *they have never abandoned the goal of making disciples who make disciples and planting churches that plant churches.*

When we change our paradigm for ministry, we must of necessity change our practices, as well.

Transforming Institutional Phase churches in the Global North is a much slower process, however, because the believers in those churches have always been members of institutional churches; they don't have the immediate experience of the Unreached or Movement phases, which the church in the Global South enjoys. Therefore, such change has to be done with a great deal of care and sensitivity so as not to leave the congregation or the leadership behind.

It is more difficult—but it can be done. And it is not only possible to make this transition—it is essential if the Global North is going to see the kind of dynamic movements that we see in the Global South. The *dissatisfaction* and the *vision* must be strong enough, and the *first steps* must be clear enough to overcome *resistance* and inertia.

In the rest of this book, we will look at what some of those *first steps* are. When we change our paradigm for ministry, we must of necessity change our practices, as well. Before we do so, however, we will examine Jesus' paradigm for ministry and the instructions that He gave for disciple-making. This is the biblical foundation for DMM and the source of many of the practices associated with it.

WHAT IN JESUS' NAME IS A CHRISTIAN TO DO?

CHAPTER
7

WHAT JESUS DID . . . HIS DISCIPLES STILL DO

Jerry recently had the opportunity to spend time with a group of disciple makers who live in a dangerous area. They are not free to worship Jesus openly, so they have devised methods of worshiping and praying together secretly—yet at the same time, in the open. They also cannot openly possess Bibles and consequently are forced to memorize as much as they can, allowing them to "carry" the Word within. They had invited Jerry to join them at a retreat in an area where it was safe to meet, asking him to share some principles of the Kingdom of God as it relates to making disciples. Jerry started by asking them to close their Bibles and answer questions only from memory.

"Tell me about John the Baptist," Jerry began. "What was his message?"

"Repent and be baptized," they answered in unison without hesitation.

"And what happened next?" Jerry asked.

"Jesus came to him to be baptized," they continued.

"And what happened next?"

"Jesus fasted and prayed."

"And next?"

"Jesus went into the wilderness to be tested by the devil."

And thus it continued, Jerry leading them to remember their way through the Gospel accounts of Jesus' life and into the book of Acts. Jerry was amazed that they knew every passage by heart.

But after a little while, Jerry began to notice a subtle but growing change coming over the men and women in the group. They were becoming more excited and more animated with almost every passage about Jesus and the Kingdom. And when the session was over, every one of them jumped up and began shouting and thanking the Lord. They were clapping and laughing and rejoicing, and they continued to praise God with unbound celebrations.

Later that evening, Jerry had the chance to ask one of the English-speakers what had happened. "We finally got it!" the man exclaimed. "As you walked us through the scriptures, it was like a light slowly came on—and we began to understand: It is the Kingdom of God. What Jesus did, He wants us to do. We all knew all of the passages, but we have never seen the connection between them!"

Those men and women had an "aha" moment concerning the Kingdom of God during this session with Jerry. They knew the Bible, but somehow they had not made the connection between His Kingdom and their own country. It was almost as though the Kingdom had been hiding in plain sight.

The best part? This story is not an isolated one. These holy brothers and sisters are not the only ones to have experienced that glorious "aha" moment in unison by reviewing what was already on their hearts.

DAVID AND JAN WATSON

David and Jan Watson were missionaries to South Asia working out of Hong Kong. They were asked by their sending agency to begin a pilot project in northern India. Six young Christian workers whom David had trained and recruited to join in his work in India were martyred in an eighteen-month period. Jan tells us about this terrible time in their lives:

I watched David grieve over those young men—and I grieved over them with him. Now we know that this was at the beginning of a work, but I thought we had seen the end of it. We weren't really sure how it was going to turn out. But as I watched David struggle with it, he prayed that God would take away the call to overseas missions work—he prayed that fervently! I was praying that, whatever God wanted us to do, He would make it clear. And at some point, David realized that God was not going to take away the call. And that's when he began to pray: "God, please show me how to do this, you've got to have a better way to do it than this, sending people in to die."

Then David started searching the Scriptures for guidance on how we should proceed. He did that for several months. Then one day, God gave him what he'd been praying for.

I remember the day—we were homeschooling the children and we were together in one room. And David opened the door, and he said: "It's here, and it's been here all along. It's simply what *Jesus did* in making disciples!" He was so excited with the Scripture, and we sat down and read it together, and he was convinced that we were going to see a difference. And I was excited that he was excited, and more confident that he had found the path to get into groups— and that path was hidden in plain sight!

This is the passage that David read which changed his life and ministry:[1]

> "Stop grumbling among yourselves," Jesus answered. "No one can come to me unless the Father who sent me draws them, and I will raise them up at the last day. It is written in the Prophets: 'They will all be taught by God.' Everyone who has heard the Father and learned from him comes to me." (John 6:43–45, NIV)

The idea that no one could come to the Father unless He drew them to Himself caught David's attention. He began looking in the Gospels for ways God drew people to Himself. That led David to Luke 10 and Matthew 10, and ultimately through all of Jesus' teachings about the Kingdom and disciple-making— and he discovered that the answers to his questions had been right in front of him all along.

David discovered the centrality of the Kingdom in a new way, as well as a radically different approach to disciple making in light of the Kingdom. A brief survey of the Kingdom in the Gospels will highlight the main points.

PRELUDE TO JESUS' MINISTRY

The essence of John the Baptist's message was simply "repent, for the Kingdom of Heaven is near" (Matt. 3:2). There is a lot buried in that short statement. As we have seen, a kingdom (Greek *basileia*) is not a geographical location, rather a

---

[1] Luke 9 and Mark 6 were also important passages.

deliberate acknowledgment of royal authority. John tells us that the Kingdom of Heaven is near, and this brings us to his call to action: repent!

Repentance (Greek *metanoia*) refers to a complete change in how we think and thus in how we act, generally accompanied by sorrow and remorse for the previous orientation of our lives. The point here is stark. Everything in the physical Universe does exactly what God made it to do—everything, that is, except humanity. Human beings have moved away from Him to such an extent that the very nearness of His Kingdom requires an urgent call to change our entire outlook and mode of living. We need to turn away from our disobedience and reorient our thinking and lifestyle to align with obedience to God if we are to have a part in the emerging Kingdom. For some, this is a difficult thing; for others it is easy. But it is necessary for all.

> *Those who accept and obey the King will be rewarded; those who don't will suffer eternal loss.*

John tells us of the coming Messiah in Matthew 3:11, the one whose sandals John is unworthy to undo. He describes Him as *one who will baptize with the Holy Spirit and with fire, and by whom all will be judged.* In other words, the Kingdom of Heaven will be present when this Person arrives. Those who accept and obey the King will be rewarded; those who don't will suffer eternal loss.

And then Jesus came to be baptized (Matt. 3:13–16). This confused John, who knew that Jesus was the promised Messiah whom he had come to proclaim, but Jesus told him that it was necessary for John to baptize him "to fulfill all righteousness."

Jesus' Preparation for the Kingdom: Fasting and Prayer

Jesus was baptized and, as He was coming out of the water, the Holy Spirit came down upon Him in the form of a dove, and the Father proclaimed from Heaven that Jesus is His beloved Son in whom He is well pleased. Then something strange happened: The Holy Spirit drove Jesus into the desert, specifically so that He could be tempted by the Devil. Jesus spent forty days in fasting and prayer, preparing for His ministry and His encounter with Satan. Afterward, in what must be one of the great understatements in Scripture, we are told that He was hungry.

And only then did the devil make his move. His first temptation was to get Jesus to focus on His body and to meet His own needs by turning stones into bread. Jesus responded with Scripture, pointing to the Kingdom: "It is written, 'You shall not live by bread alone, but by every word that comes from God's mouth.'"

Hearing and obeying God—recognizing and acknowledging His authority—was more important to Jesus than food, even after fasting for forty days.

Next, the devil tried to get Him to go for attention, to shortcut His way to the Kingdom by causing a miraculous scene at the Temple and justifying it by Scripture. But Jesus responded that we are not to put God to the test; we are to do His will, not try to get *Him* to do *our* will.

Finally, the devil showed Him all the glories of fallen human kingdoms and offered them to Jesus in return for worship—another shortcut to fulfilling the promise that He would rule over the nations. But Jesus refused to substitute Satan's kingdoms for the Kingdom of God, choosing to obey and worship God alone. So the devil left Him—Luke tells us that the devil was waiting for an opportune time—and angels came and served Him.

Jesus Begins His Ministry in the Power of the Spirit: Repent

After His time fasting in the desert and His rejection of Satan's temptations, Jesus returned "in the power of the Spirit" (Luke 4:14) and began His teaching ministry. He did not go to Jerusalem, the center of the Jewish world, but instead began His work in the provinces. His message was the same as John the Baptist's: "repent, for the Kingdom of Heaven is near" (Matt. 4:12–17).

Jesus Chooses Twelve Very Ordinary People to Be with Him

All three synoptic Gospels agree that, early in His ministry, Jesus called Peter, Andrew, James, and John to follow Him. From nearly the beginning of His ministry, Jesus begins training a group of people to expand His ministry and to learn to do what He was doing. Remarkably, He did not choose the well educated, well connected, or well off. Instead, He picked ordinary people—fishermen—to be His first disciples. He did not choose to work through rabbis or "the wise and learned," but through working class people and businessmen. And with these ordinary people, He changed the world.

Jesus' ministry was not simply preaching and teaching, though He did both.

Matthew does not tell us much about what the Apostles were doing at this point, except following Jesus. We can assume that they listened to His teaching and preaching and absorbed from it all they could. They also watched what He was doing, which brings us to an important point about Jesus' earthly ministry.

Jesus Proclaimed that the Kingdom was Near and Demonstrated it in Healing and Freeing People from Spiritual Bondage.

Jesus' ministry was not simply preaching and teaching, though He did both. His proclamation of the nearness of the Kingdom was backed up by His work, healing all kinds of diseases and infirmities and freeing people from demonic oppression. It was a holistic ministry reaching the spirit (preaching), mind (teaching), and body (healing). Jesus' ministry contained no bifurcation between meeting people's spiritual needs on the one hand, and their temporal needs on the other; He healed the sick, raised the dead, cast out demons, fed the hungry, called individuals to specific acts of obedience, preached, taught, etc.

Jesus thus showed the reality of the Kingdom—God extending His rule over all things and reclaiming from the devil and this broken world what is rightfully His. And demonstrating the presence of the Kingdom gave authority to His words and won Him a hearing among the people. In fact, word of Him spread from Galilee to Jerusalem and Judea, such that great crowds began to follow Him wherever He went.

Jesus' Teaching: The Sermon on the Mount

From there, Matthew turns to the longest example that we have in the Bible of Jesus' teaching. We call it the Sermon on the Mount, though it is arguably less a sermon and more a teaching about Kingdom living.

In the context of this chapter, it is impossible to have a complete discussion of the Sermon on the Mount. We will limit ourselves to identifying the main themes in the passage, though we encourage you to read it, meditate on it, study it, and live it yourself.

Before we talk about the text, we need to make an important observation about the Gospels as a whole. The Creeds say nothing about Jesus' teaching; they skip from His birth to His Passion. The reason for this is that the Creeds were written to address specific theological questions currently circulating at the time when they were written; obedience to Jesus' teaching was uncontroversial, so the authors of the Creeds saw no reason to address it. This has had the unfortunate effect of leading many theologians to minimize Jesus' teachings in favor of the doctrines taught in the Creeds and to focus on the Pauline epistles more than on the Gospels. Yet, if we proclaim Jesus as Lord, would it not make sense to study what Jesus did and what He taught—and to obey it? We need to pay much more attention to the Gospels and to Jesus' teaching if we are going to be able to claim Him as Lord with any integrity.

The Counterintuitive Beatitudes

Jesus' overall theme in this—and in all of His teaching and preaching—is the Kingdom of God. He begins by identifying key **Kingdom values** in the Beatitudes. These include recognition of our spiritual poverty (the word "poor" refers to people who have absolutely no resources and so are forced to live as beggars), mourning for sin, meekness (sometimes translated "gentleness"), etc. The final element of the list is being persecuted for righteousness. To make this point abundantly clear, Jesus repeats it and personalizes it; it is not simply "blessed are those who are persecuted," but "blessed are *you* when *you* are persecuted." Persecution is part of Kingdom living, and it is a value and a source of blessing for those who recognize it as such.

Salt and Light: Jesus Calls Us to Become Change Agents in the Word

Jesus then moves on to principles of **Kingdom living**. He tells us that we are to preserve and enlighten the world around us with the Gospel and with our good works, which will give glory to God. Notice here the emphasis on good works; just as Jesus' ministry combined works of mercy with preaching, so are we as His disciples to do good works that demonstrate God's work within and through us.

Transformed Hearts: Jesus Says that Cleansed Hearts are Possible

Jesus then explains what this means. The key in this section is that the Kingdom involves changed hearts. External obedience is not good enough; our heart attitude must be right since God sees and judges the heart as well as our behavior. Thus, hate is murder and lust is adultery. We are even to go as far as to love our enemies.

This principle that our heart attitude is what counts before God even applies to our worship; what we offer to God must be intended for Him, not for a human audience. We are rewarded according to our desired audience. If it is a human audience, their applause is our reward; if it is God, our reward comes from Him. We need to be careful to store our treasures in Heaven.

On Earth as it is in Heaven: A Kingdom Prayer

Much of this teaching is also connected to the Lord's Prayer, which is the **Kingdom prayer**. In connection with our responsibilities to God and our neighbor, Jesus gives us a prayer in Matthew 6:9–13 which He then proceeds to teach about in much of the rest of the Sermon.[2]

The Lord's Prayer is a summary of Jesus' teaching and ministry. It also reveals His prayer priorities; the first three of which are that God's glory, God's Kingdom, and God's will be manifested where we live on earth as they are in heaven. Only after these does Jesus tell us to move on to our own needs, which are, themselves, an outgrowth of God's will for us personally.

Jesus finishes the sermon with the well known image of a house built on rock versus a house built on sand. The difference is obedience: your life is secure if you put Jesus' teachings into practice. If you don't, you are heading for great loss.

The Sermon on the Mount has been described as the Constitution of the Kingdom. It gives us, in concise form, the values, attitudes, and lifestyle that Jesus came to inaugurate in this world, and how we are to pray them into reality. These were the things that Jesus Himself lived and that He called on His disciples to live as well.

Jesus' Teaching: The Kingdom Parables

Jesus also taught a great deal about the Kingdom of God in His parables, many of which are collected in Matthew 13. First, we have the parable of the sower and the soils. The point of the parable is that Jesus expects the word to produce a harvest in our lives. Harvest imagery is used in Jesus' parables to bringing people into the Kingdom—so this is a parable focused on evangelism.

Next is the parable of the wheat and the weeds. The harvest here is the judgment, with the wheat entering the Kingdom

---

[2] Matt. 6:11 is expanded in 6:25–34, 6:12 in 7:1–12, 6:13 in 7:13–25.

and the weeds being burned. It also shows the impossibility of producing a pure church in this world, since the wheat and the weeds are so mingled that trying to pull the weeds will result in wheat being taken up as well.

Then there are the parables of the mustard seed and the leaven, both of which show that Jesus expects His Kingdom to grow and expand to influence and shape the world.

Some of the key points here are that the stakes are very high . . .

These are followed by parables that treat the Kingdom as a hidden treasure. There are two main ways of interpreting these. In the first, the parable is about how we must approach the Kingdom. Whether we stumble across it or search to find it, we must be willing to give up everything we have to obtain it. After all, Jesus tells us that whoever would save his life must lose it, and whoever loses his life for His sake will find it. Alternately, the man who finds the treasure and the one who buys the pearl might represent Jesus, who gave up everything—including his life—for the Kingdom. Given that these are parables, it is possible that both meanings are intended, and both are certainly true.

In Luke 14, we have the parable of the wedding feast, in which Jesus tells us that the people who seem most likely or most suited for the Kingdom are *not* the ones who will enter the Kingdom. He teaches us that the Kingdom will be populated by people from outside polite society—the poor, the crippled, the blind, and the lame, as well as people from the highways and byways.

Some of the key points here are that the stakes are very high; entering the Kingdom brings blessing, while missing it brings disaster. But there is a price involved: the Kingdom will cost us all that we have and all that we are; and further, Jesus expects us to produce a harvest for Him. He tells us that the Kingdom will grow, perhaps invisibly at times and certainly in mysterious ways, but in the end, it will win out over all the kingdoms of the world, as Daniel 2:44–45 prophesies.

Jesus Takes on Kingdom Apprentices

Prior to becoming Jesus' disciples, the Twelve had regular income and even owned businesses, but as apostles, they left their sources of income behind and were called specifically to be with Him (Mark 3:13). They heard Him preach and teach, were witnesses to His miracles, and handled many of the mundane tasks that needed to be done as Jesus travelled. Mostly, though, they watched and learned.

The needs that confronted Jesus in the world were great, and He chose to have His disciples assist Him in meeting those needs. He saw the crowds that were following Him as sheep without a shepherd. He knew that there could be a great harvest for the Kingdom if there were more workers, so He told His disciples to pray that God would send more workers to help.

And then He made the Twelve the answer to their own prayer and the prayers of the lost. They were sent out as an extension of Jesus' ministry, and He gave them authority to do the same things that He was doing. They were to heal the sick, raise the dead, cleanse lepers, cast out demons, and to proclaim the presence of the Kingdom.

Jesus also gave them instructions on how to go about doing the work (Matt. 10, Luke 9). They were to begin with prayer, to rely on God for provision, and to find a "person of peace" who would welcome them into the community; if they did not find a person of peace, they were to leave and go on to another town rather than staying in an area that was unproductive for ministry. They were to build relationships, and then to carry out the same ministry as Jesus by healing and proclaiming the Kingdom.

In other words, Jesus was commissioning people to extend and carry on His ministry, centered on "show and tell," demonstrating the reality of the Kingdom, and proclaiming its presence.

Jesus Asks for a Confession of Faith (Finally!) and Teaches About the Kingdom

After sending out the Twelve and getting the reports back from them, Jesus spent more time with them growing their understanding about the Kingdom. Several important events occurred during this period. They had followed Him closely for a few years and had their first experiences of the Spirit's power working through them, and Jesus finally asked them who they believed Him to be. Peter confessed that He believed Jesus to be the Son of God, at which point Jesus began to teach them about His coming death and resurrection. He promised them that some of them would live to see the Kingdom of God, and then Peter, James, and John saw His glory in the Transfiguration.

He taught them that they should not oppose other people who were working for the Kingdom, even if they weren't among the Twelve. He also taught them to have forbearance toward those who reject the message. And then He decided that it was time to expand the scope of Kingdom ministry further.

The progression of Jesus' transfer of Kingdom authority became clearer. Initially, it was just Jesus healing and proclaiming the nearness of the Kingdom, but then He gave the authority and call to the Twelve to do the same thing.

Jesus Sends the Seventy-Two to Do His Kingdom Work

Jesus then appointed seventy-two disciples (Luke 10) and gave them the same authority and mission that He had given to the Twelve; indeed, their commission is in almost the same words as that of the Twelve. Once again, there is the call to prayer in the same words that He spoke to the Twelve, there is a warning about persecution, there is the message to rely on God's provision both for resources and for the person of peace, and there is the call to heal, to cast out demons, and to proclaim the nearness of the Kingdom.

The most interesting thing about this group is that we have no idea who they were! We are told the names of the Twelve and even some of their backgrounds, but the seventy-two are completely anonymous—just a group of nameless men. They did not have the time with Jesus and the training that the Apostles did, but they were ready and willing to go and do what Jesus said.

When those seventy-two no-name disciples returned, something happened that is unique in the New Testament: Jesus rejoiced (Lk. 10:21). Why was He so excited about their return? Certainly, a part of it was His joy at the spread of the Kingdom, and part of it was connected to the broader scriptural theme of God lifting up the humble ("little children," i.e., the seventy-two) and bringing down the proud ("the wise and learned"). But another part of it was that He saw His strategy being put into practice by His disciples, advancing God's reign on earth as it is in heaven. By giving His authority to the disciples, Satan's hold was being broken and the Kingdom was advancing.

Again, Jesus' own ministry to proclaim and demonstrate the Kingdom coming on earth was being reproduced by ordinary people, who were not in his inner circle. The fact that the seventy-two had no idea how important their mission had been contrasts dramatically with the reality that a cosmic spiritual battle for God's glory and His Kingdom would now be waged by Jesus' ambassadors—ordinary people filled with the Spirit of God. And for that Jesus rejoiced!

The Kingdom Mandate and the Church's Role Today in Finishing the Task

After this, Jesus spent time teaching the disciples about future events, including His own death and resurrection. He also told them that the end of human history would not come until the Gospel was preached through all the world as a testimony to all nations (Matt. 24:14).

We need to focus on what Jesus says about when the end will come. The word translated "nations" is the Greek word *ethné*, which can mean either "nation" or "people." Jesus is telling us that the scope of the Kingdom is global, that every people group matters so much that He will not return until the Gospel of the Kingdom reaches all people groups.

To put it differently, the Kingdom is not only about individual salvation but the transformation of peoples, nations, and cultures. And even though the Gospel has been taught widely in Europe and America, there are still sub-cultures within those places that have not heard it—hidden people groups in our own neighborhoods do not have a Kingdom presence yet. We need to be on the lookout for them, and seek persons of peace who will act as a bridge, sharing the Good News to these unreached people in our midst.

Over the last decades, the Global North has become a diaspora for thousands of people groups that have historically been resistant to the Gospel. Western Christians may focus on the risks these people bring. But with a Kingdom perspective, and much prayer, we can imagine that God has also brought them in proximity so that ordinary Christians can invite them to Jesus' banquet table. In the Great Commission (Matt. 28:18–20), Jesus tells us that He has *all* authority in heaven and earth, and so we are to make disciples of *all* nations, baptizing them and teaching them to obey *all* that He has commanded, and that He will be with us until this age of the world ends. Notice all the "alls." Jesus has *all authority*, and He has that authority over *all nations*. This means that all nations—all people groups on earth—belong in His Kingdom. And it means that all people groups should be obeying *all that He commands*. Notice also that making disciples means teaching them to *obey*. Discipling is not primarily a matter of intellectual *knowledge*; it is a matter of *obedience* to Jesus' commands.

Remember, the seventy-two were average, no name disciples—just like we are.

Our English translations obscure one important point about the Great Commission: the only phrase that is an imperative in the Greek is "make disciples." "Go" is not a command; it is a participle. The meaning, therefore, is "in your going," or in common parlance, "as you go" or "wherever you go." The point is that the Great Commission is something that we should be fulfilling *all the time* no matter what we are doing or where we are. It is not something that we do only on special occasions or with special planning or preparation. It is not just for missionaries, pastors, or evangelists, and certainly not just for special events. It is something that all of us are to be obeying as Jesus' disciples. Remember, the seventy-two were average, no name disciples—just like we are.

Models of Ministry

So that is Jesus' model for ministry—both His and ours. We can summarize it as follows:

- His ministry was all about the Kingdom of God, which the Apostle Paul defined as "righteousness, peace (i.e., *shalom*, a holistic vision of everything needed for human flourishing), and joy in the Holy Spirit" (Rom. 14:17).

- As a result, Jesus' ministry combined compassion with proclamation.

- Jesus' miracles and acts of compassion showed the reality of the Kingdom, His teaching showed what living in the Kingdom looked like, and His life was entirely lived as an expression of the Kingdom—recognizing and obeying the will of the Father through the power of the Spirit.

- Jesus' model for training leaders was essentially apprenticeship. The Twelve lived with Him, watched Him, listened to His teaching, were given assignments by Him, and then given further training for subsequent assignments.

- Jesus commissioned His followers to do what He did—first the Twelve, then the seventy-two, and ultimately all of us through the Great Commission. He connected our commission with His own, "As the Father has sent me, so I send you" (John 20:21).

The question is this: *how closely does our model of ministry follow the one that Jesus demonstrated?* If we are honest, we have to conclude that the church in the Global North uses a model that is far from what we see in the Gospels.

There are elements of what Jesus did that are recognizable today, but overall, the church in the Global North over the centuries has adopted mindsets and practices that have seriously hindered its ability to carry out Jesus' Kingdom commission. We have to stop busying ourselves with social events, over-assigning tasks that exhaust our members and burdening ourselves with busy work. It is time to try something different—and following the example of Jesus' ministry would be a good start.

AN INTERVIEW WITH JAMES FORLINES

James Forlines was a young pastor in Arkansas in 1986 when he attended a Change the World School of Prayer conference; he came home with a copy of *30 Days of Praying for Unreached Peoples*. When he came to day eight to pray for North Africa, he was overcome by the realization that this home for some of the great early fathers of the faith had a near-zero percentage of Christians today. Thus began his lament for North Africa. Over the next few years, his passion for the nations led to his being appointed to Executive Director of his denomination's mission agency.

Soon James discovered the reality of Disciple Making Movements, and his heart leapt at the possibilities now in North Africa. But as he became an increasing advocate for DMM, his role as leader of the mission ended. He thought that he would never have another chance to participate personally in the liberation of North Africa. He thought that God had abandoned him. And yet, today, he is Executive Director of Final Command Ministries and is participating in the work of engaging this most challenging region of the world.

James describes his journey in terms of Kingdom of God.

People need to realize that, when you walk in obedience to Jesus' Kingdom principles, there is another kingdom, a kingdom of the evil one that is going to be mobilized in opposition to what you are doing. And that's the reason for the prayer and fasting component of this. It's not an add on; it is absolutely essential. You dare not go into this realm unless you are spiritually equipped, or it will be a very bumpy journey.

The thing you have to ask is: what is a model that will work? Which ones emulate more of what the New Testament was advocating; the model of Jesus and the early church? That change in thinking to me was not hard because I was committed to the mission, not to the strategy or tactics that were being employed at the time. And I am trying to help people get the vision of the Kingdom, to say: "we need to be committed to Jesus' Kingdom, and to His mission. Nothing else matters."

Let's re-evaluate the whole thing with prayer and fasting and sensitivity to the Holy Spirit. We can come up with biblical models of leadership, biblical models of how God works. The truth is, there will be no penetration of North Africa unless what happened at Thessalonica happens there—"the Gospel came to you not only in Word, but in power." It's something that God only can bring.

We must have that Kingdom of God paradigm shift, because it is not about my strategies and plans. I can do everything I know right, but nothing will happen unless there is a divine, sovereign work of God that breaks through with power.

Jesus healed the blind man, and then he got hauled in front of everyone. His answer was: "All I know is, once I was blind, but now I see!" You'll never convince that person that anything else has happened except that he has met the Messiah and experienced His Kingdom power. You can take him in front of whoever you want to, and he will stare down persecution, he can face anything, because all he knows is "I once was blind but now I see."

But if I hold on and say: "No, I really want God to work in a way that's consistent with what I have always understood, I want God to work within our ministry models"—well then, we are not going to penetrate the darkest areas that are left in the world. It is going to have to be a divine work of God, and I am fine with however He chooses to do that.

In this chapter we met brothers and sisters whose Kingdom values are advancing the Kingdom in a place too challenging to mention.

We met James, whose heart was turned to pray fervently for North Africa thirty years ago—a man who has lived to participate in seeing the Spirit of God birthing fruit in the desert.

We got a window into the lives of David and Jan Watson who persevered twenty-five years ago after the deep grief of their disciples' deaths, to keep trusting God's Word's to open the door to Kingdom advance in the hardest of hard places—a breakthrough that continues to ripple and expand through many hundreds of people groups that previously, had no "Jesus option."

In each case it was never about strategic plans and funding. It was about Jesus' specific Kingdom of God values, lifestyles, and prayers.

Today, the Spirit of God is confirming the Bible's truths that we have dismissed, as it moves on brand new, 2000-year-old paradigms of ministry, fresh from the pages of Scripture. The rest of this book pivots now to focus on what that looks like in practice.

KINGDOM VALUES AND THE LIFESTYLES THEY REQUIRE

YOUR LIFE WITH JESUS' VISION

Paul: *I have been faithful to the
heavenly vision.* (Acts 26:19)

In this chapter we explore the kind of journey every disciple needs to take in their walk with God—discovering His highest purpose and vision for their lives. And that process may well require multiple transitions and new assignments over a lifetime of following Him.

CABBAGES IN THE DESERT

An encouraging place to start is with Aila Tasse, the leader of a remarkable ministry in East Africa that was birthed from the literal vision of cabbages growing in the Kenyan desert:

> I was praying one day at a public campsite in the forest. It was near a place where elephants sometimes come and feed. Suddenly, the spiritual atmosphere around me seemed to change. A kind of shadow was there, and a presence—I can't describe it any better than that. In one sense, I was afraid, but in another sense, I knew that I was hearing God.
>
> Then I had a vision.
>
> God showed me a Kenyan desert, the one between Moyale and Marsabit, a big desert that takes two hours to

cross by car. God brought me to a place that I knew very well. Suddenly, a question came to me: "Can cabbage grow in this place? This land is an empty land, only rocks, not a single tree. Can cabbage grow in this place?" I said, "Why am I dreaming in the daytime?" And I stood up and stretched.

Later, I went back to pray, and the vision came to me again. The question again: "Can cabbage grow in the desert?" There is no water, it's very hot, and it's covered by rocks, so how can cabbage grow? And then suddenly the Lord led me to Isaiah 43:18–19, the verses that say, behold I will do new things, I will cause a river to flow in the desert, and this shall bring glory to my name.

I didn't know exactly what this meant. It was not only a vision, but literally I saw the cabbage—how can cabbage grow in the desert? Then God led me to Jeremiah chapter seventeen, the potter and the clay. "I am the potter, you are the clay." It was like a drama, and I could hear the sound of the person going to the potter's house. And all the time I was having this vision, I was not hearing or seeing anything that was going on around me.

Elephants had come during this time, and they surrounded me, just eating leaves. The game wardens were on the other side, and they saw me praying, and they did not know what to do, how to warn me, because it is very, very dangerous for a person to move around in the middle of a herd of elephants. But I didn't know all this, I just knew that God was speaking to me.

So I stood up to leave the place where the cabbages grew, and then I saw the elephants. The warden called out— but kind of softly, you know, because he didn't want to spook them—"Don't move," he said, "or the elephants will attack you." But I just walked away, and the elephants didn't do anything to me.

That was the beginning of my calling. And as I kept preparing, God showed me the desert of northern Kenya, where fourteen unreached people groups live.

Aila went on to plant a church in Moyale on the Kenya/ Ethiopia border, and it became a large church that began to send out teams every year into the desert, and many Muslims became Christ Followers. It also became an equipping center, training disciple makers across Northern Kenya and throughout East Africa. More than 7,500 new churches in ninety-one different people groups have grown out of Aila's response to God's will for the desert dwellers—his cabbages in the desert.

VISION STATEMENTS OR TRUE VISION?

In modern parlance, we speak about having a "vision," meaning that we have a personal goal that we want to achieve or dreams that we want to pursue. We think of it in terms of the "mission and vision statements" of businesses and other organizations. The Bible actually has very little to say about "pursuing our dreams" or about "vision statements"—but it has a great deal to say about vision, and it tells us that vision is immensely important for our lives, because, "where there is no vision the people cast off restraint, but blessed is he who keeps the law" (Prov. 28:12).

The word translated "vision" here is often used to refer to the visions that prophets receive. The NIV translates it as "revelation." Without God's revelation, we cast off restraints—a good picture of the culture of the Global North. The alternative, which brings blessing, is keeping the Law. "Law" is the Hebrew word "Torah," and it literally means "instruction." So following God's instructions, obeying Him, brings blessing; if revelation is not heard (1 Sam. 3:1) or not heeded (Amos 8:11–12), blessing is lost and decadence and decay follow.

The Bible does not tell us to seek a vision for our lives or ministries—it gives us one. Indeed, the Word of God is our

173

vision, in the sense that it provides us the revelation of God's will. And God's will for the world is clear: "The earth will be full of the knowledge of the glory of the Lord as the waters cover the sea" (Hab. 2:14). "He made known to us the mystery of his will according to his good pleasure, which he purposed in Christ, to be put into effect when the times reach their fulfillment—to bring unity to all things in heaven and on earth under Christ" (Eph. 1:9–10).

That is God's will for the entire world, God's vision: to bring unity to all things in heaven and on earth under Christ. This is precisely what we have already considered from the Lord's prayer, "Your will be done on earth as it is in heaven." God's will for us as individuals is also intimately connected with His will for the world: that we advance His glory, His Kingdom, and His will on earth, just as it is in heaven. And that means that we are to spread His Kingdom throughout the world, bringing the obedience of faith (Rom. 1:5, 16:26) to every "tribe and language and people and nation." Our will must align with God's will, including the reconciliation of the world to Him through Christ. Nothing less will do, and nothing else is worthy of beings made in the image of God. And this usually requires intentional prayer to clearly discern God's purposes for us.

But sometimes we confuse our notions of vision—our own goals, our own pictures of what we want to achieve—with God's vision, that is, God's will. We begin to get comfortable in our own sphere of ministry, or we develop our own goals and agendas for where we want that ministry to go, and gradually we begin to expect God's will to fit our own "vision statement."

This is part of what happens as a church moves into the institutional stage. It begins to think that its vision statement is the same as God's vision—which is actually saying that its way of doing things is equivalent to, or even paramount to, God's will. As our ways of ministry become entrenched in tradition, the church subtly begins to change its thinking, moving from "how does our ministry fit into the Kingdom?" to "how does the Kingdom fit into our ministry?"

How does our ministry fit into the Kingdom?
How does the Kingdom fit into our ministry?

TO REACH MY VISION, OR TO SEE MY VISION REACHED?

A veteran of God's work in South Asia, W. Allen, told us about the early years of his ministry there. He began by praying, "Lord, I want to reach India." But time passed, and he found himself becoming increasingly frustrated and dissatisfied. He gradually came to the realization that he was praying for the wrong thing. He was actually asking God to enable him to reach everyone in India, and he realized that such a request was putting himself in the forefront, rather than putting God's Kingdom first. "It took me years to realize," he tells us, "but I learned to pray better. I no longer say, 'I want to reach India;' I say, 'Lord, I want to see India reached.' I want to put God's Kingdom first, rather than my own personal ministry."

The vision, the revelation, is ultimately about God's glory and the Kingdom, and so it includes everything that we are and everything we do. And there is no cookie-cutter approach to serving the Kingdom, because the Kingdom is composed of unique individuals, each of whom has a unique role to play in God's plan. But Jesus' will is for the whole world to be His disciples, and He gives us tactics to accomplish that: "you will be my witnesses in Jerusalem, and in all Judea and Samaria, and to the ends of the earth" (Acts 1:8).

Our will needs to coincide with Jesus' will, including making disciples all the way to the ends of the earth. The challenge for us is to fully obey God's revealed will for the world, including the world around us. To do this, we need to spend time in the Scriptures, let God's word soak into our minds and hearts, and pray His priorities into ours—pray that we can make His will our will. Once God's heart for the world becomes ours, we need to pray fervently to discern how we are to fulfill our unique part of His plan to reach "every tribe and language and people and nation."

As those living in the Global North, we tend to distance ourselves from the word "tribe." Though this word has hard, fast rules and connotations in the Global South, for us, this concept a bit blurry. But it's actually quite a simple concept. Your "tribe" or "tribes" consist of those around you, those you work with, those you share hobbies, interests, and activities with. It may also include, in a greater sense, those at the same socio-economic level as you, in a group that speaks the same language, and even those who we simply gather with as friends. It is also your circle of influence. For most of us, that will mean working locally.

Additionally, we need to pray about how to bring the reality of the Kingdom to bear in unexpected places in our own area. What hidden people groups exist around us? What people has God pre-positioned in our personal mission field to provide a bridge into a community that needs the Gospel? Whatever other callings God has given us in life, we are all called to advance the Kingdom.

Here is an example of what we're trying to say.

NOT SETTLING FOR MEDIOCRITY

David Young is the teaching minister at North Boulevard Church of Christ in Tennessee. That church body had a difficult and turbulent year in 2011. A number of the elders had decided that it was time to retire; most of the staff had considered moving elsewhere; even David himself considered updating his resume. It was a time of prolonged discouragement, and the body as a whole was aching.

"I realized that I needed to get on my knees," David recalls. "I asked God: 'Is this it? This can't be all you intended for your church!' I wasn't afraid that we were going under as a church, but I *was* concerned that we were on a course of irrelevance. I was concerned that we would end up settling for mediocrity, and that would be the way we'd get through this difficult time—by embracing mediocrity."

So he went on a solo prayer retreat for a week and began to pray fervently that God would turn their present suffering into eternal gain for the Kingdom. "I know you can rescue this," David prayed. "I know you can turn this loss into a win." And the more he prayed, the more he came to the conviction that what was really missing was disciple-making— as he puts it, "we needed to be making *disciple-making* the main thing."

David felt convinced that he and the other leaders at North Boulevard needed to change the focus of their ministry—to alter their ministry to fit the Kingdom, rather than the other way around. During his prayer retreat, he remembered how the church in Antioch planted churches around the world; he felt that God was leading him and North Boulevard to do the same thing.

"If we rose to the level of God's vision," he says today, "maybe one day we could forget all the pain we'd been through—maybe we could pull together, and maybe something as big as God's vision would unify the church again. But more than anything we wanted to get God's vision—to find out what God is doing to spread the Kingdom and join that."

David met with his elders soon after his prayer retreat and put forward a half-formed—and very lofty—goal. He bravely said, "Let's plant tens of thousands of churches to become part of the multiplication movement. Let's make disciple-making the main thing." This was like opening a flood gate, and suddenly more ideas poured out. "Let's establish some schools; we can call them Schools of Christian Thought where we work on renewing our minds to think like Christ. And let's return to the prayer roots that God expects His people to have—build a house of prayer. In fact, let's build a multi-ethnic church that looks like the New Heaven is going to look, where every language, every tribe, every people, and every nation is represented!"

> . . . let's return to the prayer roots
> that God expects His people to
> have—build a house of prayer.

David spent more than an hour just pouring out a vision for the future direction of North Boulevard's ministry as the elders listened. He was fully expecting some resistance, some questioning, some challenges from the other leaders. After all, it was hardly a well-detailed plan, and some of the goals must have sounded outrageous. So he suggested that the eldership team all go away together on a weekend retreat to pray together and talk through the idea.

"No," said one man instantly, "I move that we accept David's vision." And someone else seconded the motion, and in less than a minute they had embraced his undeveloped, raw kernel of an idea.

David remembers, "They said, 'David, just do what you need to do to make it happen.' Just like that!" Then David smiles as he adds, "I was almost insulted that they didn't argue about it!"

A few months later, the plans had begun to take shape, but not all details were yet in place. "I had put together some ideas and was going through those ideas one Sunday when I got up in the pulpit." He felt that he needed to present a clear-cut goal to the members of North Boulevard, and he was wondering how to quantify God's plan for the future in measurable terms.

"I was trying to think how many new churches we'd hope to plant, and I was thinking, 'What would be a cool number? We need some truly *crazy* number!' I can't remember what number I came up with, but it was something like a couple hundred."

But when David began to preach, the Holy Spirit began to lead his thoughts and words. "I felt like God was telling me, 'Don't say that number. Say sixty thousand churches!' And as I was speaking, I was arguing inside with God: 'There's no way I'm saying that number! We'd just make fools of ourselves!' But at some point, the number 60,000 churches came out; I just said it, and there it was. And now everybody thinks it was part of a master plan, and I chuckle to myself and think, 'No, God just made that number come out of my mouth during the sermon.'"

Over the next few weeks, the leaders at North Boulevard laid out a tentative plan, and in the process, they estimated that they would need $1.6 million to get started. They took it to the church as a whole and asked if everyone would get on board to support the new direction. And as with the eldership team, the congregation's response took David's breath away.

Some people gave property; one couple donated their wedding rings. Another man had recently started his own business, and he said, "From now on, one-tenth of my proceeds will go to church planting." One fourteen-year-old boy had been saving up for his first car when he turned sixteen. He had saved $1,000 and only needed another $500 to get the car that he wanted—but he brought in the cash and gave it to the elders.

"In the end," David concludes, "we didn't raise $1.6 million." He pauses dramatically. "No, God provided us with $6.1 million!"

And David adds one more detail to this story: "We were about 12 months into it, when I began to notice that nobody was talking about the hardships and trials that we went through in 2011—not a single person. It all just went away."

And six years later most of the things presented to the church have already launched or are in planning stages:

- A House of Prayer with a growing focus on intercessory prayer for the whole church is raising the spiritual water level of prayer in the church.

- The new focus on making disciples and a staff position to advance all aspects of Disciple Making and Discovery Bible Groups is in place.

- A goal of every member a disciple maker launched in 2017 as hundreds of members have pledged to make new disciples this year.

- The first four new churches have launched:

- Hispanic and Chinese churches,

- two satellite churches in underserved areas,

- and a new university church launching.

- The School of Christian Thought (Christian worldviews) is in its third year serving the whole urban community

- The first two New Day Conferences have drawn churches from fifteen states, advancing a message to congregations to restore disciple-making as the main priority.

- A team of leaders has initiated a process of observing Kingdom Movements in the Global South, and exploring ways to partner in catalyzing disciple making and church planting where the Gospel has not yet gone or thrived.

DISSATISFACTION AND CHANGE

In chapter six, we introduced the Formula for Change:

Dissatisfaction x Vision x First Steps > Resistance to Change

The first step toward seeing the same level of God's miraculous work is for Christ Followers to become dissatisfied with the status quo of the church in the Global North, a recognition that the church in the Global North is not serving the Kingdom as effectively as it should be. This dissatisfaction also needs to be extended beyond finding fault with the church as a whole; we need to recognize that, if the church's status quo is not fully embracing God's will, it's because the believers who make up that church are not fully embracing God's will for the Kingdom.

We need to deliberately cultivate this dissatisfaction in ourselves, to stop being content with status quo and begin asking God to reveal to us all that He wants to be doing in our hometowns and neighborhoods. Dissatisfaction with the status quo is inevitable once we begin to grasp the extent of God's will for the world, once we begin to make His will our will. This was the experience of Abebe, a Christian leader in the Horn of Africa:

> We did some research back in 2005, and we looked at what was happening in terms of Kingdom-building in the Horn of Africa and compared that to what *could* be happening. As we began to count the cost, we were overwhelmed. Now, instead of asking "What can I do?" I ask "What will it take?"

David Broodryk of South Africa describes the time when God's vision replaced his limited human vision:

> I came to a place in my life where I said, "I live in a city of twelve-point-five million people. I simply will not be happy with a few hundred. I won't be happy with a few thousand. I won't be satisfied until I have significantly impacted twelve and a half million people!" Building God's Kingdom is not a technique, it's not a thing that you adapt, it's not a program—it's a passion that has to burn deep in you. I want my city to follow Jesus.

The question for us is whether we have a vision for our entire community and region that is as big as God's, and whether we are willing to ask Abebe's question "what will it take?"—and then to follow wherever the answer leads—which includes following through with anything you are called to do, even if it feels impossible

Another young man named Michael[1] was called upon to count the cost of building the Kingdom. He attended an all-night prayer meeting during his junior year in high school, and during that time of prayer he became convinced that God

---

[1] Michael is a pseudonym.

was calling him to work among unengaged people groups, and that call shaped many decisions in his life.

The next year, he won a contest put on by Dow Chemical Corporation, which gave him the opportunity for a free college education—plus a guaranteed six-figure income when he graduated college. But he turned it all down because he was determined to follow that call to take the gospel to the unengaged groups.

When he got out of college, he had a high probability of competing on the U.S. Olympic team, but he decided that it would interfere with preparing for the call overseas and chose not to pursue the gold medal. He was the valedictorian of his class at the university, but he decided not to give the valedictory address or even to attend the graduation so that he could immediately deploy overseas. Michael was determined to place God's call—God's will—above all other considerations.

Over the years Michael's laser focus for advancing the Kingdom and his understanding of what it takes to bring God's transformation to whole communities has been transferred to many hundreds of other leaders.

THE IMPOSSIBLE OPTION

God doesn't always speak through visions. Sometimes He simply guides our thoughts and decision-making. Consensus can sometimes be a sign of the Holy Spirit's leading, especially if it is between different groups working independently, and points in an improbable direction. In late 2008, for example, a foundation asked New Generations (formerly Cityteam Ministries) to provide executive summaries of three potential projects, and then to recommend one of those projects for further action. They stipulated what those three potential projects needed to be:

1. One project that could easily be undertaken with fair certainty of success;

2. One challenging project that would require faith, hard work, and God's blessings to achieve;

3. And one project that is "something impossible that you are hesitant or fearful to try."

New Generations prayed and considered this proposition, and also sent it on to two African missions organizations for their consideration. The foundation that made this unusual request had given New Generations a deadline to submit their decision regarding which of the three they would like to pursue; the foundation had also committed to select which of the three projects they would like to see the ministry take on.

Before that deadline arrived, all three parties had made their decision. The African missions organizations felt that God was leading them to select option three, "something impossible." The leaders at New Generations had also chosen option 3. And most remarkable of all, the foundation that initially posed the question had also chosen option 3.

The "impossible" task was indeed something that everyone involved was "hesitant or fearful to try." It involved a region where there are numerous Muslim people groups who have long histories of hostility toward the gospel. Group A has been Islamic for approximately 600 years, holding a dominant position within the culture, with perhaps a handful of Christian churches. Group B has been Islamic for around a thousand years, with perhaps a few thousand Christians scattered over several countries. Group C has also been Islamic for a thousand years and research could not identify any Christian churches within that group at all. A common saying in that third group was, "Not one of us will ever become a Christian and see another sunrise."

And thus it was a very sober African leadership team that made a decision in early 2009 to engage these three people groups. Intercessory fasting and prayer immediately started. Mobilizing prayer for this initiative was the primary focus for seven months among more than 500 African intercessors. They gathered regularly for all-night prayer vigils and spent countless hours in personal prayer.

It was a slow process, but God opened the doors and His people obediently walked through them. And in the following years, God has brought forth miraculous movements in all three of those people groups.

Tragically, however, these results have not come without great cost; in a period of just eighteen months, more than 200 believers were martyred in the region. But the ministries that took on this task have shown unprecedented courage in the face of horrific opposition, pressing on with underground disciple making and church planting.

DISCERNING GOD'S WILL FOR YOUR MINISTRY

In this chapter, we have seen a variety of ways that Christian leaders have embraced a new and dynamic vision for their ministries and how they fit into God's vision for the world:

- Aila had a literal vision.

- David Broodryk recognized his city's need for the Gospel, leading him to become dissatisfied with the incremental progress of the status quo.

- New Generations and its partners prayed that God would show them His vision from the choices placed before them, and they all arrived at a unanimous decision—which was also the most difficult and dangerous of the options.

🜲 David Young challenged his church during a discouraging season to change their way of doing ministry to fit the Kingdom, not vice versa.

🜲 The young man whom we called Michael counted the cost of reaching the unreached—and chose to place God's Kingdom above the riches of this world.

As we've said, there is no cookie-cutter approach to finding our role in God's plan for the Kingdom; God speaks to each of us as individuals. The starting points are:

1. Studying and meditating on Scripture, allowing God to speak to you and shape your mind and heart through His Word.

2. Prayer, bringing others with you to seek God's will.

It may take quite some time to discern what God is saying, and He may speak through other means as well, but the Word and prayer are fundamental to all that we do, which is why we must start there.

All of this requires a paradigm shift in the churches of the Global North. Business as usual is not working. Trying to maintain the status quo is a losing strategy. Instead, we need to find God's will for our ministries that will allow us to engage the lost within our community—whether it fits within our Church's predominant demographic group or not.

COURAGEOUS LEADERSHIP

The two biggest barriers to adopting a new vision are inertia and fear. Inertia, tradition, and even a ministry's self-defined identity are all things that can keep a church or ministry from pursuing a new vision.

Fear of failure, fear of people's reactions, fear of reaching out to a new, unknown community, fear of losing one's reputation in ministry—all these can lead a believer to censor or ignore God's leading, and it can paralyze a leader, causing him to reject the guidance that God has given him and to seek another, easier one. As we will see in a later chapter, there can be a heavy price for a leader who takes a course that goes against his church's tradition. Unfortunately, there isn't an easy way out—there is no Plan B in God's will for our lives.

This brings us to a critical characteristic for leaders in the Kingdom: courage. Without courageous leadership, God's will is not obeyed, change does not occur, and movements simply do not happen.

ABUNDANT PRAYER

Jesus's resurrection is the beginning of God's new project not to snatch people away from earth to heaven but to colonize earth with the life of heaven. That, after all, is what the Lord's Prayer is about.

—N.T. Wright, *Surprised by Hope: Rethinking Heaven, the Resurrection, and the Mission of the Church*

A 35-Year Prayer

In 1976, a group of ten women at the Arcadia Church of Christ in California read the book *What Happens When Women Pray*. That group began fasting and praying for their slowly declining church of about 60 people—and their prayers gave birth to many new things in the church: new leadership, new vision, small groups that brought surges of growth, and a reputation for being a praying church that served people with challenging life circumstances. The church eventually developed a strong focus on the Kingdom of God, which brought with it a powerful vision for the nations and a willingness to minister healing and deliverance to anyone in need. And the church began to grow rapidly.

In 1982, an American missionary teamed with an African colleague to begin a new ministry in his nation. It was determined that the ministry would blend three key elements:

1. Compassionate services to help communities with their agricultural and other needs

2. A clear proclamation of the Gospel of the Kingdom

3. Much prayer for spiritual breakthroughs in the country

In 1983 the two men were deployed to Africa.

As the church grew and ministered to more people, intercessory prayer became a central ingredient. In the books of Isaiah, Ezekiel, and especially Daniel, the Bible tells us that there are powerful supernatural beings ("princes") who have charge over human kingdoms and who oppose God's work.

From those passages, the leadership of the church sensed that God was inviting the church to pray something specific. They would pray that the powers of the prince of that African country be broken so the Gospel could spread.

This did not become part of the regular services held at that California church, but in small groups and corporately, its members began to pray against the powers of the darkness over their adopted country. It did not take long to discover that there was abundant spiritual warfare associated with that bold prayer, but they did not quit. Thirty-five years have passed, with dramatic transitions, but twenty-five people have never stopped praying that bold prayer, most unaware of how God was, and still is, answering it in magnificent ways.

In 2001, Hassan (whom you met in chapter 1) became the second-generation leader of that ministry and renamed it Mission for All. And it is not surprising that Mission for All's prayer disciplines call for all Christ Followers in the country to pray every week for the Global North—asking God to bring forth Kingdom movements in America and Europe.

And Mission for All has become one of the leading Disciple Making Movement ministries in Africa, planting churches in 12 countries. Its hallmark has consistently been its prayer disciplines and the dramatic transformations that have happened where a church prayed 35 years for spiritual victory over darkness.

HOW DOES PRAYER WORK?

Prayer is a mysterious thing. God is sovereign; He governs the universe and does what He will with the nations on earth. He does not need our advice or wisdom. He does not always give us what we ask for in our prayers because He has other, better, even greater plans than we realize. Yet Jesus sought God, often in prayer, and taught more about prayer than about any other subject except the Kingdom of God. He told us to be persistent in praying about our needs. Paul went further and told us to pray without ceasing, informing us that this is God's will for us in Christ Jesus (1 Thess. 5:16–18).

God can easily make things happen without us—yet He has given us the privilege to join Him in His governance of the universe. The theological background of this is found in Genesis 1 and 2. In the ancient near east, to be the image of a god meant that you were claiming to be that specific god's official representative or regent on earth, giving you authority to rule in that god's name.

This is the context for Gen. 1:26–27. Genesis says we are made in His image and that we are given dominion over the earth—we are to rule it in God's name and under His authority. Of course, sin makes this more difficult, but it is a calling that is never rescinded. In Christ, our ability to govern the world in God's name is being restored. And prayer is one way that this happens; it is God's chosen means to release His power into the world and to advance His Kingdom here.

This is why Jesus talks about prayer in the upper room discourse, His final teaching to the Apostles before His crucifixion. He says *three times* that the Father will give us anything that we ask in His name (John 14:14, 15:16, 16:23–24). The repetition shows how important it was to Jesus that we grasp what He was saying.

So what does this mean? Some people treat "in Jesus' name" as a formula to use in prayer, as if they were magic words—or the phrase is used to signal "I've finished this prayer." But the actual significance of those words is quite different. A treasurer in a corporation has the right to sign checks in the name of the corporation, but those checks must be for corporate purposes. If he writes a check for any other reason—if he uses corporate money improperly—he can end up in jail.

In the same way, when we pray in Jesus' name, we must be praying in alignment with His purposes. As we saw in chapter three, that means praying for God's glory, the advancement of His Kingdom, and the fulfillment of His will over our own. (Remember, when Jesus prayed "thy will be done," it was in Gethsemane—just before He went to the cross.) This means that we once again need to look for Scriptures to pray back to God, and also to cultivate a listening ear to hear the still, small voice of the Spirit as He guides our prayers.

Jesus is clear. He says three times that if we pray "in His name," in alignment with His purposes and for the growth of the Kingdom, our prayers *will* be answered. We still need to be persistent, but God will honor those prayers and will answer us.

If our prayers will be answered, why is persistence important? First, our prayers can be opposed by demonic forces. We see this in Daniel 10:12–13, where the answer to Daniel's prayer was delayed for three weeks because of demonic opposition by the Prince of the Kingdom of Persia to the angel who was sent to answer the prayer. Spiritual warfare is very real, and our prayers are an important weapon in the fight.

Second, God values perseverance, persistence, patience, and steadfastness. He builds these into our lives by not giving us things instantly. He also uses delayed answers to prayer to test how serious we are; if we let the prayer drop, it demonstrates clearly that this was not something that mattered much to us. This can be likened to the Jewish tradition surrounding conversion. A rabbi will say "no" to a person's conversion request until he or she who desires to convert asks three times, showing dedication through persistence.

God values perseverance, persistence, patience, and steadfastness.

Closely related to prayer is the practice of fasting. The early church fasted twice a week, and many of the churches of the Global South also fast regularly. The churches of the Global North do not typically fast at all, even though Jesus tells us that fasting brings rewards from the Father and conveys spiritual power (Matt. 6:18, Mark 9:29).

The church of the Global North needs strengthening when it comes to prayer. Fortunately, the Global South offers many prayer paradigms that can be adopted or adapted in the North.

It is no exaggeration to say that prayer is the engine that powers Mission for All's ministry and opens the door for movements throughout the region. With this much dedication to prayer and reliance on God, is it any wonder that their work has been blessed?

Few things have contributed to spiritual barrenness in the Church Christ founded as has the idea that prayer is mere quiet, meditational passivism. There is a time to be silent. There is a time to be still. To know the awesomeness of God's person and presence.

But prayer is alive. It is aloud with praise, aglow with warmth, attuned with song, aflame with power. And it is also unsettling in its violence. Not in the violence of its practice but in the violence of its impact when it is exercised with power.

—Jack Hayford
Prayer is Invading the Impossible

JEFF SUNDELL: ASIA AND NORTH AMERICA

Jeff Sundell and his wife were missionaries in South Asia where they were catalyzing Kingdom movements, but they are now doing this in North America through planting churches in multiple major North American cities. Jeff tells us his story in his own words how God has led him and his wife in a remarkable Kingdom journey in both South Asia and North America.

When the movement really kicked off in India, I was in a season of fasting and prayer, and my wife was pregnant with our fourth child. On the seventh day of fasting and prayer, my wife miscarried and ended up in the hospital. You are not expecting that out of your time in prayer and fasting. I didn't really even know what God was wanting to do with that since I was in a wonderful meeting in Assam training national leaders how to be strategy coordinators.

A Hindu high priest had become a disciple of Jesus and we were having this wonderful time of worship, celebrating what God had done. And right then God gave me a vision of a tsunami rising out of Myanmar and flowing down into Assam, through Bhutan, Nepal, and Sikkim before finally sweeping into West Bengal and Bihar. And at the same time God gave me some specific things He wanted me to do. I had been doing end-visioning as I trained missionaries and local workers . . . but this vision was just too crazy and there was not any way that I was going to tell it to anybody!

I just shared the vision in general, without the specifics because it was so unusual. I was intimidated about sharing the vision that God had shown me.

I returned back home to Nepal and for the next four months, I went through a season of very unusual and challenging chest pain, shortness of breath, and headaches. And on top of that had difficulty with my eyes, making it difficult to even do emails. Eventually my doctor warned me that I had multiple health issues and I was primed for a heart attack. A doctor in Nepal confronted me that my wife and I needed to return to America and get away from the stresses in the region, but I just walked away from him—and continued to struggle.

Then one day in a ministry gathering a lady came up to me and said: "Two weeks ago I had a dream about the most intimidating and stubborn man that I have ever seen." Then she points at me and said: "You're him!" They called me up in front of everybody and began to pray for me.

I was very uncomfortable, but when she prayed my whole body got worse. I felt like I was on fire, even opening my eyes to look at my arms to see why they were so hot.

During the prayer, God said to me, "I gave you a vision. And I told you to tell the people the vision so that they will not perish!"

It was quiet in the room, but God began to speak to me: "Tell the people! Repeat what I told you to say—that we are going to equip one hundred thousand people for a harvest of one million baptisms, in ten thousand churches." Immediately, I repented and said out loud: "Yes Lord!"

I shared that vision of ministry with all the others. Interestingly a few days later all of my health issues were under control. I went through a season of suffering because I did not share the vision, and I did not obey God's words.

In 2009 that season in Asia ended and my wife and I returned to America. All we knew how to do was to catalyze movements. That was our only skill set. By the end of the first year we had found about thirty-five homes in rural North Carolina and we were seeing people begin to follow Jesus.

You would think somebody like me, a veteran from India, should know better, but I came to America with the assumption that America would have less spiritual warfare than South Asia. So I was stunned to discover that the levels of spiritual warfare in America are much greater than any other place I have served. And sometimes it is truly hideous stuff--so out of the box that you just ask: "Where did that come from?" The spiritual situation in America is much more challenging than South Asia.

So as things happened in America, we learned quickly to stop and say: "Let's fast and pray." In one special season we fasted for 17 days as we searched Genesis to Revelation looking for everything we could find in the Bible about "multiplication." If the "grasshopper multiplied" we checked it out.

A key passage was in the first chapter of the Bible, Genesis 1:26–28 (NIV):

> 26 Then God said, "Let us make mankind in our image, in our likeness, so that they may rule over

> the fish in the sea and the birds in the sky, over the livestock and all the wild animals, and over all the creatures that move along the ground."
>
> [27] So God created mankind in his own image, in the image of God he created them; male and female he created them.
>
> [28] God blessed them and said to them, "Be fruitful and increase in number; fill the earth and subdue it. Rule over the fish in the sea and the birds in the sky and over every living creature that moves on the ground."

I had thought about God's creation of mankind in Genesis 3, but Genesis first chapter reveals the powerful linkage between the nature of human beings in "the image of God" with a divine mandate to "be fruitful and multiply," which includes "spiritual" multiplication of God's image on earth.

And in the Gospels we are connected to God's glory through Jesus' redemption and the Kingdom of God is within us. That led us to our Four Fields cycle for multiplying leaders: Entry, Gospel, Discipling, and Church Formation. We believe that there are three great ways to use your time: Reading the Word, Gospeling, and Discipling.

Eventually we sensed the Lord was asking us to set a goal of 2,500 churches to the fourth generation in a total of fifty cities. We made a decision not to call them "churches," so we didn't.

We invited some second and third generation leaders to come to a training in Houston. To this day I don't know why I did this, but I told the people that the requirement for this training would be: "You have to read the New Testament through ten times and fast and pray for forty days."

What was I thinking? It's impossible to do that in forty days, and I only got through the Biblical reading about seven times. It's interesting, but many leaders told us that the reason they came was the idea of reading the New Testament through ten times and linking it to fasting and prayer. They said: "Otherwise, we would not have come." The people who came really resonated with William Carey's words: "Attempt great things for God, expect great things from God!"

My philosophy is that our attempts to serve God ought to match the capacity we think our God has. And if we're not attempting God-sized goals, we are not believing the God of the Bible. We might as well be practicing agnostics. A church can actually be devoid of true knowledge because it does not obey God. Really, this is like saying: "Hey, when I know enough, then I'll go obey it." The better path is: "Let me obey God in all things, and as I obey I will grow in knowledge and insight."

We train disciple making in churches, and this is why. We are finding that there are people in the church who already have one foot out of the church because they're just looking for a cause, for something to be involved in. And then they discover disciple making and it clicks. Now, that is still just a small percentage of Christians, but the numbers of people who are ready for the disciple making challenge seem to be growing.

Today we are making progress in the key cities with a theme of "no place left." Now we are tracking churches in 103 cities in the U.S. We're not only tracking churches, but we also track streams of churches planting churches— about 150 streams of third generation churches. There are about thirty-five streams of fourth-generation, fifth-, sixth-, seventh-generation churches.

We are trying to redefine success in American churches. Otherwise, we just pat each other on the back when there is a baptism, or just one new church planted. So we are trying to change the way we Christians communicate in America. We want people to ask "What is a stream?" "What is generational replication?" "And what is the big deal about so much prayer and fasting?"

In all of this, identity is important. We actually were hoping we would be a little further along by now, but we made a mistake by calling the new churches "groups." That decision caused most new groups to only last about nine months. But when you call them a church there is a different identity and higher expectations. In our case, the attrition rate went from ninety percent to only about twenty-five percent, when they self-identified as a church. Before, in one year we lost almost 1,000 groups in North America. Those groups were made up of baptized people who understood Kingdom principles, and they were disciples and disciple makers. And today they are in other churches, so it is not a tragedy, but we lost a year of potential momentum of planting viable churches.

PRAYER LESSONS

From the beginning of the disciple making process, people are taught that they should pray and expect God to answer. In fact, the accountability questions in Discovery Groups ask about answered prayer. We offer training on how to pray (see chapter ten), but prayer is mostly taught using an apprentice approach, which combines seeing, learning, and doing all at the same time.

In prayer, it is important that we give ourselves completely to God and from that position learn to rely on Him and His power rather than our own. Claude King explains:

> One of the Old Testament terms translated *consecrate* comes from the image of a Hebrew priest standing at the altar to receive sacrifices. The term actually consists of two words, one meaning "an open hand" and the other meaning "to fill up." Literally, it means "to fill up the open hand." We bring our offering to God and fill up the hands of the priest with that offering, thus affirming that it all belongs to God. It is consecrated to Him. And because God is holy, this sacrifice becomes holy.

That understanding sheds new light on Romans 12:1, where Paul writes: "I beseech you brethren, by the mercies of God that you present your bodies a living sacrifice, holy, acceptable to God, which is your reasonable service."

And in that context also, there was a medieval ceremony where a king would call his subjects to him to pledge their loyalty and obedience. This Homage Ceremony happened when the King was on his throne. The vassal would approach with his hands pressed together and would place his hands inside the king's hands, and say: "I am your man." The word *homage* came from the Latin word for "man." I am yours; whatever I need to do, I am your servant.

And the remarkable thing about this symbolism is that Christians of the medieval period began to ponder the meaning of that Homage ceremony and considered that, if this was the promise that they were willing to speak to a king on earth, then they needed even more to do that for the Lord of Lords. Thus they developed a posture of prayer that was the same as the Homage posture, kneeling before God, with hands pressed together, and head bowed as they imagined kneeling before King Jesus at His throne with their hands in the middle of His nail-scarred hands. Then the Lord could express His will: "Today I want your life, not part of it, but all of it. I have purchased you and you are mine."

And so in prayer we can come as often as we need to the throne of God with a prayer of consecration. "King Jesus, I'm your man! I'm your woman! My time is yours! My possessions are yours! My career is yours! My dreams are yours! My finances are yours! My reputation is yours! My health is yours! My very life is yours! Command me today and I will obey you!"

—Interview with author and speaker Claude V. King regarding "Consecration"

Disciple Making Movements are not a program, not a strategy or a curriculum. It is simply a movement of God. Without Him, there is nothing. That is why all discussion about Disciple Making Movements begin with Prayer and Fasting. Our Sovereign God is passionately pursuing the lost to bring them to himself. Prayer and Fasting allows us to align ourselves with Him. There will be no results if we are walking in our own strength and according to our own resources. God says, "Ask me and I will make the nations your inheritance, the ends of the earth your possession." Also, "I will give you every place where you set your foot, as I promised Moses . . . ." Behind any success in planting churches and making disciples there is a lot of prayer and a lot of fasting, a lot of bending knees, a lot of crying and weeping before God. This is where the victory is won and then when you go on the field you see the results.

—Younoussa Djao, Engage! Africa video series

PRAYER AND SPIRITUAL WARFARE

Prayer is a critical element of the spiritual warfare that we face daily. It seems sometimes, that from the moment we open our eyes and open our phones to look at the news until the moment we tuck into bed at night and search for a movie to watch before evening prayers, we are inundated with sin—spiritual warfare is so commonplace that not only can we not ignore it, we hardly notice it anymore. Furthermore, the church in the Global North often ignores the reality of demonic activity, but the churches of the Global South cannot.

A man whom we'll call Gonda is a church planter in a central African country. He has seen God bring about miraculous outcomes in Central Africa, and he has survived and thrived in difficult situations. He told us that he has four principles that have shaped his ministry:

1. For him, everything depends on prayer, and listening to God's voice;

2. He searches for people of peace;

3. When he finds them he catalyzes Discovery Bible Studies;

4. And he coaches and mentors his disciples, other leaders, and new churches so that they all reproduce themselves.

Gonda had heard about a town named Hante. It was a fairly closed community that engaged in a horrific business of murder and exportation of human blood and body parts to other countries for demonic purposes. The town did not tolerate strangers very well. And Gonda's research suggested that some people had not survived a visit to that community.

So Gonda began to pray to God on behalf of this town. He knew the risk of seeking to bring the Kingdom of God into this place, but God had encouraged him in this endeavor, so the only thing to do was pray and obey—and do some more research.

He learned that the community's chief was very deep into ancestral fetishes that gave him supernatural abilities to get right into the middle of a herd of elephants, then summoning his helpers. People feared him and his mystical powers.

Gonda prayed for guidance and waited.

Soon, he met a Christian woman who lived in the town of Hante. The moment he met the woman, he sensed that the Lord's clear calling to start the process. She wanted to see the Gospel engaged there, but she worried that her community was just too much of a challenge. Gonda came up with a plan to start first with a village seven kilometers away. He figured it could be a staging place to get close enough to Hante to explore and prayer walk around the area.

Finally, on a Saturday afternoon, he made the journey to the "staging" village with two young disciples that he was coaching and mentoring, hoping to sleep there. But a former pastor happened to meet them on the way, and when he learned of their intentions, he insisted on taking them directly to Hante, to the target village itself. Gonda sensed that the pastor was a person of peace who could introduce them to the villagers, so he agreed to the change of plans.

It was well after dark when the exhausted men trudged into Hante—and it did not feel at all safe. But it helped that they were escorted by someone who was already known in the village, especially when the pastor told the people that his friends were storytellers who told the stories of the Creator God.

It was already 10:00 at night, but the people who had first gathered to accost the group of strangers now insisted that they wanted to hear one of their stories; then they would judge whether or not they could stay. The residents built a fire and the men started telling the stories of the Bible, beginning with Creation and moving through the great narratives of the Old Testament and into the Gospels, all along giving the people time to discover what it all might mean for them if it was true. Sometimes Gonda would even sing a worship song and people would begin to dance. And so it went on for a couple of hours. At about two a.m. people started to leave the fire—but not to sleep. They rushed off to awaken their families to come and hear the wonderful stories.

Eventually, approximately 150 people were gathered around the fire listening to chronological storytelling of the Bible. Gonda had never expected that people would stay awake all night to hear the stories, but he and his disciples were thrilled for this surprising development.

Later, people reported that they stayed all night because they had a deep fear of dying, and these stories about the Supreme God resonated within their hearts. There were families among the group whose ancestors had done terrible things and some of them were still doing these things. They felt cursed and afraid, but they were intrigued with the stories—almost as if the stories were the first lifeline to hope and salvation they'd ever received. Whenever it seemed like the stories might end, these families insisted that the men continue.

During the night, the elephant hunter (who was also chief of the village) fell ill. He went to a local animistic priest but there was no help for the chief. He knew that something was happening in the town but he was too sick to check on it. The disciple makers were told of the town chief's illness and they knew that some of them should go to him and pray so that he would know that there was a greater power than his fetishes. By God's grace, with the disciple makers by his side, he experienced an immediate healing, and decided to attend the early morning storytelling.

The Bible storytelling did not end at daybreak or even at noon—it went on until three p.m.—seventeen hours of Bible storying from Creation to Jesus enthroned in Heaven. During all of that time, the team of disciple makers were amazed that the people were eager to give so much time and energy to this non-stop Chronological Bible Study.

Dialogue and Discovery Bible studies went on for two weeks, after which, the chief decided to become the community's first Christ Follower. He called a gathering of the town, confessed many sins including his fetishes, brought out all of his occult devices, and destroyed them before receiving baptism. More than forty more were baptized soon after, and a church was birthed in the village. Eventually, 280 people were baptized. Then the chief travelled to the other villages in the region to tell them of the loving Creator God who heals, forgives, and changes peoples' heart. Miraculously, with each visit, more churches were planted.

Gonda reports that, in the new town, people began to explain why they had become Christ Followers, simply stating, "We have discovered the Creator God who is very powerful!" In the new town, Christ Followers continued to grow and thrive with more answered prayers and evidence of the love of Jesus. A few months later, a rebel war caused all the villagers, many of whom had become Christ Followers, to evacuate to a much larger town for safety.

The story ends there, except for one remarkable detail. In the town that the team had originally intended to use as a staging area, there was a very large temple dedicated to the town's goddess—a malevolent presence who, the residents believed, periodically caused people to die when near the temple. The pastor whom the team had met on the road, the man who had been their person of peace to enter Hante in the first place—that pastor had been emboldened by what God was doing in the region, and he spent three days of fasting and prayer. Then, one Monday morning at eight a.m., he walked to the center of that "staging area" town—and he personally burned down the temple. Most of the residents were certain that he would die, but he didn't.

Thanks to that incident, powered by God through Hante's persistent prayer, there was a surge of momentum among Christ Followers, as the worship of the goddess went into decline.

THE DESTRUCTION OF SATAN'S KINGDOM

This story illustrates that Jesus' ministry was not to deliver a new philosophy or religion; it was to destroy the kingdom of Satan. Jesus ended one of His dialogues with the Pharisees with these words: "How can one enter a strong man's house and plunder his goods, unless he first binds the strong man? And then he will plunder his house" (Matt. 12:29). It is Jesus' intent to destroy the works of Satan and his minions, and for Kingdom people to rescue others from darkness in order to populate the Kingdom of God.

LESSONS TO LEARN

Serious dedication to prayer and fasting is central to Disciple Making Movements. Nothing happens without prayer. Yet churches in the Global North are weak when it comes to prayer. What lessons can we learn from the experiences related here from the Global South?

- The best way to learn prayer is by praying with people who know how to pray. Classes and training can help, as can mentoring and modeling, but with prayer, experience is truly the best teacher.

- Use the Psalms and scriptural prayers to guide your prayer. The Lord's Prayer is particularly important for this.

- Listen for the voice of the Spirit nudging you to pray for specific things in specific ways.

- Start small. Do not attempt all night prayer, forty days of fasting, or anything else that is not sustainable, and check with your doctor before engaging in fasting. Start with a simple dawn to dusk fast once a week. As you grow accustomed to that, increase the rigor, either by expanding the time or the frequency of the fasts. Review the prayer schedule from Africa in chapter three to get ideas on how to do this. Be sure as you fast to devote extra time to prayer. You can develop a similar approach to learning to pray more.

- As an individual, you can (and should) invite others in your church or fellowship to join you in your fasting and prayer.

- Get new followers to pray.

- Along with private prayer and corporate prayer in both small groups and the congregation, take prayer walks, inviting God to bring His Kingdom reign into a community and to show you where and how to begin. Some people on prayer walks begin to prophetically rename the streets of an area to themes God puts in their hearts, like *Redemption Place* or *Deliverance Way*.

- Experiment with highly participatory prayer formats.

  For example, years ago some Korean churches began to make corporate prayer a huge priority to the extent that many Christians would spend vacations in prayer. Prayer meetings became participatory, and these kinds of prayer meetings spread rapidly in the Global South. Leaders in prayer meetings would name a specific area for prayer, and everyone would then begin praying verbally about that topic. After a few moments another theme would be announced and the group would transition their prayers to that issue.

  For some Americans accustomed to prayer meetings being quiet, led by one person at a time praying, this might at first seem chaotic. However, in much of the Global South this is a common and powerful way of keeping everyone actively engaged in the process of praying, while leaders are constantly guiding and shaping the prayer meetings with intercession themes, and then perhaps moving to praying Scriptures that transition prayers to worship, thanksgiving, repentance, times of singing, or even silence. This approach is also used in half-night and all night prayer meetings.

Spiritual warfare is real. Prayer and fasting are major weapons in that warfare. Learn to use them. In the Global North, we tend to rely on the abundant resources that we have at our disposal; the Global South lacks those resources and is forced to rely on God and His resources. As a result, the North is spiritually impoverished, while the South sees abundant spiritual resources poured out on it—resources that are available in the Global North as well, if the church would only seek them. The words of Jesus to the church of Laodicea come to mind:

"You say, 'I am rich; I have acquired wealth and do not need a thing.' But you do not realize that you are wretched, pitiful, poor, blind and naked. I counsel you to buy from me gold refined in the fire, so you can become rich; and white clothes to wear, so you can cover your shameful nakedness; and salve to put on your eyes, so you can see." (Rev. 3:17–18)

Let whoever has ears, hear what the Spirit says to the churches.

EQUIPPING ORDINARY PEOPLE FOR THE IMPOSSIBLE

J erry took a group of seasoned Christian leaders to an African country so they could see what it is like to spend time in the midst of multiple Kingdom movements happening in the same country. On the way off the plane, he told the group that they might not even get out of the airport area without running into someone who was connected to Mission for All and Disciple Making Movements.

Jerry's words had hardly left his mouth when an immigration officer, who was handling one of the customs lines, heard that his business in the country was with Mission for All. The officer smiled broadly and said, "I work here at the airport, but I am a disciple maker, and I have just planted my first church! Say hello to my brothers and sisters there." Jerry still laughs about this experience. He often jokes, "Not only did we not get out of the airport without meeting a DMM practitioner— we had not even cleared immigration yet!"

In chapter four, we looked at some of the many examples in Scripture of God using ordinary, unexpected people to do extraordinary things. We see this throughout Scripture, both Old and New Testament. Now, we might think that these are exceptions, that they occurred because of a special call of God on that individual's life, a special empowering by the Spirit, which enabled them to do what they did. But that would only be partly right.

Think about it: why did God choose ordinary, not particularly special people? Why not use extraordinary people? In part, it is to show that it is His power at work, not ours. And that points to a lesson for us: it's not *our* ability that leads to great results for God, but *Him* working *through* us. "Not by might, not by power, but by my Spirit" says the LORD God Almighty (Zech. 4:6). And with the gift of the indwelling Holy Spirit, we are *all* empowered to be potential world-changers for God.

THE PRIESTHOOD OF EVERY CHRISTIAN IS SHOCKING WHEN YOU ACTUALLY SEE IT

Many Christian traditions use the phrase "priesthood of all believers" to describe what they believe and who they are. It is a biblical concept. It is an ideal value. It honors the potential for every Christian to be a world changer.

The question is, though, whether we actually live it out in practice. Does it result in the full empowerment and deployment of all Christians to bring dramatic transformation of families, communities and cultures? Or has the church been satisfied with theories of transformation instead of the reality? Is it possible that the theological pronouncements of the "priesthood of all believers" is just an idealized theory that for some curious reason rarely reflects reality?

When Global North church leaders visit Kingdom Movements in the Global South, the single most powerful response to what they see is "everybody here is making disciples. The accountants, the custodians, the police, the doctors, the farmers . . . they all see themselves as disciple makers and church planters!

Just before the completion of this book, a Christian businessman with a passion for engaging the lost was invited to accompany leaders of his church and see Kingdom Movements in Africa firsthand. He journaled his reflections extensively, and has summarized each in simple observations. Here are just a few:

> We cannot add disciple making and church planting to what we're already doing. It has to be what we're doing. And we have to stay with it and not move on.
>
> God doesn't need us to start movements for Him. He needs us to humbly join the one He's already begun. It's about getting onboard the global train that's already left the station.
>
> All we have to do to plant thousands of churches in a decade is . . . pray, fast, and praise. Trust the Living Word more. Preach less. And allow God to raise the occasional dead person.
>
> Pray without ceasing. There is no planting movement without first a prayer movement. And planting continues only as prayer continues. And the vigor of one reflects the other. You take the measure of a city by walking it. You take it for Christ when you walk it in prayer.
>
> When we added padding to the pews, we quit finding it more comfortable standing up to praise God, kneeling down to honor God, and leaving the building quickly to spread God.
>
> Saying it won't work here ensures that it won't work here.[1]

---

[1] Nelson Eddy, excerpts from *On Walking with Christians in Africa*.

EQUIPPING THE SAINTS FOR THE WORK OF MINISTRY

Jesus sent out ordinary, unnamed people to be the catalysts of His Kingdom coming in many places in Israel. Historically, there is some evidence that ordinary Christians have much better social networks to utilize in planting a church than most clergy.

But that is counter to Christian strategies today wherein only ordained professionals are trusted to open a new community to the Gospel. Christians in the Global North may agree that evangelism and church planting is their job, but they do not do much of it. The most common reason they give for not sharing the faith is that they do not know enough—which unintentionally suggests that evangelism actually *is* best left to the pros.

Churches can feed into this mentality by treating their services not as times of equipping the saints for the work of ministry, but as times to attract visitors to Jesus and to His church. Whether intentionally or not, this leads many Christian congregants to bring people to their church with the expectation their pastor will then win them to Christ through teaching.

Admittedly, that can sometimes work. But this approach takes power and responsibility away from the common believer. No matter how much personal evangelism is emphasized, the sharp distinction between clergy and laity will always make most Christians see winning people to Christ as the responsibility of the clergy, and in the worst cases, impossible for anyone who isn't a clergyman. No matter how many evangelism training opportunities are offered, the overall ethos of most churches communicates the message that evangelism is the clergy's job.

A *Transformational Discipleship Assessment* by LifeWay Research indicates that sixty-one percent of Christians who are attending church reported that, over the last six months, they had not attempted to share how to become a Christian with anyone.[2] How much would change if pastors embraced their role as coaches, trainers, and mentors, equipping their congregants to do the work of ministry—including disciple making, as discussed in chapter four?

If you are an ordinary believer with no Bible college or seminary training, you need to ask yourself, why not me? If you are a pastor, you need to look at your congregation and ask yourself, why not them?

However, this does not mean that some type of training is unnecessary. Jesus picked ordinary people for his Apostles and the seventy-two, but He also worked with them to enable them to carry out the tasks that He had assigned them. Jesus' approach was to take them on as apprentices.

In traditional crafts, an apprentice lived in the master's household, watched and learned from the master, was given increasingly complex tasks to do, had the work evaluated and corrected by the master, until eventually the apprentice had all the necessary skills to become a master and take on apprentices himself.

In the same way, the Apostles were called first to be with Him. They listened to His teachings, watched His way of life, and learned. Then He sent them on assignments, ranging from collecting a donkey on Palm Sunday, to preaching tours, to baptizing, to participating in miracles such as the feeding of the 5,000—the only miracle of Jesus recorded in all four Gospels. And when they came back, Jesus took the time to debrief them and give them further teaching.

---

[2]   http://www.lifeway.com/Article/research-survey-sharing-christ-2012

It's important to note that Jesus' approach to leadership development was primarily on the job and relational. It had a teaching component to be sure, but because of the parabolic nature of His teaching, the explanations were given privately to the Twelve, often in answer to their questions. And in the end, Jesus refers to them as His friends, not His servants (John 15:15).

The training was also integrated with ministry, and thus was contextual; they were given instructions on what to do, they did it, and then they got together afterward to report on what had happened and to get further coaching.

We see Paul using this same approach. He took Timothy with him on his missionary journeys; then, when he was ready, Paul sent him as his representative and ultimately as a pastor/leader in the important church in Ephesus. And then he told Timothy to do the same: "And the things you have heard me say in the presence of many witnesses entrust to reliable people who will also be qualified to teach others" (2 Tim. 2:2). Remember, this was Jesus' approach for training ordinary people. Remember as well that Jesus told us to make disciples, a word that means "apprentices."

Not every disciple got the level of training of the Apostles, of course, and not everyone in every church is going to emerge as a leader. Different people have different gifts. Nevertheless, every member should be a disciple, being coached and mentored, and should, in turn, be passing on to others the things that they are learning and doing. This requires a radically different concept of "the ministry" (i.e., the pastoral role) and of the responsibilities of the average church member than what we usually see in churches, especially in the Global North. The average church member must recognize this and be willing to participate accordingly.

Although this may seem impossible to some, fortunately, we have an example of someone who made this transition and who has had a tremendous impact on movements around the world. John King was a pastor for twenty-four years before encountering Disciple Making Movements in 2003. He put DMM principles into practice by starting a movement in the county jail, and since has shifted his ministry completely to the DMM model. He has coached organizations on four continents, and he refined the template used in Discovery Groups around the world today. The following are John's reflections on equipping congregations to do the work of ministry.

JOHN KING:
THE JOURNEY FROM A PASTOR TO A MOVEMENT CATALYST

Ephesians 4:11–13 haunted me! What I encountered in this text was not what I was schooled to do, and I never had the privilege to even apprentice under another pastoral leader. Speaking of Christ, Paul wrote:

He gave some as apostles, meaning to impart kingdom culture on earth as in heaven;

and some as prophets, to communicate heaven's vision here on earth;

and some as evangelists, to share the good news with the passion of Jesus;

and some as pastors and teachers, to build divine community and to train skills;

for the equipping of the saints for the work of service, to the building up of the body of Christ; until we all attain to the unity of the faith, and of the knowledge of the Son of God, to a mature man, to the measure of the stature which belongs to the fullness of Christ.

The purpose for these grace gifts—these equipping gifts—is to build up the body so that all reflect the character of Jesus and look, act, and sound like our heavenly Father. To the extent that they exist, the laity is equipped and empowered by the clergy to do ministry!

We become men and women of honesty and integrity. We use our speech to build people up rather than tear them down. We work, rather than cutting corners or stealing from others. We forgive as freely as we have tasted God's forgiveness. We all become servants who minister with compassion and proclaim the kingdom, like Jesus did (Ephesians 4:14–32).

Disciple Making Movements especially focus on the apostolic. Core DNA centers around bringing the reign of Christ into reality—especially where His name has not yet been heard. Doing more of what the Global North church has been doing will not bring us into the obedience called for in the Great Commission.

Making disciples of all the nations was honestly not on my radar. I had accepted too small a role in the kingdom—maturing some of those who had come to follow Jesus, but how can we follow him if we are not making disciples? No one makes these shifts all at once. I sure didn't!

That's why many of the best catalyst-people in Africa rebuffed what is now called DMM when they first heard it. Maybe it piqued the imaginations of one or two, but the whole was so different than what any of us had previously experienced.

The first shift for me was accepting that "whatever you do has to be reproducible by the people you train." "Can they replicate this?" is an earth-shattering question to force yourself to answer. My four-year Bible degree and two master's degrees argued that you have to have a Bible Dictionary and a Concordance at a minimum. How can you equip people for ministry if you can't train them to feed themselves spiritually? I mean, they could all purchase a Concordance and Bible Dictionary here in the U.S., but what about people in churches where there was only one copy of the Bible?

Discovery became the answer. How do we get people to slow down and listen to what the Word says? How do we get them to answer basic questions which go a bit farther than general reading comprehension—but not too much further? Many of my earliest attempts were far too complicated and demanded too much technology, but that nagging question kept popping back in my brain: "Can they replicate this?" Of the sixty whom I attempted to train, five could not read and write. How do you make the Word and Discovery accessible to oral learners, too?

They could all purchase a Concordance and Bible Dictionary here in the U.S., but what about people in churches where there was only one copy of the Bible?

What if a relatively new disciple came to you and asked, "Which of those Grace gifts has Jesus given to me to use to equip others?" How do you help him discover the answer? How do you help him explore where God is already at work in his life and join Him there?

Recently I discussed this very point with a man who wrote me, "I would love to come out of a study with confidence concerning my own gifts and how to use them. I have always felt a little unsure when it comes to this topic."

Be warned, though: discovery is demanding. The easy way forward is to just tell someone which ones of these gifts you have seen the most in his life. But what if you are wrong? What if there is another which they have not yet attempted? I choose instead to ask him to explore. Which of the following excites you more? Which scares you more?

- Planting kingdom **culture** where the name of Jesus has never been heard.

- Communicating God's **vision** for living differently.

- Telling other people **good news** which lifts their defeated spirits.

- Calling disciples to experience the **community** that Jesus enables us to have.

- Becoming confident and competent in exercising **skills** that a community needs.

What do you need to see yourself being settled into one of these that you do not already have?

- Is it a clearer picture of what it will look like?

- Is it the courage to take risks?

- Is it a new way to see yourself?

- Is it a passion for a group of people that you do not care for, but you sense that God wants you to have His heart for them?

Then I ask him some additional questions:

What gives you great joy in your spiritual walk?

What spiritual questions, concepts, or skills are you most likely to think about when you are showering or mowing your lawn—the ideas that you are not forced to think about by schedule or need, but things that percolate without effort?

When have you found learning new skills hard but rewarding?

What life experiences repeatedly cause you to feel shame? (These can be strongholds that the enemy uses to hold us back from daring to step into God's calling for us.)

What accomplishments, completed projects, or experiences give you great joy?

Answering similar questions can help one begin to discern where God is already working, and can become prayer points for intentionally joining in with what He is doing!

This questioning process is part of good coaching in a Discovery approach. Disciple Making Movements demand that catalysts learn to hear from God and apply what they discover to their life in concrete actions—appropriate obedience. Legalism is applying a list of rules that someone else gives us. Obedience is being responsive to God's directions. Good coaching models an incredible trust in the Holy Spirit. It acknowledges that God produces better outcomes than the coach can. It believes that the resources are in the harvest. The kingdom-advancing force will arise from God's harvest field, if we will disciple others in the disciple-making style modeled by Jesus Himself.

> *Disciple Making Movements demand that catalysts learn to hear from God and apply what they discover to their life in concrete actions—appropriate obedience.*

Training entails learning skills. Coaching and good training work well together, but in the DMM world, much of our training is intentionally done to find the few who are willing to be coached. Most in the Western Church are not willing to be coached.

Finding a Person of Peace becomes the greatest hook which reels in those of us who have been "captured" by Movement thinking. "Taste and see" may be the opening invitation. Seeing the joyful transformation in the life of a Person of Peace following a Discovery path is intoxicating.

Helping ordinary people experience breakthroughs in making disciples gives me great joy! Doing an exposure training in facilitating Discovery Groups with people who have a passion to reach Chinese university students holds out great promise. Coaching them to explore meaningful ways to connect with these students and to engage them in spiritual conversations advances the cause. Guiding them into discovering why a small Discovery Group format being reproducible back in China makes it the better option for here, too—and this pushes essential paradigm shifts.

Floyd McClung has said, "Apostolic people take the church to the world; they don't wait for the world to come to the church." We need apostolic people to reach the large percentage of Americans who are not coming to our existing churches. Maybe the Great Commission's call to "go, make disciples" will produce better results than our cultural shift to "build it and they will come"!

Many of us become pushy and impatient right after we experience an internal paradigm shift. We so desperately want the people we love to go with us on this exciting journey, but they need us to help them envision new possibilities and new ways of getting there. Trust the Spirit to produce dissatisfaction.

Mentoring expands potential. It requires a depth of relationship which is rare in the West. Good mentors not only lower the drawbridge over our moat, but they also unlock the inner rooms of their castle, allowing others to be with us as we truly are. Rare indeed is the Western leader who takes away all masks and becomes truly transparent. But such vulnerability is essential to guiding others beyond their inner limitations.

What happens when people are equipped and released for ministry? God uses them in remarkable ways, even in improbable and dangerous situations. We see this in the story of a woman from a closed Muslim country.

ZAHRA: THE MUSLIM STREET VENDOR

During the last weeks of writing this book, Jerry spent a couple of days with a room full of Disciple Makers from one of the world's most intensely Muslim countries. They were not in their home country and their worship was amazing—remarkable because only when they cross a frontier can they switch from snapping with their fingers and singing in whispers to joyful, loud music, with singing, clapping and dancing before the Lord. And they related to themes of the Kingdom of God with a passion and excitement that is beyond description.

They had endured some major challenges from the secret police in their home country, but they were so excited to share stories of what God was doing that the translator could barely keep up.

One of those stories was about a street vendor in a major city, a woman whom we'll call Zahra. She was introduced to a Discovery Bible study in early 2016 and eventually surrendered her life to Jesus. After that, she moved to the north of her country to be near her family, and then set about learning to read well enough so that she could easily share any part of the Bible.

She even started developing her own biblical story sets for different people and situations because she wanted all of the Discovery Bible Groups that were forming to learn to follow and obey God in any situation. She was starting groups when she was just six months into her time in the Lord.

One of the women who discipled Zahra said in the interview, "When we were doing traditional study groups, we made *converts*, but in Disciple Making Movements, we make a lot of *disciples*. The difference is their obedience, and that they have trust in God, not in us—they have crazy experiences with God that we can't even dream of!"

Zahra had been separated from her husband for fifteen years. In one Bible study, the obedience element that she got from the passage was to choose to love her estranged husband, and she began to cry because she was still so bitter. With tears in her eyes, she went to reconcile with her husband in the city where he lived. Now they are together again, and she commutes because of her work selling products on the street. And since reconciling with her husband, her business has improved. She had one hour when she sold her whole inventory—making as much money as she typically earned in a whole month before she was saved.

Zahra said: "This blessing is the glory of Jesus because I obeyed Him. Now I am learning how to give tithes. I have a piggy bank now. Before I didn't have money because I am just a vendor on the street. This is all God's money, and I can give to people. Before I give, I say to God: 'This is your gift for your people.' I have a lot of fire now for the Lord. I couldn't read very well, but now I can read well and tell His stories."

The groups that Zahra catalyzed are now at three generations—in a place where every new group has to learn how to avoid the secret police and still multiply.

Zahra shows the incredible things that average people can do when they are given the tools, coaching, and mentoring that they need as they need it. If churches in the Global North are going to see movements like we see in the Global South, we will also need to provide training, mentorship, and *permission* to ordinary people to advance the Kingdom.

THE HOLY SPIRIT: MANIFESTING THE KING'S CHARACTER AND AUTHORITY

In hundreds of places across the six continents disciples are returning to their original design. The DNA of Jesus' discipleship is emerging fresh. Disciples are making disciples. Churches are starting churches. Leaders are maturing into their God appointed roles. The Book of Acts is happening again and again and again. At the core is not a method (though simple, biblical methods are important). At the center is not a discipleship process (though life-on-life interaction is critical). What is driving and sustaining the explosive growth of God's kingdom is the age-old Spirit walk God designed us for. Disciples are learning to keep in step with the Spirit of the Almighty God who knows no boundaries, opens every closed door, and produces fruit that lasts for eternity.

—Steve Smith, *Spirit Walk*

There is a call of God on the African church in the 21st century. Following the flow of spiritual power, we are discovering that God has infused and engaged people groups with remarkable disciple making. We can see mighty movements spreading across the entire continent bearing the fingerprint of God. It encourages us that the continent will be "filled with the knowledge of the glory of the Lord, as the waters cover the sea." (Hab. 2:14)

We want to be clear about one thing—a Disciple Making Movement (DMM) is not a program; it is not a strategy or a curriculum. It is simply a movement of God. Without Him, there is nothing.

Our Sovereign God is passionately pursuing the lost to bring them to Himself. Prayer and fasting allow us to align ourselves with Him. There will be no results if we are walking in our own strength and according to our own resources. God says, "Ask me and I will make the nations your inheritance, the ends of the earth your possession."

—Younoussa Djao

Engage! Africa video series

THE HOLY SPIRIT AND MOVEMENTS

Training isn't everything.

Even with the best models for coaching and mentoring, nothing happens without the Spirit.

Jesus told His disciples to wait in Jerusalem until they received power when the Holy Spirit had come upon them (Acts 1:4–5, 8)—and He did this *after* giving them three years with the greatest Teacher that the world has ever known, *after* they'd done preaching tours that included healings and deliverance, *after* having baptized people in His name, and *after* receiving the Great Commission.

In his Upper Room Discourse, Jesus looked past His death and resurrection to the ascension. He told the Apostles that it would be *better* for them if He left, because then He could send them the Spirit who would be with them forever (John 16:7).

Why is it better to have the Holy Spirit than Jesus' physical presence? Isn't being with Jesus in eternity the nature of our hope?

The Holy Spirit—and Jesus through the Spirit—goes with each of us wherever we go.

The answer is directly connected to God's plan for us to spread the Kingdom throughout the world. The Holy Spirit—and Jesus through the Spirit—goes with each of us wherever we go. The gift of the Spirit enables Jesus to be with us as we carry out the Great Commission.

Jesus describes the Spirit as their *paraclete*, a very rich word whose range of meanings includes "advocate," "counselor," "helper," "encourager," and "exhorter." He promised the Apostles that the Spirit would teach them all truth and remind them of the things that Jesus had told them (John 14:26). The Spirit will bear witness to Jesus (John 15:26) and will convict the world of sin, righteousness, and judgment (John 16:8–10).

The Spirit is thus critical for the Christian life. As the *paraclete*, He guides us, encourages us, and exhorts us in living out our relationship with Christ. He is responsible for our growth in conformity to the image of Jesus, as shown by the fruit of the Spirit (Gal. 5:22–23). The Spirit is also critical for evangelism, both by bearing witness to Jesus and convicting the world of their need for Him.

Christians in the Global North frequently gloss over the idea of the Spirit bearing witness to Christ. This is due to the assumption that Jesus meant simply that the Spirit would work through and empower our witness. That is certainly true, yet the context of John 16 suggests something more: that the Spirit would actively bear witness Himself to the truth of the Gospel. And we see that happening in the miracles performed through the Apostles in Acts.

We also see this in the Global South. It is impossible for any researcher to visit all 500 movements today, yet every catalyst of Kingdom movements that we know strongly affirms that the miraculous is abundantly obvious in a high percentage of the new churches being birthed—including raising the dead.[1] Jesus told the seventy-two to heal the sick, raise the dead, and cast out demons, and Christians today are doing those same things, as the Spirit bears witness to the truth of the Gospel.

Steve Smith had seen some miraculous healings and deliverance in his ministry in Los Angeles, but when he got to China, he realized that far more extensive miraculous intervention was needed there. This is due to the fact that the Chinese

---

1 For examples, see Jerry Trousdale, *Miraculous Movements* (Nashville: Thomas Nelson, 2012), p.134–140; Pat Robertson et al., *The Father Glorified* (Nashville: Thomas Nelson, 2013), chapter 12.

were largely held captive by demonic forces deeply entrenched in the culture. So he turned to the Scriptures and prayer:

In my first couple of years overseas, I read the book of Acts at least once every month. I would say to the Lord: "What you have done, please do it again," not requiring God to act certain ways, but remembering what the horizon holds for God to act if He so chooses. Then it is just a matter of living in the faith of saying: "God, please do what you want to do here."

In the first 190 churches that I could document in the movement in China, every one of them had some miracle in the early evangelism phase of their existence. God was doing it to prove His power and presence, and to reveal Himself.

THE APOSTOLIC ERA VS. TODAY

This does not align with the theology of many Christians and churches in the Global North. Some groups believe that the "age of miracles" ended with the death of the last Apostle, or that miracles were given solely to authenticate the word of the Apostles. Since we now have the Bible, the argument goes, no further authentication is needed, which is why miracles no longer occur. They do acknowledge that God sometimes answers prayer and heals people, but believe that is not a "sign miracle" of the same type.

At the same time, these theologians will typically also affirm *sola scriptura*, the idea that Scripture alone is our source of theological truth. Yet they cannot point to any passage of Scripture other than a tortured eisegesis of 1 Cor. 13:10 that could lead them to the idea that miracles ended with the Apostles or the New Testament.

If such "sign miracles" have ended, then the witness of the miraculous church multiplying in the Global South must be dismissed either as a misunderstanding, a lie, or counterfeit miracle done by demonic power. The last is a very dangerous charge, since it is exactly the context of Jesus' teaching on blaspheming the Holy Spirit.

The only remaining possibility is that the miracles happening in the Global South are real. And if the Spirit is bearing witness to Jesus through miracles in the Global South, shouldn't we look for Him to do the same in the Global North?

PREACH AND HEAL

Charles Fielding has written a significant book on the theme of Jesus' mandate entitled *Preach and Heal*. Recognizing the complexities of the question of whether God still does miraculous healing, he suggests imagining yourself standing before the Judgment Seat of Christ and finding out that you were wrong:

> If I had spent my life stubbornly believing that there were no modern-day miracles but found myself to be wrong, how would I feel? If Jesus asked me, "Charles, why did you never obey my command to use the power of the Holy Spirit to heal?" what would I answer? Although Jesus will completely forgive me, I will still be ashamed. To find that I had disobeyed Jesus would bring me much grief.
>
> On the other hand, if I spent my life stubbornly believing that supernatural healings were a possibility and prayed for Christ's healing on many occasions, how would I feel at the judgment seat if I were wrong? Jesus would say something like, "Charles, my commands to heal were only for the

disciples of that day. Why did you pray for the power of the Holy Spirit to heal in your day?"

In this situation, I would also be wrong but at least I wouldn't be as ashamed . . . In the first situation, I would be guilty of disobedience but in the second situation, I would only be guilty of being wrong, something that I am more comfortable with as my age advances. At my judgment, I expect to find that I was wrong about many things. During this life, though, I endeavor to live in such a way that the judgment will reveal fewer instances in which I had been disobedient.

SURPRISED BY THE MIRACULOUS

Fortunately, the Holy Spirit *does* work in and through us, regardless of our theology. In 2015, Jerry was asked to visit Team Expansion to spend some days with their senior field leaders. The following story is about Terry and Amy (referred to in chapter 5), veteran missionaries who adopted Kingdom Movements in their work among Muslims in West Africa. Terry asked Jerry if he would review their tracking data and evaluate their work. This is Jerry's account of what followed:

> Their outcome tracking was excellent and it only took two or three minutes to discover that they were seeing phenomenal growth among some difficult people groups.
>
> The realization that this had happened in less than 18 months was stunning. Over the next few minutes, I pumped Terry for details and the overall picture was encouraging. The "bad news" was that they were growing faster than their leadership training could keep up with. They needed some emergency help to get all of the training, coaching, and mentoring elements up and running more efficiently.
>
> Eventually, I put the charts down and said to Terry, "I have rarely seen growth this fast in these kinds of people;

this usually means that miracles are abounding. Terry, are you and Amy seeing miracles every day?"

He shook his head and said, "No, not really."

Something was wrong here. I asked again: "So you are not seeing miracles happening in the new groups forming?" Then Terry's eyes brightened and he said, "Oh yes, we hear the stories of miracles all the time. It's amazing. I thought you were asking about just Amy and me—we grew up cessationists!" It was a great answer.

Veteran missionaries were humbly watching God do the heavy lifting in a very hard place and seeing their long-held dreams for these unreached peoples now coming to pass—and being transformed themselves in the process.

"Those in whom the Spirit comes to live are God's new Temple. They are, individually and corporately, places where heaven and earth meet."

—N.T. Wright, *Simply Christian: Why Christianity Makes Sense*

SEAN STECKBECK

Stories of miracles on the mission field have been circulating for years among evangelicals. They are almost invariably from a part of the world that is inaccessible to us and is under-developed, populated by animists or other people-groups with magical beliefs. The stories of these groups often come to us by word of mouth with no documentation, making them almost like Christian urban legends that may or may not have any basis in fact. It is easy to be skeptical about these stories, or even to naively accept them.

But the story of Sean Steckbeck is a different matter. He is a mentor who is working in Israel—a highly developed part of the world that is more or less integrated into the Global North socially, politically, and economically. The story of his call to Israel and his ministry there illustrates the work of miracles and the centrality of the Holy Spirit in Kingdom movements.

Sean was just a year away from graduating from his theological studies in preparation to serve in Southeast Asia. He was working at a restaurant in Pensacola, Florida, and a woman whom he had never met walked up to him and said: "I don't know you, but I was on a 40 day fast, and the Lord told me to break my fast and to walk into this restaurant. He said that I'd meet a young man in there who is being called to Israel."

She was certain that Sean was the person she was supposed to invite over to a house of prayer. Curious about all this, Sean agreed to go.

At the house of prayer that day, intercessors prayed for Sean, and he still remembers what happened:

> As they prayed over me, I felt like fire coming over me, and I heard the Lord saying, "Yes, I am calling you to Israel." That was strange for me, because I was set for Southeast Asia. So this experience was a complete 180-degree shift. I began to prepare my heart to obey that calling.

That day, at the house of prayer, Sean also met Ayelet, an attractive Israeli woman who quickly caught his eye, and eventually captured his heart.

After graduation, Sean headed to Israel. He and Ayelet began their relationship and were married in 2003. Sean tried many different kinds of ministries. Youth ministries were difficult because of legal constraints, so he trained Christian youths to reach out to others.

At that point, he had not heard about Disciple Making Movements but he had already sensed that it was important to disciple people in the context of their culture. In 2005, Victor Choudhrie became a mentor to Sean. It was then that Sean says he read James Rutz's *Megashift*, David Garrison's *Church Planting Movements*, and Neil Cole's *Organic Church* and began to sense the direction that he needed to go.

Sean started down this path in 2005, making mistakes but learning from each one. He started by meeting strangers on the street and trying to find people of peace just by a sense that God had something for him to share with them—what the Bible calls a "word of knowledge." He recalls, "That did not get us into a lot of homes, unfortunately." But in 2007, Sean and Ayelet's first year in Beer Sheva, he started a new approach: Praying for strangers whom he met. That produced a remarkable wave of signs, wonders, and healings—almost unheard of in Israel at that time. For a while, it was just Jewish people who were healed, and then it spread to Muslims. It was an exciting time for Sean, as he began to see some momentum as groups began to form.

If we function according to our ability alone, we get the glory; if we function according to the power of the Spirit within us, God gets the glory. He wants to reveal Himself to a watching world."

—Henry T. Blackaby, *Experiencing the Spirit: The Power of Pentecost Every Day*

But back in 2005, Disciple Making Movements[2] were just beginning to be recognized in the church, and many of Sean's colleagues in Israel were suspicious about what he was doing. He was misunderstood, he lost a lot of his supporters, and he even had to leave the organization that had sent them to Israel.

His colleagues were also uncomfortable because Sean had a vision of laypeople ministering. He did not know yet how to do that, but the fact that he advocated empowering laypeople for ministry was a big issue since it was so rarely done, if ever. Sean explains:

Our network had clear leadership—we believed in good leadership. But I had a vision that:

- we could release lay leadership;
- we could release the entire body of Christ;
- everybody could plant a congregation;
- everybody could make disciples;
- everybody could baptize;
- everybody could take the Lord's Supper by themselves;
- and you don't need to be ordained leaders or recognized leaders to do these things.

Biblically, Jesus commanded us to do these things. Every believer is not merely *allowed* to do them, they are actually *commanded* to.

That brought a lot of fear into the hearts of leaders. They felt like we were creating a rebellious movement against an institution, but we felt like we were releasing people into obeying Jesus.

---

[2] At that time, they were called "Church Planting Movements."

Thankfully, over the years, these wounds have been healed and Sean's vision and his initiatives have been generally accepted. However, this does not discount the fact that there were painful times early on.

Sean reports that the next phase came when he read *Miraculous Movements* and met Jay Judson (pseudonym). We will pick up this narrative in the next chapter. Though it would be unwise to risk identifying them in this book, you should know that God has used Sean and his colleagues to launch multiple house churches in different segments of Israeli society.

One thing that is abundantly clear is that the testimony of God's work through Sean and Ayelet has confirmed—a thousand times over—the power of a word birthed in God's providence and spoken between perfect strangers years ago in a Florida restaurant.

NOT IN CHARIOTS OR HORSES

> Some trust in chariots and some in horses,
> but we will remember the name of our God.
> (Psalm 20:7)

These words of the psalmist are still important today, "In my view of the world, what do I trust as my source of security and success?" In many aspects of life, prudence, restraint, and the counsel of wise people are altogether appropriate and praiseworthy. However, in matters of the Kingdom of God—which should comprise the totality of our lives—there are many times when our King invites us to stretch our faith; he asks us to engage a task as His ambassador of the Kingdom or as a steward of Kingdom resources. Restraint and human limitations are not the currency of the Kingdom of God.

In many aspects of life, prudence, restraint, and the counsel of wise people are altogether appropriate and praiseworthy.

The Kingdom of God is manifestly upside down and backwards—tasks don't get done nor is our wellbeing secured the way we assume it is. The Kingdom of God is a realm that is as real as the ground beneath our feet, but it operates more like the wind that blows through our hair.

> "I tell you the truth, no one can enter the Kingdom of God unless he is born of water and the Spirit. Flesh gives birth to flesh but the Spirit gives birth to spirit. You should not be surprised at My saying, 'You must be born again'. The wind blows wherever it pleases. You hear its sound but you cannot tell where it comes from or where it is going. So it is with everyone born of the Spirit."- John 3:5–8

Participating in the Kingdom of God requires ongoing faith in and dependence on the Holy Spirit. This requires an entirely new paradigm for how we think about and plan our ministry.

CHRISTIANS AS STRATEGIC THINKERS: Shall we trust our vision of what God can do based on what we have seen Him do before, or on what He has invited us to ask Him to release to us?

CHRISTIAN PRAGMATISTS: Shall we set goals that we have seen happen before, or trust Him for what seems impossible?

CHRISTIAN RESOURCE GATHERERS: Shall we trust our development team's strategy, or the storehouse of heaven, which cannot be seen with human eyes?

CHRISTIAN LEADERS: Shall we trust our ability to sell a program to people and make it work, or shall we trust God to shape our programs completely by Kingdom values?

The measuring stick for what is possible is God, not us.

So he answered and said to me: "This is the word of the Lord to Zerubbabel: 'Not by might nor by power, but by My Spirit,' says the Lord of hosts." (Zechariah 4:6)

UNBRANDED KINGDOM PARTNERSHIPS AND CATALYSTS

[T]he Lord appointed seventy-two others, and sent them two by two ahead of him to every town and place where he was about to go. Luke 10:1 (NIV)

Behold how good and how pleasant it is for brethren to dwell together in unity! It is like the precious oil upon the head. Running down on the beard of Aaron, Running down on the edge of his garments. It is like the dew of Hermon, descending upon the mountains of Zion. For there the Lord commanded the blessing— Life forevermore. Ps. 133: 1–3 (NKJV)

UNBRANDED AND UNLEASHED: ONE BODY, MANY MEMBERS

Over the last twelve years of working with many hundreds of partners, we have seen a few organizations, some large, who try to focus on or stick to their "brand" (i.e., their organization, denomination, or ministry) in the middle of executing a movement strategy and come up far short of their goals.

On the other hand, we have seen hundreds of ministries, and even single churches, that participate in the process in close partnership with other ministries quite different from theirs, and they experience a level of fruitfulness that they had never experienced before.

Unbranded ministry does not guarantee success, but in the context of replicating movements, attempting to stay within the confines of a "brand" more often than not leads to failure. Emphasizing a brand takes the focus inward, thus dulling the drive for the mission at hand, and creates surface partnerships that splinter easily.

In the Upper Room Discourse, Jesus tells His disciples how people will recognize them as His followers: "By this everyone will know that you are my disciples, if you love one another" (John 13:35).

When the unchurched in the Global North think about Christians, love is not the first thing that comes to mind. Culturally, a segment of society intentionally tries to marginalize Christians and, in those circles, Christians are identified more for what we are against than what we are for. The Protestant world is especially known for the divisions that have beset it since its beginnings, 500 years ago.

We divide over baptism, Communion, or proper church structure. We quibble over the gifts of the Holy Spirit. We debate theological ideas, which we typically agree do not matter for salvation but, somehow, think are important enough to drive us apart. We divide over styles of worship or building programs or over a host of things that do nothing to advance the Gospel. And all this division serves to destroy our witness to a watching world because we are not exhibiting love for one another, according to Jesus' prophetic words (John 13:35).

This is not a new problem. Jesus himself faced it with the Twelve:

> "Teacher," said John, "we saw someone driving out demons in your name and we told him to stop, because he was not one of us."
>
> "Do not stop him," Jesus said. "For no one who does a miracle in my name can in the next moment say anything bad about me, for whoever is not against us is for us. Truly I tell you, anyone who gives you a cup of water in my name because you belong to the Messiah will certainly not lose their reward." (Mark 9:38–41)

The same story is told in a shorter form in Luke 9 between the sending out of the Twelve and the seventy-two. It is even possible that some of those driving out demons were among the seventy-two that Jesus was about to commission. None of them were part of the Twelve.

A related problem is the all-too-human tendency to promote our church, our ministry, our denomination to the extent that it looks a lot like spiritual rivalry. We come up with a wide range of high-minded excuses for this but, unless these include rejecting the genuineness of someone's commitment to Christ, the refusal to work in harmony with them violates Jesus' commandment to love one another, as well as His prayer for the unity of all those who follow Him so that the world might know that God sent Him (John 17:20–23).

The question we have to ask is how can we bring everlasting Kingdom impact into a society. It may be people groups or a geographical area, but as long as we are proactive in keeping the DNA of a movement, it is only about two things: God, and lost people. If we think it is about us it will not last.

So when we think about leadership we think about disciple-making—something that will live on whether I am there or I am not there. It will be impactful and the fruit is everlasting.

One of the challenges in the world in Africa is people-centered movements with someone's name attached to them. I think that takes the glory away from God.

The Kingdom is the Kingdom of God. It belongs only to God. And it is for rescuing and transforming lost people.

—Aychiluhm Beyene, Engage! Africa video series

Divisions and dissension among Christians, churches, and ministries is bad and damages our witness to the world. It is simply antithetical to Kingdom values.

DIVISION VS. DIVERSITY

But if division is a serious problem, unity in diversity is a profoundly beneficial thing in God's economy. God loves diversity. The universe testifies to this as we look at the bewildering array of things that God has created, all of which work together in a great cosmic harmony, demonstrating God's creativity, His wisdom, His beauty.

No two human beings are identical, and our bodies have a diversity of parts. Paul tells us in Romans, 1 Corinthians, and Ephesians that the church is like that: there are many members with diverse gifts, but only one body. Further, every gift is necessary for the body to function properly. Since no single person has all the gifts, we need each other; the diversity of the gifts contributes to the unity of Christ's disciples.

We can look beyond the local church to the universal church as well. God has blessed churches and ministries that have every conceivable structure, wildly divergent (though orthodox) theologies, different views of baptism and communion, various worship forms and styles. If God has worked in and through organizations with all these differences, shouldn't we be willing to do the same thing?

The nation of Israel had different tribes with different traditions, yet they were unified around their common identity as a people and their common worship of God. In the same way, the church can have different denominations with their own traditions, theological nuances, liturgical approaches, and so on, and yet still be united in our common mission in the world and in our worship of God.

We see this especially in the Global South. Organizations that typically don't partner in projects in North America work in close partnership outside of America. In those cases, you usually see that they tend to enjoy their partnership, and they observe God blessing the process. It is fairly rare for a Disciple Making Movement to start with only one organization doing everything.

In New Generations's current experience, out of more than 500 engagements with people groups and urban affinity groups in the Global South, there are typically more than 700 different partners who became involved with New Generations and with each other at any moment in time. Most are Global South organizations, but not all. Sometimes there are seven or eight partners working in unity among the same people groups.

However, we have seen one tragic thing happen that nearly always has dire consequences. Sometimes Western denominations that do not catalyze movements find a few hundred churches that had been birthed in a Disciple Making Movements and offer to provide funds for pastoral salaries and for church buildings. But they offer one condition—the churches must formally become part of their denomination. That action almost always stops replication and momentum. It is the church's choice to make, so there is no issue there, but their momentum as multipliers is now lost. The denomination may genuinely think that they have been helpful, not even realizing the damage done. But introducing money into the situation—especially in exchange for something like this—takes away the organic nature of the movement, and as a result, it stalls out.

> Who then is Paul, and who is Apollos, but ministers through whom you believed, as the Lord gave to each one. So then neither he who plants is anything, nor he who waters, but God who gives the increase. Now he who plants and he who waters are one, and each one will receive his own reward according to his own labor. For you are God's fellow workers; you are God's field.

—I Cor. 3:6–8 (NKJV)

1. STRATEGIC CATALYTIC PARTNERSHIPS AMONG WESTERN WORKERS AND ORGANIZATIONS

Jay Judson (pseudonym) and Sean Steckbeck

Jay Judson knew that God had called him to a life of ministry because he wanted to proclaim the Gospel. And after taking the Perspectives on the World Christian Movements course, he knew that God was inviting him to take the Gospel somewhere it had yet to reach.

Jay had the amazing privilege of being mentored for a year by Dr. George Patterson, an early pioneer in Disciple Making Movements and a passionate advocate for obedience-based disciple making. Jay was determined to make good use of what he had learned from Dr. Patterson. He applied to a mission agency, which agreed to send him to Burma, a closed country with some people groups who had millions of people with no "Jesus options" at all. Jay's dream was to see Disciple Making Movements there.

The first breakthrough was the day when a distinguished Myanmar man known as "the Major" knocked on Jay's door and announced, "I have heard that you want to reach my people for Jesus. I follow Jesus, but I don't know how to make disciples, so will you be my friend?" Jay was stunned and amazed that God would send him such a partner in ministry. That day, they both knelt and thanked God for bringing them together. Jay knew that the Lord had just provided a great resource who would be key to launching the ministry.

The Major got his nickname from his military career, but he had also been a military lawyer and a former political activist. For that last pursuit, he had spent years imprisoned in the notorious Insein Jail of Burma, known for poor conditions and abhorrent treatment of inmates. There, he had access to a Bible, and became a Christ Follower through reading it.

The Major had not had another Christian disciple him, and so he asked Jay, a much younger man, to help him grow in his walk with Jesus. Jay's response was: "Can I come to your house?" Jay wanted to make the Major's journey with Jesus so simple that anyone could do it. They engaged the process together, and within six months, a handful of new churches provided the foundation of what was yet to come.

During this time, Jay began feeling pressure from missionary colleagues to abandon Kingdom Movements. He was told that movements were just fads that would blow away when the next fad came along. It was very difficult to resist the pressure of his peers. But then he met David Watson. David coached and mentored Jay and the Major in Disciple Making Movements, and the two friends soaked up what they were learning as they grew in understanding the biblical foundations of movements.

Then God gave Jay another disciple who started seven churches within six months. But just as that momentum was beginning to grow, Jay experienced renal failure and was evacuated to a hospital in America. There, he had eleven different doctors working on his case, and all were asking essentially the same question: "How could this happen to a healthy young man?" He gave each the same answer, "This is the devil."

"No, seriously," the doctors would retort, "what's going on here?"

"Satan," was Jay's consistent response.

During his two weeks in the hospital, news came that seven churches had grown to eleven. And by the time that Jay recovered six months later, there were thirty. Afterward, he attended a meeting of his denominational mission and some people were asking him if there were lots of miracles happening in Burma. That question actually irritated Jay. He told them that he just shares the Gospel and makes disciples.

About that time, Jay met Sean Steckbeck, whom we met in the last chapter, and he was interested to learn about his work in Israel. Sean was equally fascinated to hear how Jay learned to be a catalyst, finding and developing leaders who, in turn, could be catalysts for rapidly multiplying movements—something that Sean had never learned how to do. Jay explained his ministry model and began to share concepts learned from Patterson and Watson.

Eventually, Jay asked Sean what his "Gospel bridge" was to get access to Israeli people. Sean replied that, since he had limited ministry funds, his access was walking through Israel's markets and shops asking God to show him people with whom to start a conversation; he then found out about their needs and prayed for and with them. That didn't cost anything. And God frequently answered those prayers with healing, which easily turned into a Bible study.

Jay was not subtle; he bluntly replied: "Sean, I just don't believe in that." So Sean patiently started telling Jay the stories of people that he prayed for who were healed and then became people of peace.

Jay's response was a challenge. His wife was back in the hotel with a serious infection which had proven resistant to treatment for several weeks. So Jay told Sean, "If this is as real as you say it is, prove it! If God heals my wife, I'll change my view of miracles." That is not the kind of challenge that regularly invites God's cooperation, but Sean readily agreed. He immediately began to pray for Jay's wife, and she later shared that she was feeling something like electricity and heat in her body. And within a few hours, all signs of infection were completely gone.

If Jay's challenge had been a bit cynical and cheeky, his response to what happened was remarkable: "Please disciple me in the things of the Holy Spirit. And come to Burma and teach all of my leaders how to pray for healing and deliverance."

Sean decided to make it a two-way partnership. "I will, if you will coach and mentor me on the principles and practices of replicating Movements." And that is how this story became a model of God's Kingdom math, where 1+1=11. Today, Sean and Jay have formed an organization together, they support each other in their giftings, and in each other's fields, and God is blessing both of them with new fruitfulness.

Some of Jay's coworkers were from a Buddhist background, and Sean introduced them to the biblical principles of praying for the sick and demon-possessed. It not only revolutionized their ministry, but the movements grew from 20,000 Buddhist-background Christ Followers to 126,000 baptized believers in 4,300 churches by 2017.

And in response, Jay has coached Sean how to restructure his paradigms of making disciples and church-planting so that generational processes are happening in three different affinity groups in Israel.

2. STRATEGIC CATALYTIC PARTNERSHIPS AMONGST GLOBAL SOUTH AND GLOBAL NORTH TEAMS

What New Generations Has Learned about Global North and Global South Teams

Over the last twelve years, New Generations has been an organization with both Global North Missionary leaders and Global South leaders. Almost all of the Global North leaders have, in years past, catalyzed church planting cross-culturally, but their roles today are very different. The Global South leaders are the most critical element in the process of launching more than 100 Disciple Making Movements (defined as at least 100 churches to 4 or more generations), many among previously unengaged people groups.

The Global North leaders for the most part do not have direct leadership roles in Global South initiatives, but typically provide strategic support instead. In two cases, both spanning approximately twelve to fourteen years, New Generations's Global North leaders have been deeply involved in gathering and supporting teams of Global South catalysts whom God used to launch Disciple Making Movements in their regions of the Global South. Those leaders are now New Generations's senior regional directors.

New Generations believes that what they have learned from these symbiotic partnerships may be helpful for other ministries trying to be more effective in the Global South. The headlines are:

- For a wide variety of reasons, cultural insiders are much more effective as disciple makers than cultural outsiders.

- Global South leaders are much more effective at mobilizing faithful intercessors than Global North leaders.

- Global South leaders report that they find Global North colleagues are often especially valuable in developing strong research methodologies, strategic analysis, tactical planning, and helping local leaders develop a bigger vision for what God can do through them, especially in engaging unreached people groups. Local churches often need help seeing over their existing horizons to what is possible with God.

- While Global North ministry models are typically too expensive to replicate in the Global South, Global North missionaries can often mobilize resources for high value projects.

- Global North missionaries need to spend their time finding the "right" indigenous people, empowering them, coaching them, and releasing them to do what is needed;

There are amazing and wonderful men and women who have dedicated their whole lives to sometimes challenging mission fields, and they are heroes and heroines. At the same time, it seems that the Lord is opening a new season with the potential for new and powerful roles, where He is calling Global North missionaries to become supporting catalysts and partners instead of prime movers.

While there are a number of additional lessons that can be gleaned from New Generations's experience, the key point is obvious: in interactions between the Global North and the Global South, each side brings strengths and weaknesses, and as they work in collaboration the greatest results are seen. If either side insisted on branding ministries rather than collaborating with each other, the progress of movements in the Global South would be much slower or non-existent.

CATALYTIC KINGDOM NETWORKS AND LARGE PARTNERSHIPS

One of the most astounding statements in Scripture occurs in Jesus' High Priestly Prayer, in which He prays that we would enter into the very life of the Trinity, and that this unity with the Godhead would be exhibited in our unity with each other (John 17:20–24). The persons of the Trinity live in seamless unity, harmony, and love; since our unity with each other is founded upon our union with the Trinity, so we should also live in unity, harmony, and love with each other.

Living out this unity means "being like-minded, having the same love, being one in spirit and of one mind." We are called to "do nothing out of selfish ambition or vain conceit. Rather, in humility value others above yourselves, not looking to your own interests but each of you to the interests of the others." We are, in short, to live like Jesus,

> Who, being in very nature God,
>   did not consider equality with God something
>   to be used to his own advantage;
> rather, he made himself nothing
>   by taking the very nature of a servant,
>   being made in human likeness.
> And being found in appearance as a man,
>   he humbled himself
>   by becoming obedient to death—
>   even death on a cross!
> Therefore God exalted him to the highest place
>   and gave him the name that is above every name,
> that at the name of Jesus every knee should bow,
>   in heaven and on earth and under the earth,
> and every tongue acknowledge that Jesus Christ is Lord,
>   to the glory of God the Father. (Phil. 2:2–11)

This reminds us of an important aspect of Jesus' teaching: the road to greatness in the Kingdom is humble service—not putting ourselves first or trying to build up our reputation in the eyes of people, but playing for an audience of One and looking only for treasures in heaven. Disciple Making Movements are almost always driven by teams of people connected by relationships to God and to each other, working out of their unity in the Spirit. Just as God blesses churches by giving diverse spiritual gifts to individuals, He also blesses strategic partnerships in ministry.

A PROPHETIC KINGDOM VOICE FOR UNITY

Few people in the last twenty years have been as influential in changing the DNA of the world Christian enterprise as Phill

Butler. His idea of getting mission agencies around the world to work together in harmony has elevated the spiritual water level of the church around the world.

Phill sat down for an interview for this book during an annual gathering of more than 500 Christian leaders serving in a single unreached part of the world. He recounted the story of the first meeting of this group in 1997. That meeting started a process that has changed the world of missions in every corner of the earth. He spoke about the challenges of that first meeting in this conversation:

Coming to ministry from a media and business background, I was simply asking the question in that first meeting of fourteen representatives of different ministries: "Among sixty million people in this part of the world who have very few opportunities to discover the God who loves them, what is God's idea of a good market share? Would one percent be pleasing to Him?"

The room went silent, and we almost had to lock the door to keep everybody there! At that first meeting, we had Pentecostals and anti-Pentecostals. We had very cerebral, scholarly types, and intuitive and energetic media folks. It was a real challenge, and we did not finish until 9:00 every night.

By Friday, we had come up with twenty different things that needed to be done in the Muslim world—*but they could only be done collaboratively*! So that was a great breakthrough! But the problem was that Christian ministries had never achieved even one of those twenty. So in the next five hours, we had to scale those down from twenty to eleven, then to seven, and then to four.

Within five or six years, we began to see radical differences beginning to happen in the region. I have realized that, in the Kingdom of God, it is never a game of guns and money, but a unique releasing of the Holy Spirit among God's people.

No one knew it at the time, but that was the first meeting of what would become the organization Interdev, which ushered in a new dynamic in the global Christian enterprise, one where the default priority is always for organizations to find ways to strategically work together.

A CLARIFYING QUESTION FOR EVERY MINISTRY

Dr. Paul Gupta of the Hindustan Bible Institute provides a pointed example of the need for cooperative ministry. He issued a challenge to Christians working in India. In order for the country to be reached, he said, it would take a million churches: one church in each of the 600,000 villages in the country, and one for each of the 400,000 colonies in the urban centers.

When Dr. Gupta issued this challenge, people were excited because it was such an incredible goal. But it was also overwhelming for a single church or ministry to even imagine. How do you mobilize people to accomplish a vision like that? This takes us back to the two mutually exclusive questions, posed in a previous chapter:

1. Do you want to reach India?

or

2. Do you want to see India reached?

Every Christian leader has to ask this question: Do I want to reach my community, or do I want to see the community reached? If it's the former, you are building *your* empire, not the Kingdom; if it's the latter, you have to be willing to work with others to see the community reached—Kingdom growth cannot have your brand on it.

W. Allen, the veteran cross-cultural catalyst we met in chapter five, explains:

> The key to multiplication is, get yourself out of the equation, to envision a future without *you* there. In India, there are 1.3 billion people; three percent of the population are Christian; ninety percent of them come from 25-percent of the population. After nearly 2,000 years of Christian presence in the country, we all must admit no one has figured out how to reach the other seventy-five percent.
>
> I will never be an Indian or fully understand the culture. Even after studying India for twenty-five years I still feel like I have not yet even entered kindergarten. I seek to find people who do understand at least some part of the country, but I have yet to find any Indian who understands *all* of India. So, I feel it is vital to develop leaders who also understand that it's not going to be done by them either.
>
> I'm looking for people who are willing to actually say: "You are right; we can't do it by ourselves!" I want to look at their lifestyle. In looking for such leaders, I want to see how they unleash people. And when they leave the room, do their people know that there is something that they can do, and they don't have to go and ask for permission? These are leaders who are looking beyond themselves to next generations of leaders. They understand what it looks like to get out of the equation.
>
> That to me is the kind of leader that I am trying to raise up. And when you talk about the sacrifices that a leader has to make, one of them is trust. Trust is an issue of sacrifice, because you have to be willing to say that I'm going to entrust this thing to somebody who might fail.
>
> And I'm still going to be willing to have my name attached to it, even if they didn't do a good job. I will sign my name to it, because I'm a builder. If you are at an architect

level or at a foreman level, you have to sign off on every person who contributed to the creation of that building. That's a leadership issue—you have to be willing to say, "I stand behind the work of my people." And that's exactly what Jesus did with His disciples!

Movement leaders have to find ways to make themselves dispensable. We need to mentor leaders and get out of the way as quickly as possible, allowing the movement to take place on its own. This is the only way a movement perfectly suited to that culture will catalyze. We have to trust our people. They will make mistakes and may not do some things as well as we could have done them, but we must allow them to *make* their mistakes, mentor them on how to *learn* from those mistakes, and trust that the Holy Spirit will work *despite* their mistakes—as He always did despite ours.

If we try to take ownership of the movement and control it, we will kill it. Only when we open it up to others can it develop. This is how God works in the Global South, and it is how He has even worked in America.

A DISCOURAGED PASTOR WITH A KINGDOM-MINDED PRAYER

When you talk to Pastor Juan Pablo of Sonoma, California, you quickly sense that there is very little varnish on the story that he is about to share. Right after he says "hello," he'll tell you:

A few years ago, I began to know that I was not going to fulfill my dream to pastor the largest church in our city, and I was discouraged and depressed. Like other pastors I have known, when discouragement with our goals comes, I felt that I had failed. All I could do was to ask God what to do. So I entered a season of fasting and prayer, because I did not know anything else to do.

In mid- 2013, Juan began to understand what God was telling him, and it was quite remarkable. In the past, he had wanted to outgrow all of the other churches around, but now God began to encourage him pray for other Christian leaders, not just in his church but in all the churches of Sonoma County and the surrounding regions. He did not know why, but he decided to obey God and began to pray what God had instructed him to pray.

At just that time, Juan reconnected with a friend whom he had not seen in many years: Ricardo Pineda, a veteran Disciple Making Movement leader and trainer with Cityteam Ministries' One53 Network. Juan shared his journey with Ricardo and asked him to come visit his church. Eventually, Ricardo spoke at the church about obedience-based discipleship, and it resonated with Juan's prayers for his church and the community. Juan was ready to start training and implementing it immediately. There was just one problem: his church had been a cell-based church, and they were just not that interested in doing anything differently.

Juan realized that God had told him to pray for other churches, so he began meeting with some other pastors to pray over the local cities for God to prepare a harvest among them. Once they did a prayer "fly over" across the city in a helicopter. Sometimes they would have thirty or more vehicles driving through the local towns with bottles of anointing oil, pouring them over the ground across the region as they prayed for the people of Santa Rosa, Petaluma, Sonoma, and other towns.

They had done this sort of thing before, but now it had a focus of engaging lostness by making disciples who make disciples.

At the same time, Juan and Ricardo were beginning to train pastors and their members from different Christian traditions to catalyze disciple-making movements. They were thinking that it would take a year for people to begin to implement what they were learning, but some pastors were taking a five-day training and going back to their churches where they began to implement it immediately. Over a few months, there were four key pastors in four different cities and about twenty total pastors from different denominations who began Discovery Groups, encouraged and coached by Juan with Ricardo's help.

Some churches began to test different access ministries to find people of peace. They started by doing neighborhood events in the church, and then moved outside the church to do Thanksgiving and Christmas neighborhood celebrations and occasional medical programs, prayed for people who were sick, and did whatever else came to mind.

One of the four key leaders was a pastor named Nelson who had come to Pastor Juan several weeks earlier to tell him that some people had left his church. He was so discouraged that he was thinking about giving up. Pastor Juan asked him why he was crying about forty people who had left his church, when there were 10,000 lost people to go and find in his community. He helped Nelson see what might be possible in obedience-based discipleship, and Pastor Nelson became energized. He started right away and, within a week, seventeen people were in Discovery Groups. It did not take Nelson's church long to begin launching Discovery Groups among different groups of people, including some Catholic sisters who began Discovery Bible Studies in their parishes.

Angelica, a leader of a church in the area, taught people how to find people of peace and launch Discovery Groups outside the walls of the church. This was encouraging, but despite her success, Angelica was still concerned that many of the people in the church were not showing enough interest in making disciples. Ricardo and some of her pastoral colleagues suggested that her church could become an equipping center for training, so that all members would get a chance to find out how they could be involved in the new wine of disciple making that the Lord was producing.

In 2014, Angelica began to make the very long drive from the Bay Area to Guadalajara to introduce Disciple Making Movements there. Now, three years later, there are four generations of disciples making disciples. And one stream of that momentum has launched groups back into the American Midwest.

In 2014, Pastor Juan went to Cuba to do a Disciple Making Movement training with Norlen, another Christian leader. The response was overwhelming, and over the last three years, more than 5,000 groups and churches have been planted. Most of the churches are in the fourth or fifth generation, and they have even seen places that have reached to the ninth generation of disciples making disciples! Today, Pastor Juan continues to find creative ways to make reproducing disciples, most recently in the form of a new Disciple Making-centered recovery center that is breaking addictions and releasing people from bondage into freedom and deliverance.

Juan reflected on his journey by saying that, once a Christ Follower tastes the fruit of transformation in individuals, families, and communities, there is no going back to traditional ministry. He still celebrates the fact that God told him what to pray for, and then He answered that prayer—not only for Juan and some other discouraged pastors, but for many, many new Christ Followers.

When we are more concerned with building God's Kingdom than advancing our reputation, and when we want to advance the cause of Christ by supporting others, powerful spiritual momentum can enter our lives. Scripture tells us that amazing things happen when we work together in unity and in obedience to Him. Leviticus 26:8 tells us that five will put a hundred to flight and ten a thousand; Deuteronomy 32:30 is even more extreme, saying that one will put 1,000 to flight but two 10,000. Psalm 133 tells us the reason: when God's people dwell together in unity, the Lord himself commands a blessing! Perhaps this is the reason why Jesus sent his followers out two by two.[1]

When pastors are praying for the other pastors in their town, and when they are extending resources to other churches to support their growth, then it is likely that this community is on a Kingdom of God trajectory that just might lift the spiritual climate for everyone.

DEVELOPING COOPERATIVE MINISTRIES

Churches and ministries in the Global North need to find ways to cooperate. They must work together to advance the Gospel, regardless of whether or not it grows their own organization or whether there is agreement on all matters of practice or theology. Without that, Jesus tells us that the world will not know that we are His disciples, or even that God sent Him.

---

[1] This also partially explains the significance of the person of peace. When the disciple makers and the person of peace work together, it opens the entire community to the Gospel.

But how do we begin?

The first step, as with all things related to the Kingdom, is prayer. We need to dedicate ourselves to praying that God would open Heaven and begin a movement among us, regardless of who gets the credit. We need to pray for a vision for the Kingdom among all the Christians and churches in the area, and for cooperative alliances with other ministries to develop that will enable us to reach our community and the hidden unreached people in our midst.

Many communities have meetings of the ministers of local churches. If you are a pastor, use these to find ministers who might be willing to partner with you in building Kingdom movements. Look for access ministries that meet needs in the community. These are good opportunities to develop relationships with other churches and show the reality of the Kingdom to the people around us. Ideally, these should not be "one and done" projects; the most effective access ministries build ongoing personal relationships between the churches and the unreached community. Without that element, the outreach may lead the community to think that the church is just checking a box and isn't doing it from a genuine place of love or advancement in His name.

Share everything that you learn with ministry partners. The more you give away, the more the Lord will work through you. This may also decrease suspicion that cooperative ministry is a cover for sheep stealing.

And above all, be patient. Building relationships between churches often takes time.

THE KING'S BARRIER-BREAKING RESOURCES

My most spectacular answers to prayer have come when I was so helpless, so out of control as to be able to do nothing at all for myself. . . . God is trying to get a message through to you, and the message is: "Stop depending on inadequate human resources. Let me handle the matter."

—Catherine Marshall
"The Prayer of Helplessness," *Adventures in Prayer*

21st-CENTURY BARRIERS OF TOO LITTLE CASH, AND TOO MUCH CULTURE

It is not easy to be a leader in a 21st-century Christian church in the Global North. It is expensive to get into the ministry today. Consider just a few of the things that pastors face:

- Many pastors will have one degree or more in theology in order to be able to teach the Bible with excellence.

- Most will also study disciplines such as Christian education, Counseling, Spiritual Formation, Worship, Cross-Cultural Ministries, Pastoral studies, Administration, etc.

- Once in a church, pastors face challenging cultural head-winds that push back against unpopular elements of faith and practice.

- The hours are long and expectations are high for every member of a church staff.

- In small churches, the pastor is expected to fulfill many tasks without the benefit of enough staff or volunteers to help.

Churches in America are expensive operations. Some estimates suggest that traditional churches spend eighty-two to ninety-six percent of their financial resources on maintaining themselves.[1]

And a major research program in 2001 reported that, "aggregating all costs of American churches, the total expense per baptism in the United States is $1.55 million."[2] The sad part? Though American churches are very expensive, they are also not very good at making disciples.

On an international level, American churches spend more on their annual audits ($810 million) than they do on all their workers in the non-Christian world. That is in part because ninety-two percent of all Christian outreach and evangelism

---

[1] David Olson, *The American Church in Crisis: Groundbreaking Research Based on a National Database of over 200,000 Churches* (Grand Rapids, Mich.: Zondervan, 2008), 29–43.

[2] David B. Barrett, Todd M. Johnson, Christopher Guidry, and Peter Crossing, *World Christian Trends, AD30-AD2200: Interpreting the Annual Christian Megacensus* (Pasadena, Cal.: William Carey Library, 2001), 520–529.

ministry targets populations that are already sixty percent Christian. The hardest places are still not fully engaged.

Global North missionaries are highly trained, dedicated professionals. But that training is, once again, expensive, and standard missionary models cannot produce enough leaders to reach the unreached people of the world.

Most of the rapid growth that we noted in Chapter 1 comes from the progress of the Global South's churches—ministries and missions that do not have the resources we enjoy in the Global North, and so cannot follow the same expensive strategies. So what are the big issues contributing to the Global North church's inability to keep up with population growth, much less make a serious contribution to fulfilling Great Commission?

There are at least two big problems that rise above most of the others, both of which can be solved by adopting a new model that relies on God's resources rather than our own.

THE FIRST BARRIER:
WORLDVIEWS AND CONTEMPORARY CULTURE

When we look at mission fields, we quickly recognize both cultural and worldview barriers that stand between the Gospel and the lost. What we often do not recognize, however, is that the same is true in the Global North. Cultural mindsets, values hostile to the Kingdom, alternative worldviews, stereotypes, misunderstandings, bad experiences with churches or individual Christians, and a host of other issues create barriers to disciple making that leave both churches and believers unsuccessful in engaging their neighbors with the Gospel.

Christian values and worldviews are being marginalized at an alarming rate in universities, the news media, entertainment media, and popular culture. Biblical worldviews are categorized as "bigoted," "uninformed," or "hateful," and so Christians are excluded from important discussions about society. We are becoming a marginalized minority with the cooperation of many so-called Christians who adopt ungodly values in the name of being "open-minded."

Millions of Americans have rejected our religion but, when they discover the person of Jesus in the Bible, they are drawn to Him. The trick is finding ways to get a hearing with these people.

Outside of America, cultural issues are the most difficult hurdles that missionaries must overcome; in America, the issue is exactly same. Christians don't speak the same language as the general population. We often don't dress like they do. Sometimes we don't live in the same space as they do. So we need a way to get those people to come together and discover Jesus on their own.

The difficulty that we face is finding people who are open to hearing the Gospel, and more, who can be "Bridges of God" into communities and social networks that are ripe for the Gospel. Fortunately, Jesus gave us instructions on precisely how to do those things.

BARRIER BREAKER #1
PEOPLE OF PEACE: GOD'S PROVISION FOR ACCESS INTO AN ALIEN CULTURE

"When you enter a house, first say, 'Peace to this house.' If someone who promotes peace is there, your peace will rest on them; if not, it will return to you. Stay there, eating and drinking whatever they give you, for the worker deserves his wages. Do not move around from house to house." (Luke 10:5–7)

> Don't try to kick in the door—
> let someone inside open it!
> —Harry Brown

Jesus sent the Twelve and the seventy-two (two-by-two) on their healing and preaching tours, telling them to look for a person of peace, someone who, knowing they represented Jesus, would nonetheless welcome them into their village, house them, feed them, and introduce them to the community. The person of peace was thus to be someone who showed spiritual interest and who had a circle of relationships within the larger community.

Remember: Jesus also told them that if they did not find a person of peace, they were to leave, though they were to tell the residents that the Kingdom had come near them—perhaps to lay the groundwork for future engagement. Jesus was clear that if the Father is not drawing them, they are not going to come to Jesus. But if the Father *is* drawing them then, in effect, while you are looking for them, they are looking for you. This is why a level of spiritual interest is so important in identifying persons of peace.

This strategy is followed everywhere that Disciple Making Movements happen in the Global South. Because the person of peace ministry model is so practical and effective, some Global North churches and ministries are adopting it in their outreach programs. Still, many churches in the Global North are not yet aware of it. There are several reasons for this.

Global North churches base their evangelistic approach more on their reading of the book of Acts than on Jesus' words. They see this in terms of proclamation, which generates individual responses of faith. This model underlies crusade evangelism, evangelistic preaching in churches, and even most systems that teach personal evangelism.

Yet a closer reading of Acts shows evidence that persons of peace were involved in spreading Christianity through opening social networks to the Gospel. Examples include:

- Aeneas, Acts 9:32–35
- Cornelius, Acts 10, esp. vs. 24, 44 (Note "all.")
- Lydia, Acts 16:14–15 (Note "household.")
- Philippian jailer, Acts 16:32–33 (Note "all his family.")
- Titius Justus, Acts 16:7 (Note that Paul stayed with him.)
- Crispus, Acts 16:8 (Note "entire household.")

This shows two things: The apostolic church made very effective use of persons of peace to introduce the Gospel to new social circles, and conversion was often not a purely individual matter. Sometimes in the Global North, we miss opportunities to utilize the power of close family relationships because, in our highly individualized understanding of "salvation," we don't think in terms of a family and/or social network moving together toward the Kingdom of God.

Households and affinity groups become Christ Followers together when a catalytic Kingdom agent introduces the Word of God into a person of peace's family or social network. Not only have we seen this happen in families, but we've also seen this among co-workers, sports teams, and even (now former) criminal gangs.

This process is how billions of the people of the world make major family or communal decisions. A half-century ago, Donald McGavran coined a name for this reality: *Multi-individual, mutually interdependent decisions,* the phenomenon that moved whole communities to abandon animistic and other religions to become faithful disciples of Jesus. McGavran later simplified this to "People Movements."

This is much more than an imaginary, spiritual group-health concept, where one person gets a job and everybody in the family is spiritually covered. It is a blending of the power of family and community in making a Kingdom choice that will redefine future generations. As Hassan, the African DMM practitioner, says, "The Gospel still flies best on the wings of relationship."

The person-of-peace principle is a simple way for any Christian to assess the spiritual hunger of people whom they already know or meet casually and to determine their interest in self-discovering the Bible in their own home. The reality is that there are many, many people just waiting for someone to extend that invitation. Any organization is able to double its impact when it adopts Jesus' person of peace principle in its strategies rather than using a mass-media, cold-calling, or door-knocking approach to ministry.

> *The reality is that there are many, many people just waiting for someone to extend the invitation.*

So a Person of Peace is really a person that God has prepared in the community to receive you. Somebody that God has placed in that community somehow, by his own divine arrangement that will receive you. A Person of Peace is a local of a community, lives within the community, knows the community, understands the community.

A Person of Peace is a person that opens his door voluntarily to you. It's a person that wants to listen to you and hear your story. A Person of Peace is willing to introduce you to the community and if possible will become your advocate to the community. A Person of Peace, also, is a person that is willing to take the gospel that you bring. But what normally we say is that, if you go to any community, if you can't find a Person of Peace you have to move on. No person of Peace, no church-planting.

The Person of Peace can be a man/woman. Can be young/old. And can be someone very bad in the community.

—Younoussa Djao, Engage! Africa Video, Person of Peace

So how do you identify persons of peace in a community? Before Jesus sent out the Twelve and the seventy-two, He told them to pray. Similarly, in our efforts to make disciples, we need to begin with prayer. This is always the vital first step to all Kingdom work. We need to pray for guidance and discernment to identify the persons of peace whom God has placed in our personal mission field, and to pray for our interactions with them.

To put it simply, people who spend a lot of time in prayer are the ones who are most likely to find people of peace.

Part of the reason for this is that people who are searching and open to hearing the Gospel tend to be attracted to people with an active and vivacious spiritual life. Christians who naturally and unselfconsciously introduce spiritual themes into their everyday conversations attract the interest of those who are spiritually open. According to David Watson, people of peace find disciple makers rather than the other way around.

That said, we need to place ourselves in positions where we can connect with persons of peace. These can be almost anyone, male or female, young, old, or somewhere in between. They can be educated or uneducated, respectable in society or not. They can be drug lords, drunks, community or religious leaders, business people, students, or teachers. They can even be hostile (at first) to the Gospel. It's important not to prejudge anyone, or to predetermine the kind of person who will be a person of peace. The only prerequisites are a spiritual hunger and a divine call on their lives, both of which are invisible to us.

Access ministry (sometimes called compassion ministry), discussed in chapter fourteen, is one important approach used in the Global South to connect with persons of peace. This is readily adaptable to communities in the Global North. But this is just one approach.

For example, Sean Steckbeck often approaches local shopkeepers and asks them, "If you could ask for one thing from God, what would it be?" He then prays with them about it, and comes back later for updates. Other questions are also useful such as: "What do you see as the greatest need in the community?" "What can our church do to help the community?" "What can we do to help you?" Once you hear the answer, pray with the person you speak to, and then follow up, taking whatever action is appropriate.

As you build a relationship with the person, it opens the door to asking about needs and challenges in his or her own life, which in turn can open the door to a Discovery Group using Scriptures that address the person's (or community's) needs. This last step is part of an approach that Jimmy Tam teaches his congregation in Los Angeles. This is only one example of an approach that has been successful. Every situation is different just as every person is different, so a measure of creativity is necessary. Use these ideas as a jumping off point to help kickstart your thinking.

How much would change if churches taught and pastors modeled simple ways to identify persons of peace and catalyze their families, friends, or co-workers into a simple Discovery Group? Kingdom movements occur because ordinary Christians become Kingdom catalysts—causing or accelerating a reaction that can multiply into hundreds of new Christ Followers if given the chance. In New Generations, we have tracked up to twenty-seven generations of Discovery Groups becoming churches that plant other groups, which also become churches, and so on. There is every reason to expect further generations of churches to be founded by the same method.

THE SECOND BARRIER: THE RESOURCES TO DISCIPLE BILLIONS OF LOST PEOPLE

The second barrier is the resources needed to partner with Jesus in a harvest that looks barren to us but fruitful to Him. It looks impossible with our resources because it is—if we follow the old model. In reality, the advancement of the Kingdom of God does not require money as much as it does God's spiritual resources, stored just behind the curtain of plentiful prayer. They must simply be released in the lives of obedient disciples, and are held in escrow for courageous Kingdom men and women. These are the things that release the Kingdom storehouse, full of everything needed for Jesus' Kingdom to advance where it must go.

BARRIER BREAKER #2
JEHOVAH JIREH

Don't Trust Human Resources for God's Kingdom Outcomes

> Freely you have received, freely give. Do not take along any gold or silver or copper in your belts; take no bag for the journey, or extra tunic, or sandals or a staff; for the worker is worth his keep. Whatever town or village you enter, search for some worthy person there and stay at his house until you leave. As you enter the home, give it your greeting. If the home is deserving, let your peace rest on it; if it is not, let your peace return to you. (Mt. 10:8–10)

In Matthew 10 and Luke 10, Jesus addresses issues of resources. He told the Twelve and the seventy-two the same things. His last words spoken on earth were:

> All authority in heaven and on earth has been given to me. Therefore go and make disciples of all nations, baptizing them in the name of the Father and of the Son and of the Holy Spirit, and teaching them to obey everything I have commanded you. And surely I am with you always, to the very end of the age. (Mt. 28:18–20)

Jesus said nothing about money here. He simply said that He had all authority in heaven and on earth, and that His disciple-making command could be achieved. But we know that it costs a lot of money to make one disciple in the traditional Global North model. So is Jesus' task impossible, or is the issue that we have Christian institutions that can add but not multiply? Is a soul for whom Jesus died worth $1.55 million? Without a doubt—and even more. But does this formula have any chance of finishing the task that Jesus gave us? Of course not!

So if we were able to become 100 times more efficient than we are now in making disciples, we would see a cost of $15,000 per baptism. That would be so much better. But can we finish the Great Commission if it costs $15,000 per person? The cost would be far more than America's national debt.

The traditional Global North paradigm costs so much because most of our funds are spent on buildings, staff, and programs that don't make replicating disciples. It is obvious that we need to look for biblically grounded paradigms that are proven to work.

In the movements happening today in the Global South, the cost is far less than $50 for each new Christ Follower—and a high percentage of those people are from Muslim or Hindu backgrounds. Is that because everyone doing DMM is a strategic genius? Absolutely not. How is this possible, then?

Throughout Scripture, God provides for His people. This is a living reality for those involved in Disciple-Making Movements, and this provision frequently follows well-established patterns from the Bible.

> *In the movements happening today in the Global South, the cost is far less than $50 for each new Christ Follower . . .*

One of the most beloved names of God in the Old Testament is Jehovah Jireh, the LORD provides. This name came from Genesis 22:1–14, where Abraham was called to sacrifice his son Isaac. At the last moment, God provided a ram as a substitute for Isaac, and so his life was spared. For our purposes, there are two things that we need to notice about this story: first, Abraham obeyed God's instructions because he trusted Him, even though they made little sense and brought great personal cost; second, God did provide the substitute, but He only did so at the last moment, *after* Abraham obeyed.

During the Exodus, God provided food for His people in the form of manna, but He set very specific rules for how it was to be gathered. Space does not permit us to include the entire chapter here, but please read through Exodus 16 for the full context. In doing so, you will notice that God *did* provide for His people's needs, but that provision was contingent on their obedience. Further, the provision came just in time, on a day-by-day basis.

Rather than allowing them to store up for their long-term needs, God wanted them to live dependent on Him each day. Moses explains the lesson to be drawn from this by saying, "So He humbled you, allowed you to hunger, and fed you with manna which you did not know nor did your fathers know, that He might make you know that man shall not live by bread alone; but man lives by every word that proceeds from the mouth of the LORD" (Deut. 8:3). Obedience leads to life and, as we obey, God provides for our needs.

GOD'S PROVISION IN THE GOSPELS

When Jesus' disciples came to Him on the mountainside, He taught them about God's provision for them (Matt. 6). He said they were not to be concerned about:

- what you eat
- clothing
- what you drink
- tomorrow
- your body
- in short—life

When Jesus sent out the Twelve on their preaching and healing tour, He gave them specific instructions about their needs:

> Provide neither gold nor silver nor copper in your money belts, nor bag for *your* journey, nor two tunics, nor sandals, nor staffs; for a worker is worthy of his food.
>
> Now whatever city or town you enter, inquire who in it is worthy, and stay there till you go out. And when you go into a household, greet it. If the household is worthy, let your peace come upon it. But if it is not worthy, let your peace return to you. (Matt. 10:9–13)

He gave very similar instructions to the seventy-two:

> Carry neither money bag, knapsack, nor sandals; and greet no one along the road. But whatever house you enter, first say, 'Peace to this house.' And if a son of peace is there, your peace will rest on it; if not, it will return to you. And remain in the same house, eating and drinking such things as they give, for the laborer is worthy of his wages. Do not go from house to house. Whatever city you enter, and they receive you, eat such things as are set before you. And heal the sick there, and say to them, "The kingdom of God has come near to you." But whatever city you enter, and they do not receive you, go out into its streets and say, "The very dust of your city which clings to us we wipe off against you. Nevertheless know this, that the kingdom of God has come near you." But I say to you that it will be more tolerable in that Day for Sodom than for that city. (Luke 10:4–12)

Once again, we see the same principles at work in God's provision: those whom Jesus sent out were to follow His directions, living by faith, and their needs would be met as they went. They were not to rely on their own resources—notably their own financial reserves—as they proclaimed the Kingdom, but on the resources that would come to them day by day on the way.

GOD'S SUPPLY

All of this points to the dictum attributed to Hudson Taylor, British missionary to China: "God's work done in God's way will never lack God's supply." And it is God's supply, not ours, that is important for His work. Taylor continued, "The branch of the vine does not worry, and toil, and rush here to seek for sunshine, and there to find rain. No; it rests in union and communion with the vine; and at the right time, and in the right way, is the right fruit found on it. Let us so abide in the Lord Jesus."

As we have seen, the churches of the Global North have abundant resources to draw from. We have money, far more than is available in the Global South; we have pre-packaged programs; we have management, marketing, and media gurus who can advise us on how to attract the kinds of people we are looking for; we have an abundance of things that we can rely upon rather than the Spirit's power and provision to advance the work of the Kingdom.

God might choose to bless any or even all of those things, at least to some extent. But those resources don't require stepping out in faith, and they aren't the ways that God has provided for people doing His work, either in Scripture or over the course of church history.

The point is clear: as we step out in faith and in obedience to God, we cannot rely on human resources; we must instead rely on God. And we will find those resources day by day, on the way, and frequently in the harvest itself. If we put God's Kingdom first, ahead of our own reputation and our preferences, and if we give our lives to honoring and obeying His perfect will and seek to be faithful followers of Jesus, then the things that we need will be provided by God day by day, because He knows our needs.

To break this down:

- we need to approach our service to God with the right attitude: we should be humbled by the privilege of serving;

- we need to be focused on God's Kingdom, not our brand— we have to be careful never to touch His glory;

- we need to recognize that we are His bond slaves and, at the same time, His friends;

- we need to emphasize His will and His priorities, not our own;

- we have to rely on His provision and protection.

We also need to do the right thing: we need to love Jesus enough to obey Him in all things. As His disciples, we need to learn to obey everything that He commanded.

As we do this, He will provide for our needs in the disciple-making process.

DMM AND RESOURCES

Some of these needs are tangible and obvious to us, such as funds, transportation, food, lodging, supplies, and equipment. It is certainly prudent to plan and budget for these expenses, but we still need to pursue the ministry opportunities that God places before us, whether or not all of the resources are in place. William Carey's motto was: "Expect great things from God, attempt great things for God."[3] If we are going to do this, we will

---

[3] As quoted in the *Baptist Herald and Friend of Africa* (October 1842) and "The Missionary Herald" in *The Baptist Magazine* Vol. 35 (January 1843), p. 41.

need to step out in faith. And that will sometimes mean relying on God to provide what we need when we need it.

We see this in the life of Elijah, where containers of meal and oil were miraculously replenished to feed the prophet and the widow with whom he was staying (1 Kings 17:13–15). We see it again with Elisha, where a jar of oil did not run out until it had poured out enough oil to save a widow's family (2 Kings 4:1–7).

The account of the Feeding of the Five Thousand, Jesus' only miracle that is recounted in all four Gospels, is an illustration of relying on God to provide. After teaching the crowds all day, Jesus was concerned that, if they didn't get something to eat, they might faint along the way home. This is a good indication that many of the people who came to hear Him were poor, but it also demonstrates that Jesus is well aware of our needs and that He does not fail to meet them—even before we ask. The disciples didn't have the resources to feed the people; there was only a young boy who had five small loaves of bread and two fish. Jesus blessed the food, put it in His disciples' hands, and that boy's lunch was miraculously multiplied to feed 5,000 men, plus women and children—and leave baskets of leftovers.

The principle is the same in all cases: God can take a very little and multiply it in His disciples' hands to advance His Kingdom and glorify His name. But He does more than that: He prepares persons of peace to open the door into new social circles and communities; He frequently attests to His presence through the supernatural work of God's Spirit, healing and breaking the power of Satan in people; as Discovery Groups begin to meet, He raises up new leaders, so that people with interest and gifting to plant new Discovery Groups emerge; and He provides the people that are needed for a movement to grow.

TEACHING THE THEORY OF TYPING

Coming back to Hassan's story again, in the early years of his ministry, his homeland suffered a season of intense violence, displaced people, and a breakdown of infrastructure. As it drew to a close, a small window of opportunity opened to demobilize and disarm the warring factions and begin the season of reunifying the country.

One of the elements of that effort was to give all of the combatants an opportunity for vocational training for a productive livelihood. It required a bold "seizing of the moment" to get a mass of fighters to turn in their guns while also fulfilling the promises made in the process. But the NGOs were not fully equipped to provide all of the resources that the government had promised to deliver to combatants who gave up the fight.

The needs were immense. Almost the entire rural population that had escaped to the cities for security now had to find a way to resettle back in villages or to develop new skills. Many schools and medical facilities had been destroyed. Churches were overwhelmed with needs and did not have time to recover themselves from the trauma of displaced members and tragic losses.

Hassan heard about the government's offer to fund trade schools for ex-combatants, and he felt a very strong leading from the Lord to start two of those schools and to provide vocational training in carpentry, sewing, tailoring, tie-dying, typing, and basic computer skills. He opened both schools as the first soldiers were being mustered out of the national army, and soon former enemies from multiple warring factions were warily learning to get along. A couple of months after that, Hassan took Jerry on a tour of the schools.

It turned out that Hassan had not found any support for launching those schools. In his view, if God said to open the schools, then God must also have a plan to supply the resources.

On the tour, Hassan first took Jerry into the typing classroom. In front of each student was a neat piece of paper with a drawing of a computer keyboard showing every letter and character—but there was not a single typewriter. Not one!

"Where are the typewriters?" Jerry asked.

"They are here!" Hassan replied. "They are here—by faith! We have promised the students to have typewriters by the next semester [only two months away]." Then he smiled. "For now, we are teaching the *theory* of typing."

Next, he took Jerry to the carpentry class, where twelve to fifteen young men were in a room with an instructor and a toolbox with a couple of hammers, some wrenches, a few screwdrivers, and a saw. Compared to the typing room, it was a state-of-the art workshop. The students made a joke that, just a few weeks before, they held AK-47s and were trying to shoot each other, but now they just had a hammer or two to throw—yet nobody had felt an urge to fight.

The next stop was a sewing class, and sticking with the emerging pattern, there were no sewing machines to be seen. Once again, Hassan explained they did not need machines to teach "Sewing Theory." And those machines were also "there— by faith." The rest of the tour was the same, and the second school was just as fully equipped ("by faith") as the first, and just as lacking in hardware. But beyond all these things, the young men were being taught more than just "theoretical technical skills"—they were being carefully discipled concerning the Kingdom of God.

When Jerry's congregation in Tennessee heard this story, there was an outpouring of support for Christian technical schools teaching former warriors the "Theory of Carpentry" and "The Love of Jesus." By the second semester, just about everything that the schools needed had arrived—just in time! And this faith experiment increased Hassan's vision of schools that achieve excellent vocational, academic, and spiritual outcomes for all kinds of students across the country.

This was the first access ministry of dozens that followed. And Hassan affirms that, of the thousands of communities that they have engaged with some kind of access ministry, almost every one of them has eventually resulted in a church—and often multiple churches—being planted. At this writing, God has multiplied many times that original faith commitment to provide schools for the militia and soldiers. But they have gone beyond that target group. The ministry has launched start-up primary schools across the country in partnerships with communities of unreached people—even some that have martyred Christians—often starting an entire school for less than $800. In the process of believing God for two schools, God has also raised up twelve Secondary Schools, two Trade Technical Schools, and an accredited college with a School of Business and School of Theology.

Some of those schools have won national awards. All of the schools, including the college, hold Discovery Bible Studies for all students, even non-Christians in the School of Business. Thousands of students and their families have become Christ Followers.

Regarding the original wartime trade schools, many of those ex-combatant men and women prospered by launching their own businesses, and a high percentage became Christ Followers. Several became pastors—living testimonies of the power of a Kingdom vision, courageous leadership, and faith that outcomes worthy of the risks would be seen.

STEWARDS OF GOD'S RESOURCES

At the time of writing, the number of movements (DMM, CPM, T4T, Four Fields, and others) being tracked in the world is more than 650, with more than fifty million new Christ Followers. A dozen years ago, there was excitement about even a single credible rumor of a promising new move of God happening somewhere. Today it requires complex databases for some ministries to keep tabs on the incredible momentum.

Why is this happening? Without a doubt, it's because both human catalysts and divine power are involved. It is impossible to quantify divine guidance, empowerment, transformation, and replication; it is also impossible to miss its presence in every movement. This is evident simply in the limited resources that have been expended in catalyzing these movements, especially when compared to the costs involved in traditional approaches to missions and ministry in general.

In strictly human and financial terms, movements are incredibly cost-effective. The return on investments to plant a church, to make a single disciple, or even to see a Muslim church of twenty-six people planted in a restricted country look bogus in comparison to traditional ministry costs. We know of hundreds of people groups, the majority of them categorized as "unreached," where the financial investment averages less than $600 per new church planted. The finances are small, but the sacrifices of the people engaging lostness in hard places are sometimes extreme—just as Jesus warned.

In other words, as we look at movements in the Global South, the data demonstrate that DMM approaches require a very small expenditure of resources, producing oversized result. This kind of return on investment is the kind of ministry model that it is going to take to fulfill Jesus' final words. Why? Because Kingdom values that Jesus spoke about are taken seriously.

> *This kind of return on investment is the kind of ministry model that it is going to take to fulfill Jesus' final words.*

There is a practical element in this, as well. If a movement is going to start, it must be self-sustaining; if it relies too much on investment from the outside, it will never take off, since that outside investment is non-replicable. The resources must come from within the community itself if the movement is to be replicable and scalable. Additionally, in a traditional missionary engagement, missionaries typically return home. When they do, they leave a physical worship structure behind and a few trained people to fill roles found in typical churches in the Global North. Sadly, these structures are often not sustainable. So the shockingly high costs return relatively small impact over time.

Because, in the Global North, church planting is generally a very expensive proposition, it is impossible to plant as many churches as are needed to reach the unreached in America, let alone the world. If we are to see the Kingdom expand in the Global North, another model will be needed, one anchored in Scripture and in wise stewardship of our resources.

DMM models from the Global South can point the way forward. When we follow Jesus' instructions on how to make disciples by the power of the Holy Spirit and the Storehouse of

Heaven, then we enter a world where everyone has the potential to be a world-changer, regardless of funding. And we can jettison dependence on most of the institutional and financial limitations of Global North paradigms of how ministry happens.

If you want some tangible examples of these things, you may consider going to a country where multiple movements are happening. There, you'll be able to see on full display the Kingdom values that Jesus invited His first disciples to live out in prayer, vision, spiritual authority, provision, obedience, transformation, and multiplication. But for now, perhaps the following testimony will provide a window to one woman's discovery of the God of All Resources.

AN AMERICAN MISSIONARY IN SOUTHEAST ASIA

I read *Miraculous Movements* during my first year in Southeast Asia, and the testimonies written in that book gave me the faith to pray some big prayers. Handcuffed by language and cultural barriers, my husband and I prayed for 100 disciples that first year, and I thought we must be crazy. But I learned soon enough that God can't *not* answer prayers that will bring glory to Him and His church. We were able to train a small group of believers that first year, who then went out and discipled many others. One of the young men trained an entire village: 103 in attendance for several days of DMM/DBS training. That village then made a plan for how to send out groups of four to every surrounding village for the rest of the year to share the same message. God answered our prayers and then some.

I work for a human trafficking ministry and have worked closely with our outreach staff. I led them through a seven-week DBS course last year, and I was given a vision from the Lord to pray for entire brothels to be shut down and converted to churches (rather than focus on individual girls being pulled out of the sex trade). I've prayed (albeit with weak faith at times) for this end, and last week our local director came to me with news that an entire brothel— eight people total, including the owner and his wife—had professed faith in God.

So many stories I wish I could share openly. So many stories I can't wait to tell friends in person when I see them . . . about our Father who is alive and well. I could elaborate on all this, but you know how Great our God truly is.

HOLISTIC KINGDOM MINISTRY PT. 1

COMPASSION AND HEALING

We have lived for many years now with "Kingdom Christians" and "cross Christians" in opposite corners of the room, anxious that those on the other side are missing the point, the one group with its social-gospel agendas and the other with its saving-souls-for-heaven agenda. The four gospels bring these two viewpoints together into a unity that is much greater than the sum of their parts. . . . In fact, what we call "politics" and what we call "religion" (and for that matter what we call "culture," "philosophy," "theology," and lots of other things besides) were not experienced or thought of in the first century as separable entities.

We have allowed "atonement" to be narrowed down to "forgiving sins so people can go to heaven," leaving unaddressed the (to us quite different) problem of "evil" as an abstract thing. That was a dangerous mistake. And of course the reason the Enlightenment has taught us to trash our own history, to say that Christianity is part of the problem, is that it has had a rival eschatology to promote. It couldn't allow Christianity to claim that world history turned its great corner when Jesus of Nazareth died and rose again, because it wanted to claim that world history turned its great corner *in Europe in the eighteenth century.* "All that went before," it says, "is superstition and mumbo-jumbo. We have now seen the great light, and our modern science, technology, philosophy, and politics have ushered in the new order of the ages."

—N.T. Wright, *How God Became King*

JESUS ON KINGDOM COMPASSION AND HEALING

Before Jesus sent the Twelve on their preaching mission, Matthew tells us what was on His mind:

> When he saw the crowds, he had compassion on them, because they were harassed and helpless, like sheep without a shepherd. Then he said to his disciples, "The harvest is plentiful but the workers are few. Ask the Lord of the harvest, therefore, to send out workers into his harvest field" (Matt. 9:37).

Jesus' motivation for sending us out is His compassion for the harassed and helpless. This includes their eternal salvation, but also their wellbeing in this world. This is why he told both the Twelve and the seventy-two to accompany their proclamation of the Kingdom with acts of compassion: heal the sick, raise the dead, cleanse lepers, and cast out demons. These miracles did more than simply authenticate the disciples' message; they continued and extended the ministry of Jesus Himself, who did all of these things because of His compassion for the suffering.

The Gospel of the Kingdom is holistic by its very nature. Jesus is Lord of all, and thus He is concerned with all aspects of our world and in every area of life. As Abraham Kuyper said, "No single piece of our mental world is to be hermetically sealed off from the rest, and there is not a square inch in the whole domain of human existence over which Christ, who is Sovereign over all, does not cry: 'Mine!'"[1]

This is why, wherever the Gospel has gone, hospitals have followed: the body is important. Jesus healed the sick, and we should emulate Him in any way that we can. That means that we ought to pray for the sick, cast out demons, and seek God's blessing on the harassed and helpless.

In the Global North, it is particularly important to recognize the reality of spiritual warfare and to take the authority that Jesus gives us to deal with it. The worldview in the Global North tends to downplay, ignore, or reject the idea of demonization, but Scripture is very clear that it is real and that Jesus has given us the means to deal with it. But even in the absence of miraculous intervention, we should still do what we can to bring relief to the suffering and health to the sick.

Schools also have followed wherever the Gospel has gone, because the mind is also important. Jesus is the *logos*, the source of all wisdom and knowledge, and so study is (or ought to be) a sacred activity. Christians founded primary schools to spread literacy and enable people to read the Bible and other sources of the Christian faith; they also established many of the great universities around the world as an expression of their faith and to the glory of God.

---

[1] Inaugural speech for the Free University of Amsterdam, cited in *A Centennial Reader*, edited by James D. Bratt (Grand Rapids, MI: Eerdmans, 1998), 488.

Along with hospitals and schools, Christians today dig wells, install water purification systems, run food banks and soup kitchens, and engage in a wide range of other compassion ministries at home and abroad. And yet all the polls indicate that this type of work is not what Christians are typically known for in the Global North. Why is that?

Part of the reason may have to do with Jesus' instructions in the Sermon on the Mount not to do your good works in front of people in order to be praised by them. Another part of the reason may have to do with the fact that in the Global North, these things are so readily available to most that they aren't seen as needs—they are seen as rights. Though compassion ministries exist, they are not the norm. This is simply because these needs are not viewed as "the norm;" it is just assumed that everyone in our pews has everything they need.

A more important reason, though, is that many churches send people on short-term mission trips overseas to do some sort of ministry there, but neglect needs in their own communities. And when they do decide to do something, whether locally or farther afield, it tends to be "drive by" ministry, meaning the work is done and the missionaries leave. This one and done approach (hopefully) fixes a problem but does not involve a long-term commitment of resources or time. More importantly, it does not require building relationships with the people in the community. Thus, once the project is over there is no plan for following up and making sure the good work is (or stays) done. Even longer-term commitments, such as running a Bible study in prison, suffer from a similar problem: it is relatively easy to get volunteers to go into prisons but, once inmates are released, it is very difficult to find people or churches willing to commit to aftercare. The risks and the demands are much higher, and so the willingness to help is more difficult to sustain.

But Jesus calls us into holistic ministry, and that is always best done in a context of relationships. Churches in the Global South use "access ministries" to open doors into closed communities. These are generally compassion-based ministries that identify needs in the community and look for ways to meet them. In the process, relationships are established, persons of peace are identified, and disciple-making can begin.

Churches in the Global North that want to see movements should focus on engaging in this kind of entrepreneurial ministry, identifying needs in their community and finding ways to address them—always with a mind to establish relationships and identify persons of peace. In this way, we can show that we share Jesus' compassion for those in need and can bring His solutions to the problems in the world around us.

PART 1

KINGDOM PEOPLE BRING KINGDOM COMPASSION ON EARTH AS IN HEAVEN

You know of Jesus of Nazareth, how God anointed Him with the Holy Spirit and with power, and how He went about doing good and healing all who were oppressed by the devil, for God was with Him. (Acts 10:38 NASB)

The New Generations regional Disciple Making Movement leaders throughout Africa, South Asia, and Southeast Asia whose voices are heard throughout this book have earned the right to speak to the Global North church, not by virtue of the impressive results they have had in hundreds of very challenging people groups in more than thirty countries, but because their ministry models are completely holistic, including compassion and healing—they make obedient disciples who bring replicating transformation to whole families and communities.

Their Kingdom credibility is also established by the quality and quantity of genuine Kingdom compassion expressed in extreme sacrifices that manifest the love of Jesus. In many Muslim regions of the world where Disciple Making Movements are common, the lands are susceptible to droughts and famine. This is always a heartbreaking and deadly problem. In some places in Africa, droughts have been mitigated by strategic water and food resources from DMM ministries, resulting in the formation of Discovery Groups that became simple churches in these regions.

Working in refugee camps provides another example. It is hard to describe the tragedies that can overwhelm these camps today. Some people marooned on the Sudan and South Sudan borders are still facing ethnic violence, aerial bombing, and terror on a regular basis. Christian responses to these tragedies have addressed some of these challenges, and in the process have opened doors for people to engage in Discovery Bible Groups and begin the journey into God's Kingdom.

Access to a community is often gained by doing something that will help develop a trusted relationship with community members. Most of the time, it will be meeting needs in a community. Remember, it is vital that the focus not be on your team and what you are providing—the focus must be on what God is providing through you. By meeting needs in the community, at least three things will happen:

1. Bringing peace;

2. Showing love;

3. Gaining trust.

Once trust has been achieved between you and the community, you can move to the next step in the process.

> The Great Commission can be fully obeyed through Disciple Making Movements. Our goal and passion is to faithfully respond to Jesus' commission to make disciples of all people groups. If we are going to build significant relationships with an unreached community, we need to connect with people who already have meaningful relationships. The gospel records that Jesus proclaimed the message of the Kingdom, and He went around doing good. His acts of compassion opened the heart of the people to the message. The good news of God's grace is shown in healings, deliverances, and feeding. Today we want to create openings for significant personal relationships to begin. We meet needs as a way to look for Persons of Peace. Our goal is to see entire families reached and, through them, to see entire communities reached.
>
> —YOUNOUSSA DJAO, African Director of New Generations Engage! Africa video series

Pat Robertson, the President of Cityteam Ministries when it adopted Disciple Making Movements in 2004, tells us why he thinks that God used a Rescue Mission to launch Disciple Making Movements around the world,

> There was a sense that the Spirit of God was prompting us and that, in a sense, you can choose not to do this, but if you choose not to do this, the eternal consequences of that will be very significant.
>
> In terms of courageous leadership, I think it is the realization that God is calling, that the potential outcomes are significant enough that it is worth gambling on. It's worth a

big investment, and it's worth a big push. To be really honest, it's a commitment to obey and follow Jesus' leading every step of the way. And it is not *our* brilliant leadership, it's not *our* great strategy.

In retrospect this is the passage that explains our call:

> *Brothers, think of what you were when you were called, not many of you wise by human standards, not many were influential, not many were of noble birth, but God chose the foolish things of the world to shame the wise; God chose the weak things of the world to shame the strong, He chose the lowly things of this world and the despised things, and the things that are not--to nullify the things that are, so that no one may boast before him.* (1 Cor. 1:26–30, NIV)

I think, if you read between the lines, He chose people who were not great leaders so that He would get the glory, so that no one may boast before Him. I think that's my final word on this. It was really about Jesus making this happen in spite of us. There's lots of great leaders that God could have chosen to do this, but He skipped over them.

I think God looked around and said, "Ah, here's a rescue mission that's willing to hug people who have poop in their pants for days, they are willing to hug drug addicts and total losers in society and to believe that God's power is sufficient to transform their lives. And they've got a very mediocre leader. This is the perfect group. I can do things through them that I couldn't do through others.

WHAT CAN GLOBAL NORTH CHRISTIANS DO?

It is true that most of the Global South stories we tell are about extreme compassion and sacrifice for the sake of people in traumatic and critical situations. But most people also respond to less intense situations where someone demonstrates God's grace and love toward them.

The reality is that American and European churches and ministries are always finding ways to be compassionate and help-ful neighbors, whether it is by helping families that have suffered disasters, supporting worthy causes, refurbishing community centers, or hundreds of other creative expressions of God's love. What might happen if Global North churches were as inten-tional as their Global South neighbors not to let those acts of kindness be the end of the story? It is a very small step from demonstrating genuine compassion to starting a simple spiritual conversation that may result in a Discovery Bible Study with a person or family of peace. That is almost always how it happens in the Global South. That's why we *know* it can happen here—even more than it already is.

PART 2

KINGDOM PEOPLE BRING HEALING AND DELIVERANCE ON EARTH AS IN HEAVEN

[Jesus told the seventy-two,] "Heal the sick who are there and tell them, 'The kingdom of God has come near to you.'"

The seventy-two returned with joy and said, "Lord, even the demons submit to us in your name." (Luke 10:9, 17)

As we noted in chapter eleven, there are many Christians today who believe that the "sign gifts," including healings and deliverance, have ceased. There are many more who act as if they have.

But over twelve years of research among hundreds of CPM, DMM, and other Kingdom Movement practitioners, and leaders, we have met and interviewed hundreds of movement catalysts. All have reported that signs and wonders are a major element in the success and rapid growth in the movements they serve.

For the last six years we have polled the New Generation regional leaders to help us understand the true impact of the miraculous on church planting. The most recent analysis from each region produced a collective estimate that seventy to eighty percent of the churches planted met human needs, confirmed the truth of the Bible, and could be directly related to some sort of manifestation of the power of God.

Additionally, some regions of the world report that the majority of families who become Christ Followers are influenced by some other supernatural experiences during their journey of discovering God in the Bible: dreams of Jesus, the Holy Bible, or judgment; a dramatic answer to prayer; a broken addiction. When these people discover Jesus' command to pray for God to manifest His Kingdom in people's life situations, they just do what Jesus said to do. And they do it a lot!

The key element of all such movements is encouragement of individuals to adopt a lifestyle of reading the Word of God and obeying whatever it says—it is doubtful that Satan is at all pleased with that outcome!

TAKING TIME TO PRAY FOR PEOPLE WHILE SEEKING GOD'S DIRECTION

In the Global North, people are frequently nervous about praying for sick people or, in some cases, being prayed for. And then there is the prayer itself. What to say, what not to say? What level of intensity is appropriate? Should it be short and sweet because God already knows the need anyway? Or should it be long enough to cover all the possible themes that would trigger God's answer?

By now you have probably noted several Kingdom values repeatedly weaving through this book. Perhaps the biggest one is that, in all Kingdom outcomes, God invites disciples of Jesus to participate as catalysts, asking God's Kingdom authority to be manifested where we live—but with God always the senior partner. It's as though we contribute a penny to the process, and the storehouse of Kingdom outcomes brings forth a thousand dollars. He always supplies all the resources, but He still awaits our faithful participation. He is training all of us as disciples, learning on the job to reflect His image, to be His ambassadors, and to steward His special purposes in our unique lives.

Prayer is no different. God is the senior partner, and we are catalysts to pray three specific things down to earth: God's glory, God's Kingdom, and God's will as they are already established in heaven. So what does that have to do with how we pray for healing for someone? Why not ask God's Spirit to direct the prayer? That may take a few minutes of quiet reflection, and likely an occasional dialogue between the person praying and the person in need of prayer.

He always supplies all the resources, but He still awaits our faithful participation.

Asking questions that the Lord seems to bring up may seem awkward, but it often pinpoints the barriers that need to be broken inside a person's soul. If you pray like this regularly, you will rarely pray the same prayer twice. You will pray what God nudges you to pray. When God is invited to be the leader of a prayer meeting, He does not say "no."

When we take the extra time to listen, God will sometimes speak to the person whom you are praying for and they themselves will discover a sin to confess or a discipline to engage, which can be the pathway to healing. Sometimes the person being prayed for may hear from the Lord about unforgiveness toward someone, or some other issue holding them prisoner. Over time, you will probably find that half of the barriers, sicknesses, and bondages in peoples' lives are rooted in unforgiveness. In those cases, dealing with the issues that God brings up can be taken care of in a gentle time of encouragement and counsel, and then the prayer is sometimes answered before it is verbalized—because the Holy Spirit has led the prayer time.

If you are intentional in praying with people, you will often see higher and higher levels of success because you have learned to listen to the Lord and trust His voice. And you will be comfortable exploring what you sense the Lord is revealing for this person's healing. If you ask that person if they are sensing something from the Lord and they confess a sin or acknowledge some traumatic event in their lives that is still blocking their spiritual health, inviting God into the prayer time makes all the difference, especially if, with the person's permission, you focus prayer on the very incident or sin creating the blockage.

Deliverance

There is not a lot of difference in praying for healing and praying for deliverance. When praying for people who may have some level of demonic oppression, realize that all people live on a continuum in relation to temptations that we tolerate lingering in our mind. Some just need to be confessed and repented, while others remain in bondages that we can't seem to break without spiritual help. You don't have to have spend years in witchcraft to have some strongholds that must be confessed and swept out of the house. Some deliverances are relatively gentle processes of simply confessing whatever is revealed, and then being cleansed by the power of Jesus name. Others can take hours or even longer.

The Kingdom of God is a treasure for which we should sell everything that we own because, like the Apostle John, we discover that the Lord of the Universe is our best friend. And we get the privilege of participating with God in making known the Glory of God where we live, releasing the Kingdom of God where we live, and portraying the obedience and transformation of God in our family and community.

JIMMY TAM

Jimmy Tam was born and raised in Hong Kong in a family that worshipped idols and ancestors. When he was 16, he came to California and became a Christ Follower within three years. Nothing gave Jimmy more joy than sharing his testimony and watching God transform lives.

So it was no surprise when he chose to study theology at a prominent seminary before being ordained in an evangelical church. In 2000, he started Sunrise Christian Community in Southern California, and the church grew slowly for the first fourteen years, averaging about five or six new people per year.

By 2013, Pastor Jimmy was feeling that there must be something more effective than what he was doing to engage non-Christian cultures. Then a little later he met Sean Steckbeck (whom you met in chapters eleven and twelve) at a conference in Hong Kong. Sean told him about Disciple Making Movements and the approach resonated with Jimmy.

Jimmy asked Sean how to find people of peace and, instead of teaching him, Sean took him into Hong Kong streets to show him. Pastor Tam was shocked as he watched Sean find likely people of peace, doing just what Jesus told His disciples to do. He followed Sean into stores and watched him find a person or two and ask them simple questions: "Do you consider yourself a spiritual person?" "If a miracle can happen today, what would you want that miracle to be?"

An elderly gentleman who managed one store said, "I have a lot of body pain. I would definitely want prayers if they really work." Sean prayed, and the shopkeeper said, "I do feel a little better." And then Sean told him the story of Jesus and Zacchaeus. The man asked more questions, but it was his niece, who was sitting quietly next to him, who was most interested. She had not been prayed for, but she wanted to know more. So they arranged to come back.

Pastor Jimmy was stunned at what he saw an American do in a couple of hours—an American in Hong Kong who spoke no Chinese. That night, he realized that God has many people who are interested in spiritual realities—you just have to find these people and let God do what He will with them.

In October of 2014, Pastor Tam started a "love your neighbor campaign." It was not very complex; he just asked his church members to go into their neighborhood and say, "Jesus commands us to love our neighbors. And I haven't been doing that too well because I don't even know my neighbors. So is there anything that I can pray for you?" It was just that simple.

People began pouring out their hearts. One person began to weep when Pastor Tam prayed with her about a cancer diagnosis. One young man said, "I was looking for God, so I went to a church, but I didn't feel like I fit in. I couldn't understand what they were talking about." Today that man is baptized, growing as a disciple, learning how to pray for the sick, and making new disciples at McDonalds.

Pastor Jimmy asked his members to increase their commitment to disciple making in the first weeks of 2016. At the time, there were about fifty people in the church and he invited all of them to come join him in this. He understood that this was going to be a dramatic change for the church. Nobody was used to doing this, so he trained them how to do it and about ten people committed to the pioneer team. They tried different things in different neighborhoods and discovered that Hispanic people responded well to some questions, and Chinese responded well to others. They were learning how to be good biblical neighbors.

As time went on, Pastor Tam discovered that some members of the church were praying for a lot of people, praying with very simple faith. Some discovered that they had a gift of intercession, and God was honoring their prayers. People would have financial challenges; they would pray and, a week later, they would report what God did. Sometimes they would see God move dramatically in fifty or sixty percent of their prayers.

The situations were exactly what you would expect from families whose lives were torn by pressures and struggles beyond their control. One woman asked for prayers for her daughter who had a difficult situation relative to custody of her daughter. During the process of prayer the woman and her daughter began to discover the Bible and were eventually baptized outside of their house.

That woman's next-door neighbors saw the baptisms and asked the church members if they were Christians. Upon hearing that they were, they asked if they could pray for evil spirits in their house. They were regularly seeing moving shadows where there should have been none, and lights were turning on and off by themselves. Their young children were having frequent nightmares, and certain parts of the house had the strongest manifestations.

The people from Pastor Tam's church said: "Sure, we can pray for you and your house." And so they went throughout the house into every room, breaking the power of demonic influences and casting them out. As a result, every manifestation stopped.

Ordinary people were finding Kingdom solutions to the ordinary challenges of Californians just by asking if they could pray for them. One woman who, in her professional life, spent her workdays with people in the midst of trauma and crisis, was herself healed of a health condition. So she began to pray for her clients about their circumstances, and God began to answer those prayers. One of her clients, a woman on dialysis and in great pain, was healed dramatically, and she and her friends wanted to come to the church. But Pastor Tam suggested that they start a new fellowship in the community. They did, and that church has become a strong center of prayer.

Pastor Tam chose seven different Bible stories that anyone could tell to people they met, depending on their life circumstances, in order to bring the truth of God's word into their lives. This way, they can remember the stories of the Bible even if they aren't able to read. He also began to teach his members that they don't have to bring everyone to the church. Some people are simply more willing to worship where they feel at home— Jimmy recognized that offering this option may make discipling even more effective.

Jimmy comments about this:

> I knew that everyone in the church used to see bringing people to the church as the ultimate goal. Even as the first step of

bringing people to faith, people thought that they must first come to a church. That is where they will hear about Jesus. Even though they may pray for people, in order for us to feel like we are really being obedient to Jesus, we have to bring people to the church.

I think that was one of the most challenging mindsets that had to shift. I spent a lot of time trying to shift that mindset, by creating videos, by teachings and sermons, and by changing the terminology we use. We changed the name of the Sunday service to Celebration and Training. I changed the name because, if you get training, it is to help you carry out your mission more effectively out there, not in the Sunday service.

What is happened out of this time is more important than what happened during a Sunday service. The Sunday service is only two hours, but what you do for Jesus out there is more important, how you share Jesus with people, going to people's homes, is more important than bringing them here. We spent a lot of time and worked to change that mindset. The church was not resistant, just hesitant in the beginning, because we are Christians who have been sitting in the church for years.

And they felt that bringing people to the church is a must. That is the hardest thing to shake. So with about fifty people at the beginning of 2016, we set out to change.

One of the church's leaders named Simon was disappointed that he had not made any disciples after the first year. He had not found a real person of peace. He had been persistent, he had been praying for the Lord to use him to make a disciple, and he asked for prayers that God would give him one disciple. Pastor Tam prayed for Simon to find the person God wanted him to disciple.

After that Simon, met a stranger, Will, at his son's preschool. He sensed that Will had an interest in Jesus, so he took him to dinner. During the dinner Simon shared his testimony how the Lord delivered him from gambling addiction. Will reflected on what he heard and said, "This is amazing. I am exactly like you. Right now I am stuck in a gambling addiction that I cannot get out of. Your story is just like my story, but you've already experienced the change, and you sound so normal now!"

So Simon baptized Will and his wife on Christmas day, and they came out of the water shouting together: *Yes! We want Jesus!* After the baptism, Simon prayed for Will: "Father, fill him with the Holy Spirit to bless a lot of people."

And that very Christmas night, Will was shopping on eBay and struck up a conversation with a seller. As they were chatting about Ebay business, the seller went to Will's Facebook and said, "Oh! You follow Jesus, and you just recently got baptized?" "Yes, I just got baptized today." And the seller said, "Yeah I want to know about Jesus!" So immediately Will started sharing Scripture story sets with him. At the end of the conversation, the seller said, "I have been interested in Jesus. I've been waiting and waiting for somebody . . . and somehow I met you!"

Will ended his story saying, "God is already using me, just one day after I got baptized. Simon prayed for me, and I am now doing what Simon did for me."

So how did it go in 2016 for Pastor Jimmy's church?

By the end of 2016 there were still about fifty people attending the church. However, there were also another fifty people who were worshipping in new house churches in the communities. He had experienced a 100% growth year. And by mid-year 2017 another forty or so people had been added to their numbers.

THE GOSPEL OF THE KINGDOM
IS MORE THAT WE HAVE IMAGINED

From the first chapter of Genesis to the New Testament Epistles, the consistent theme of God's Word is that God's people are to be a chosen generation, a royal priesthood, a holy nation, His own special People (I Peter 2:9 NKJV), to be his ambassadors and representatives on earth to advance God's reign of Peace.

To bifurcate the Gospel is to choose to represent only part of God's nature and to advance only our favorite parts of His Kingdom purposes. To align with God's holistic intent is to enter the realm of God's highest purposes and the fullness of His purposes on earth.

HOLISTIC KINGDOM MINISTRY PT. 2

OBEDIENCE AND TRANSFORMATION

But the fruit of the Spirit is love, joy, peace, longsuffering, kindness, goodness, faithfulness, gentleness, self-control. Against such there is no law. And those *who are* Christ's have crucified the flesh with its passions and desires. If we live in the Spirit, let us also walk in the Spirit.

—Galatians 5:22–25 (NKJV)

THE DISCOVERY BIBLE STUDY IN A DRUG DEN

Val Kadalie is president of Cape Town City Mission in South Africa. She and her husband Charles began a disciple-making ministry there in 2007, and most recently among some of the country's most dangerous criminals. Here is the story of one of those men named Hani.

HANI'S STORY

I was born in a township were there were no positive role models in my life or in my community. The guys I looked up to were criminals who were committing various crimes in our communities and our City. One of these criminals that I admired and looked up to as a hero was Sibu.

Hani turned to violence and crime at an early age. By the time he reached manhood, he was committing armed robberies. He spent time in prison, but that only hardened him and gave him connections to other men of violence and, when he got out of jail and back on the streets, he was more prone to criminal activity than ever.

I followed the footsteps of criminals in my community and dropped out of school at an early age. I started to steal and do petty crimes. Later this progressed to armed robberies, which landed me in prison. I was sentenced to eight years' imprisonment, but I only ended up doing five years.

My father passed away while I was in prison and I could not even be at his funeral. I was released after five years and just continued were I left off in my life of violence and crime.

I became a drug dealer in my community because the money was good, I thought, and the risk was lower. I dealt with drugs on a big scale. During my dealings with drugs and gangsterism, because young people in my community were becoming seriously addicted, many of them were terrorizing the community doing armed robberies, house break-ins and other violent crimes. The community began to lay the blame on me for all the problems of crime in our community because I was the one who was selling the drugs.

In our community we use the term "mob justice." One evening the men in the community formed such a mob. They were determined to permanently end the "Hani problem," and they came very close to doing so. I was blind drunk in a stolen car. Armed with clubs and machetes, the enraged mob dragged me out. They beat me mercilessly, breaking bones, disfiguring and carving up my face, knocking out teeth, all the time stabbing me repeatedly with machetes and even gouging out one of my eyes. The mob finally left me for dead.

I was unrecognizable, but one of my friends recognized me by my shoes and he managed with others to drag me away and rescue me. God had other plans for me. It wasn't time for me to enter eternity.

I ended up in critical condition in hospital. By this time Sibu was out of prison and he was now a follower of Christ and had been discipled by Charles and Val. Sibu heard what happened to me and he came to visit me in hospital. He encouraged me not to give up on myself. He said as long I'm still alive I can change my life. He told me it doesn't matter what I look like on the outside but what matters is my soul.

I was eventually discharged but I was badly disfigured. Sibu arranged for me to do some training at a centre for visually impaired people. But when that ended, I continued selling the drugs because I was hopeless and I thought that no one would employ me because of the way I looked.

I returned to my same neighborhood and started selling drugs again from a shack. Then one day Sibu came into my life again. He found me sitting on the corner of a street waiting for my clients to buy their drug supplies. That's where the conversation started that would eventually turn my life around.

Sibu asked me how I was doing. I told him that things were not well with me. After all did he not see what my face was like? He asked me what I thought the problems were that plagued this community. I told him what I knew and rattled off the problems. It did not occur to me that I was a big part of the problem.

He asked me if I realized that I held the key to change in my hands. That the community could change if I changed. I laughed at him. "Me change? I will never change. What— you think I'm going to get a job? Hmmm? Work in a store all day?" Hani leaned forward again. "And just who would hire me, looking like this?" But Sibu was not frightened because he saw the opportunity that he'd been praying for. "Do you have friends?" he asked. I said "I have friends. "They're all my customers or my drug-runners, but there's plenty!" I realized Sibu was not joking when he said, "Can you invite them next week so that we can chat about life." I called them, and we met together in my wood-and-iron shack later that week.

And that was how Sibu gained the trust of his drug-dealing friend, and it was how Hani moved from being a man of violence to being a person of peace. They began a Discovery Bible Study right there in Hani's drug shack, a Bible study that was frequently interrupted by people coming to buy drugs, and once in a while, one of those people would decide to stay and listen. Sibu very deliberately followed the same format at each study, opening with questions, moving into reading a passage from the Bible, discussing it, and asking more questions. We will explain this format in detail at the end of this chapter, but what matters here is this: these actions began to build a "DNA of the Kingdom" into Hani right from the beginning. And after a few weeks, Hani would sit in the shack, now with his Bible open beside him for most of the day, reading and pondering it in between dealing with his drug customers. His questions and struggles to understand the Bible passages were many.

Hani continues:

> While I continued with my drug trade, I attended a three-month introduction to computers course at City Mission. This is used as an access to difficult to reach groups, and each class was followed with a DBS run by Sibu relating to our lives and struggles. I was fiercely resistant to any talk about God and the Bible. I challenged everything because I said it was a white man's religion and it went against our culture. So I challenged and pushed back, but Sibu allowed me

to do that and calmly had me read from the Bible for myself the answers to my fiery questions.

Then he invited me to join a weekly nighttime meeting of ex-offenders where Charles and Val prepared a meal and talked about their struggles to exit a life of crime and gangsterism, again, reflecting on what God says about this.

At the end of that evening, again with my push back and questions, Val told me there was no pressure on me to make any decision, that I should go on opening God's Word and listening to what He was saying to me. Suddenly I knew that I wanted this more than anything. I heard myself saying. "I'm ready now to follow Jesus."

Sibu continued to disciple and walk with me. I continued to sell drugs for a short while because that's all I knew. Sibu encouraged me to learn to obey what God was telling me. One late night, God did just that. He told me that all the profit I made that weekend from selling drugs could be translated into many destroyed lives and families. I had to choose.

I chose the Bible. I chose Christ.

Whatever Sibu told me about God and His Word, I was doing the same to my girlfriend because we were living together. By now I was fully committed to Christ as my Lord and my Saviour. I led my girlfriend to Christ and I also baptised her. We got married. Today it's three years and I'm doing the very same thing Sibu did in my life, to others.

I was transformed in my own community in front of their very eyes. Today they call me coach. I am on staff with City Mission, working with guys who were just like me. My wife received a scholarship to study Community Psychology at a Christian university. She just completed her first year successfully. How big is our God!

Hami and Sibu are only two of the men whose stories Charles and Val Kadalie love to tell. Today, both are serving God in South Africa with City Mission, reaching back into the darkness where they once lived to bring in the light of the Kingdom.

THERE ARE NO MOVEMENTS WITHOUT OBEDIENCE BASED DISCIPLE MAKING

Any form of "discipleship" that is not based upon obedience is no form of discipleship at all. Obedience is the foundation of discipleship, which is precisely why the Lord Himself commanded that we build our discipleship strategies upon it: "Therefore go and make disciples of all nations . . . teaching them to obey everything I have commanded you" (Matt. 28:19–20, NIV). Yet somehow, the church in the Global North has lost sight of this command, or has subtly changed it from "teaching them to obey" into "teaching them good doctrine"—or even "teaching them to feel good about themselves."

The church in the Global North has come to tolerate many who call themselves Christians but who treat the commands of Jesus as optional extras that they can pick and choose from when convenient. Some express serious doubts about whether objective truth exists, and so they never share their faith with non-Christians because it might not be "their" truth. Humanistic worldviews have dominated the culture for so long that hardly any Christian can escape pressure to compromise the values of God's Kingdom on a daily basis. This means one thing for Christians—we are in trouble.

The answer to a humanistic worldview is not a *Biblical Worldview for Dummies* crash course. It is an opportunity to discover God in the Bible and simply see what happens when people obey. God Himself has made promises about what He will do when people seek Him and obey Him. And the Holy Spirit regularly begins to transform hearts and bring conviction into the soul of anyone who obeys whatever they discover in the Bible.

Such is the power of non-legalistic, self-discovered obedience to God—it is the power of *transformation*.

The biblical term "transformation" tends to be co-opted today to refer to any activity that adds value to human existence. Now, just to be clear: we strongly affirm the importance of compassion ministry, as we stressed in the previous chapter. Nevertheless, compassion on its own is an incomplete expression of true discipleship. The United Nations might use the word "transformational" to describe purely humanitarian projects that do not affirm the love and lordship of God, but we should not confuse the intent of this language with transformation in the Kingdom of God.

God Himself has made promises about what He will do when people seek Him and obey Him.

Consider Romans 12:2. Biblical transformation is more than simply not conforming to the world's thinking. Biblical transformation requires the renewing of our minds, and that begins to happen only when people intentionally align their lives with God's will. Indeed, Paul is telling us that we can only understand God's will in the first place by having our minds renewed—and that can only be done through the power of the Holy Spirit. Biblical transformation is the work of the Holy Spirit, bringing our lives into alignment with Jesus' teaching.

Animists, Muslims, Hindus, Christo-Pagans, and others report that their lives are beginning to change along with their worldviews within a few weeks of beginning to discover God in the Bible. The process of discovering God's Word for oneself, led by the Holy Spirit (whether or not the participant is aware of His involvement) inevitably leads people from every background to confront the question of obedience to God in their own lives. Sooner or later, Discovery Bible Study leads to the realization that it is impossible to be a citizen of God's Kingdom and not have a life committed to obeying what Jesus taught. It is also impossible to be a citizen of the Kingdom for which Jesus died, on the basis of "works righteousness." There is no spiritual wholeness on the margins of the truth that Jesus is Lord. We have to honor Jesus' ongoing acts of grace and mercy extended toward us by loving and obeying Him in response.

THE AMAZING TRANSFORMATIONS OF CHOOSING TO OBEY GOD'S WORD

Evangelicals have almost always affirmed that the Bible holds a unique status among all other sacred books as a source of spiritual power and dramatic transformation—yet most have treated it as if the Bible had to be interpreted for ordinary people to understand it and experience it. While good biblical scholarship is important, this attitude seriously discounts the unlimited power of Spirit-led Scripture reading, whether read by PhDs or heard by illiterate people. Around the world every day, untold thousands of people are experiencing the power of the Bible almost immediately beginning to transform worldviews, demeanors, and actions.

Leaders of Disciple-Making Movements consistently observe that when people obey the Bible—even lost people—the Holy Spirit begins to validate the truth of the Bible and to demonstrate its power to transform their lives:

> For the word of God is living and powerful, and sharper than any two-edged sword, piercing even to the division of soul and spirit, and of joints and marrow, and is a discerner of the thoughts and intents of the heart. (Heb. 4:12)

And in the presence of the Holy Spirit, Scripture brings conviction of truth and need for forgiveness:

> Now when they heard this, they were cut to the heart. (Acts 2:37)

And beyond that, Jesus gave an incredible number of promises that were dependent on loving and obeying God. Far from being a legalistic *quid pro quo*, the promises represent the fruit of our gratitude and commitment to obey all that we know of Jesus' will. When people who do not yet fully understand the God of the Bible nonetheless respond in obedience to truths discovered in Scripture, it shows that they have begun a journey toward God—and that they are sensing that the truths of the Bible contain the secret to joy and peace.

John 14:15–15:16 contains *twelve promises that accrue to those who love and obey God*. These promises show that God's love language is something that even lost people can begin to sense as they discover new aspects of His character and His promises. The list below includes all references to the the blessings that come from obedience to God's commandments.

- 🕊 **14:15–17:** If you keep my commandments I will send you the Helper, who will abide with you forever.

- 🕊 **14:18:** I will not leave you orphans; I will come to you.

- 🕊 **14:21:** He who loves me will keep my commandments.

- **14:23:** We will come to him who obeys and make Our home with him.

- **14:26:** The Holy Spirit will teach you all things and remind you of my words.

- **14:27:** Do not be afraid—I give you my peace.

- **15:7:** If you abide in Me, and My words abide in you, you will ask what you desire, and it shall be done for you.

- **15:8:** My Father is glorified when you bear much fruit.

- **15:9–10:** If you keep My commandments, you will abide in My love.

- **15:14:** You are My friends if you do whatever I command you.

- **15:15:** I no longer call you servants, but friends.

- **15:16:** You did not choose me; I chose you—that you should go and bear fruit, and that your fruit should remain.

The lives of lost people are often transformed as they obey God's Word, even before their Discovery Groups get to the New Testament. And transformed lives are the catalyst of multiplication in the world of Disciple-Making movements. Consistent obedience to God's Word can begin to reconcile feuding spouses and make mean people nice—and we gain God's version of attractional evangelism in the process. When we let God's Word do what it promises to do, then God's Spirit begins to transform even the most horrible people into the image of Christ—and this leads many *other* people to wonder how to learn more about God.

The early pioneers of Kingdom movements were mainly desperate missionaries whose agencies gave them permission to try non-traditional methods where nothing was working. And when obedience-based discipleship was made the centerpiece of the strategy—precisely because Jesus' last command said that we are to teach people to obey Him—then it became obvious that obedience has always been the key to the Kingdom of God. Remember, as we saw in chapter two, the definition of a Kingdom is obedience to royal authority. Without obedience, by its very definition, the Kingdom is not present.

Jesus said that He was giving the 1st-century church "the keys to the Kingdom of Heaven," and in the 21st century we can rediscover the keys that will open the doors of the Kingdom of God to the lost. The following story illustrates this reality.

"BURN THE BOOK!"

Ayele is a teacher and church planter in the Horn of Africa. He became a Christ follower in 1998 and within a few years the Lord had matured him and grown his ministry to a remarkable degree. He was instrumental in the planting of three churches in the early part of this century, and he began a growing ministry throughout a widespread area in Ethiopia and Kenya.

God gave him a gift of healing, and he began preaching and teaching the Gospel in a great many towns, healing the sick and casting out demons. There were many miracles during this time. The blind received sight and the lame walked—and Ayele began to keep a journal. He found that he was having trouble remembering names of the people among whom he ministered, so he began writing those down. Then he wanted to remember their prayer requests, so those went into the journal as well. Then he began to record specific miracles and signs that the Lord revealed through his ministry—and those details went in too.

Eventually, that journal contained the names and information on 10,000 individuals! Every page was a treasure to Ayele, a written indication that God had powerfully used him to produce dramatic results. Even the details themselves were helpful, calling back his mind to where people lived and when he'd met them and what they were prayed for and how God had wrought the miraculous. And gradually that journal helped to define Ayele's ministry and how he did God's work—and even, in some measure, who and what he was in his own eyes.

And that was when the Spirit of God called him to a new task, a very difficult and costly task: burn the journal.

Ayele explains, "The Spirit seemed to be saying to me, 'You are only doing half the job—and I want you to do the whole job!'" He had been diligent in ministering to the physical and corporal needs of others, but he had never done anything to make disciples. He would pray for healing, lay on hands, pray the sinner's prayer—then move on to address the next need. It took some time, but God made it increasingly clear that He wanted Ayele to learn to minister to the whole man, the spiritual as well as the physical aspects, in order to carry out the Great Commission in full rather than in part.

And so, in obedience, Ayele burned his journal. It was a symbolic act, he now explains, but the symbolism was important for him. It represented a deliberate decision on his part to forsake his ministry methods, abandon his traditional approach to ministry, and take a leap of faith in a whole new direction. And this was both huge and new for him. "I finally understood the Great Commission," he says, "to 'go make *disciples*'—but the problem was, I didn't know *how* to make disciples."

Fortunately, there was a ministry in the Horn of Africa that was training people to make disciples in the same way that Jesus taught the Twelve and the seventy-two. Ayele soaked in everything he could learn and immediately put it into practice. He then took a job to support his family and began the process of making disciples.

Eventually, he took six of his colleagues from local churches into his home and devoted six months to training them in the things that he'd learned. Over the previous years, these men had planted three churches; now, those churches became *sending* churches, as new church planters trained at all three churches went out to make new disciples. And, in the next three months, they planted thirty-seven churches. And to this day, Ayele continues to lead this ministry while supporting himself with a full-time job.

. . . salvation has two parts, justification and sanctification, and they are accomplished through different processes.

In late 2010, Jerry brought a research team to the community where Ayele lives, and he invited them to be his house guests for two days. They had the opportunity to walk in a baptismal parade through the town and to witness the baptism of scores of new Christ Followers. And that night, they returned to Ayele's home to meet seven generations of leaders in the stream of disciple making that he has catalyzed.

Jerry and his team spent the two days interviewing some of those seven generations of disciples, and the stories were stunning. Some were drug cartel members a few years prior who had become legitimate businessmen—and disciple-makers. Another former leader of a criminal enterprise now spends his life helping people find full-time jobs. The most memorable interview was with a policeman who said that law enforcement had become fairly boring because the whole town had been transformed by the Gospel, so there was not much work to do anymore.

Seven years later, as this book is being completed, Ayele's work has led to two different movements among two different people groups, totaling 670 churches with more than 40,000 Christ Followers. His team is careful about tracking generations, and they are now seeing 27 generations of disciples making disciples and churches planting churches. This is indeed fruit that remains, and it grew out of the burning of a single book—the day when Ayele obeyed God's call to transition his from a healing ministry to a holistic ministry, fully embracing obedience-based disciple making.

A Word about Obedience

One concern that people have about obedience-based disciple making is that it suggests works of righteousness, as if our obedience was the cause of our salvation. To clarify this, we need to recognize that salvation has two parts, justification and sanctification, and they are accomplished through different processes.

Our *justification* comes by God's grace alone; we have absolutely no part in it. We are not justified by our actions or our attitudes or our learning; we are not justified by our obedience to God's Word or to church creeds or to anything whatsoever—we are justified by the grace of God and absolutely nothing more.

But our *sanctification* is very different; we most assuredly *do* have a significant part in our sanctification—that is to say, our *holiness*. Holiness includes our actions, so the things that we say and do matter. Our obedience to the Word of God and our cooperation with the Holy Spirit is integral to the process of personal sanctification. We work with God's grace through obedience, leading to the transformation of our lives. Such obedience is not legalistic; it is a response of love and trust to Jesus, not a matter of conformity to external rules.

Remember, Jesus talks in the Upper Room Discourse about the importance of obedience. He tells us that if we love Him, we will obey His commands; conversely, if we obey His commands, we are demonstrating that we love Him (John 14:15, 21). He also says that if we obey Him, we will remain in His love and are His friends (John 15:10, 14).

Then Jesus goes beyond this. He makes a clear connection between our obedience and the gift of the Holy Spirit (John 14:16), between our obedience and the love of the Father (John 14:21), between our obedience and our joy (John 15:11)—even between our obedience and the very revelation of Jesus to us (John 14:21). Can there be any serious question about how important obedience is to our Christian life?

We can only grow to be more like Christ by growing in obedience to Him. The New Testament tells us again and again and again that Jesus *obeyed* the Father. Growing into the likeness of Christ therefore means growing in our obedience to the Father. These two concepts are inseparable; indeed, they are not two concepts at all, but simply two ways of saying the same thing:

> We become more like Christ by obeying the Father.
> Obeying the Father makes us look more like Christ.

Many Christians in the Global North seem to think that transformation is a purely internal matter, accomplished through studying the Scriptures and perhaps through prayer.

This reflects the knowledge-based model of discipleship common in Global North evangelicalism. We certainly don't intend to downplay the importance of studying and meditating on Scripture—but it is equally important to *obey* it. When Jesus discusses the last judgment, He does not tell us that He judge us based on whether we pass a Scripture quiz; He tells us that He judges us based on how we live our life.

TRUE ATTRACTIONAL EVANGELISM

As we have already stated, we learn to be like Christ simply by learning to obey. Similarly, we learn to love simply by loving others. This does not happen overnight, of course; growing in obedience is a lifetime process. In nature, fruit develops gradually; in our lives, the Spirit works with us to develop His fruit in our lives over time as well.

But as our lives become increasingly conformed to Christ, we will attract others. People see the evidence of changed lives and are drawn to the beauty of Jesus. This leads to transformed communities, which in turn attract other communities to the Gospel.

American evangelicals frequently think in terms of attractional models for the church. They look for ways to get people to attend, typically through choice of music, or the amenities that the church provides, or even by creating an atmosphere that isn't like church at all, with large nightclub-like services that trade making disciples for gaining members. This approach disempowers the average churchgoer as we have suggested already—but there are also some deeper problems. It feeds an entertainment mentality in worship; it conforms the church to the consumerism of today; and it attracts people to the *event* rather than to the *Kingdom*.

By contrast, a biblical attractional model is built around attracting people to the Kingdom through the evidence of transformed lives. And people who are attracted to the Kingdom this way become disciples who grow in depth, since they want to experience the same kind of transformation in their own lives. Once again, this is not theoretical; we have many examples in the Global South that demonstrate the attractional power of transformation through obedience.

It is for these reasons and many more that Discovery Bible Studies focus so intently on obedience. As we have already said many times, the idea is to establish a DNA of discipleship right from the beginning of a person's involvement in the disciple-making process—well before the person has become a Christ Follower, before he has begun to read about Jesus of Nazareth, before he even has a rudimentary understanding of the Bible itself, he has begun to grasp one fundamental principle: he is called upon to obey what he learns in the Bible. A few stories will illustrate how this works.

THE WOMAN ON THE PLANE WHO HATED BIBLE-THUMPERS

Jerry was on an airplane a few years ago when a fellow passenger introduced herself with a lengthy monologue, beginning with her Ivy League credentials, moving on to her ownership of a large consulting company, and then throwing in this bombshell: "I am Jewish and I sort of admire Jesus, but I don't like Christians—especially Bible thumpers. Them I *really* hate!" She continued her stream of talk for a few more minutes, then paused for breath—and, as if she had suddenly become aware of Jerry's presence, she added, "But what do *you* do?"

Anticipating that question, Jerry had already been praying for what to say, and so he answered, "I help people discover God in the Bible."

That caught her attention, and for a moment she was at a loss for words. Then, with just a trace of sheepishness, she asked, "What does *that* mean?"

"Well, I can show you if you like," Jerry said. "Since you are Jewish, I wonder if you have a favorite passage from the Hebrew Scriptures?"[1]

She looked a bit confused for a moment, not quite sure what to say or where this might be leading, but suddenly she brightened and smiled. "Yes I do—it's the Shema. I like the Shema."

"I love that passage, too," Jerry exclaimed. "Did you know that it is a very important passage for Christians also? So can you recite the Shema?"

This time, she looked openly embarrassed for a moment, as though she had just said the first thing that came to mind—but she quickly recovered her aplomb. "Well," she said, "I can remember *parts* of it, but I can't quote the whole thing."

Now, Jerry had his Bible in his carry-on bag right at his feet, but he did not get it out because he sensed that it would intimidate her. After all, he didn't want to appear to be thumping on it! But then the Spirit gave him some inspiration.

"I wonder if, between the two of us, we could remember enough to piece the Shema passage together and figure it out?"

"Sure, let's try that!" she enthused. And for the next fifteen minutes she and Jerry went intently back and forth, each adding a phrase or two from the Shema passage until they had pieced it together from memory. She was pleased with

---

1   Deuteronomy 6:4–9

herself and thought that this exercise was over. But Jerry had another question.

"So, what did you discover about God in the Shema?"

"Wow, that's a good question," she said with a thoughtful expression. And without any apparent fear that Jerry might start thumping on a Bible, she entered into a deep discussion about the attributes of God's character revealed in Deuteronomy 6.

After a time, Jerry asked, "and what do you learn about yourself—about human nature in general—from the Shema?" She smiled and said: "That's also a really good question." By now, this woman had warmed up to the topic, and she was genuinely engaged in digging into the Scripture and reflecting on what it meant to her in the 21st century.

Note, this is the very process which we've been discussing throughout this book, of building a DNA of obedience and personal application to Bible study, right from the very beginning of a person's exposure to Bible study. And by this time the woman would probably not even have described their conversation as "Bible study"

Then, Jerry asked the most important question, "So if all these things in the Shema are true, how would you obey what you have discovered in this passage?" Jerry describes what happened next in his own words,

> Our conversation had been relaxed and comfortable up to that point; we'd just been going back and forth and occasionally laughing and frequently pondering together. But she suddenly snapped around to face me directly—even though we were jammed side by side in airplane seats, she snapped right around and said, 'I—don't—*do*—obedience!' Very emphatic like that, like she was underlining each word.

I was a little taken aback, but then the Spirit came through again, and I asked her, 'Well, how would you describe how the Shema should impact your life?' I basically asked the same question again, I just left out that word 'obedience' that had set her off." To my continued amazement, she now leaned back, reflected a moment, and said, "I think I could respond to the God who created me and has a purpose for me."

Then, she opened up with some honest and private reflections. It was clear that the power of a nearly forgotten Scripture had taken her to a vulnerable place with God—along with her new friend the 'Bible-thumper.' I was so pleased that this woman, who just an hour before had been making harsh comments about Christians, was now deeply engaged in her own Bible study!

This had nothing to do with technique; it had everything to do with the power of God's Word to touch her heart, and she started to ask herself questions about what her favorite Bible passage actually meant in her life.

As the passengers buckled in for the landing, she turned to Jerry again. "You really do help people discover God in the Bible," she said thoughtfully. "This was a very remarkable experience. Thank you."

This woman had been through her first Discovery Bible Class—albeit a somewhat more spontaneous one than most. But this approach continues to be the standard way that millions of Muslims, Hindus, Buddhists, Chinese Traditional Religionists, Animists, and Christo-pagans are discovering God and becoming ambassadors of the Kingdom of God. All of the different worldviews above profit from starting with different beginning Scripture sets for the first 15–25 Discovering Bible Group meetings, but all of them use the same basic process.

THE DISCOVERY GROUP PROCESS

> Can you think of a time when you had that "Ah-ha" moment, that you feel that God dropped something in your heart? You discovered it for yourself and you saw it for the first time. People can often reference several times when that happened, years back in their lives. So they can remember those times when they saw something, when their eyes were opened, when they discovered something. But they can't remember much when it was presented in a monologue form. *David Broodryk Engage! Africa video series*

A Discovery Group is a group of lost people, gathered by a person of peace, to discover and obey God's Word, and to begin living out the core elements of a Christian community in a context where it has a high probability of becoming a church. Throughout this process, individuals are being discipled by the Bible toward conversion and toward being disciple makers. Becoming a church of baptized believers who gather together for fellowship, worship, nurture, and discipleship, and who leave the gathering to obey all that God has commanded, is a very natural part of the progression.

John King, whom you met in chapter ten, created the following template in 2010, which, building on David Watson's work, has become a standard description of a Discovery Group world-wide.

The basic approach to a Discovery Group is as follows.

- **Ask Question One:** "What happened this past week that you are thankful for?" Allow each person to answer briefly. This step is *discipling toward praise*, meaning that it helps to engender the DNA of giving thanks to God for His blessings.

🜚 **Ask Question Two:** "What challenges are happening in your life, family, or community?" Allow each person to answer briefly while the facilitator takes basic notes. (These are helpful in follow-up meetings when we get to Question Eight below.) This step is *discipling toward intercession*, building the DNA of praying and caring for one another.

🜚 **Ask Question Three:** "How did you obey / share / meet a need after last week's group?" This is actually a follow-up to three questions (numbers 6–8 below), and there is flexibility here on how to ask it. This step is *discipling toward accountability* because it builds the DNA of mutual accountability.

   Study the Bible: This step is *discipling toward reading God's Word in order to obey it*. The method used is Discovery Bible Study. It is broken into several sub-steps:

- **Read the passage aloud.** English-speaking groups can read it from two or three different translations, but if oral-learners are present, ensure that at least one of the readings is clear and easy to understand.

- **Ask a volunteer to re-tell the passage.** This is done from memory without using the Bible for prompting. The person should tell it in his own words.

- **Have the group fill in details.** There is generally some detail that will be missed, or perhaps some detail where understandings differ within the group.

- **Remember that this entire step is not a quiz or test with right and wrong answers.** It is intended to engage everyone in the process of reading, paying attention to, and caring about the Word of God—nothing more. Our job is to facilitate Bible study; understanding, application, obedience, transformation—those are the job of the Holy Spirit.

🕊 **Ask Question Four:** "What do we learn about God in this section?" This builds the DNA of *reading the Bible in order to understand God*.

🕊 **Ask Question Five:** "What do we learn about the human race from this section?" This builds the DNA of *self-examination*, recognizing that the Bible's teachings still apply today.

🕊 **Ask Question Six:** "How will your life change if you put this passage into practice?" (The facilitator should take notes, as the answers here are re-addressed in the next session with Question 3 above.) This builds the DNA of *obedience*. Sometimes, facilitators will prime the pump for this question by asking lead-in questions first. One model for this follows the acrostic SPECK:

- Is there a **S**in to confess or avoid?

- Is there a **P**rayer to pray? A **P**raise to give to God? A **P**romise to claim?

- Is there an **E**xample to imitate?

- Is there a **C**ommand to obey?

- Is there **K**nowledge to gain?

🕊 **Ask Question Seven:** "Who do you know who needs to hear this lesson?" This asks each group participant to plan on sharing the Bible with someone outside the group; it is *discipling toward making disciples*, as it builds the DNA of sharing the gospel and making disciples. (The facilitator should take notes again, as the answers here are re-addressed in the next session with Question Three above.)

⟩ **Ask Question Eight:** "How can we help with one of the challenges that were shared earlier?" This refers back to Question Two, where participants shared what challenges they are facing at present. The group selects one of those challenges and brainstorms together to develop a concrete plan to bless one of the group participants. This step is *discipling toward ministry*, as it builds the DNA of "one another-ism"—that quality of caring for one another which is so essential to the long-term life of a church. (The facilitator should take notes once more, as the answers here are re-addressed in the next session with Question Three above.)

From these discovery questions, what kind of churches are started? They are obedient; they bring transformation in the community and in the families. They pray. And they are culturally relevant, because they discover truth in the Word of God and then they will struggle with obeying that in their context. So this will produce sound, biblically and culturally relevant churches in the community.

—Younoussa Djao Engage! Africa Video series

Every Discovery Group meeting thus includes the personal Bible discovery process, along with mutual support, prayer, and accountability to specific goals to obey God and to share last week's Bible theme with someone else. It has most of the biblical elements that you would find in a healthy church, but you're seeing it in a group of people who have yet to learn about the redemption offered through the blood of Christ—indeed, you begin to see the DNA of healthy churches in the lives of people who have not yet even come to an understanding of their need for salvation. It is discipling people in a way that gently moves them toward conversion.

The process of Discovery Bible Study demonstrates a couple of important principles that the church in the Global North needs to recognize. First, the Word of God is not just a collection of information about God to be learned and obeyed; it is a living document (Heb. 4:12) with the power to change even the most skeptical people from the first moment that they discover truth in its pages. While teaching plays an indispensable role in the church, "self-discovery of truth" and "self-actuated obedience to truth" are proving to be dramatically more powerful in transforming people's lives, families, and communities than "teaching only" models.

The Word of God and the Holy Spirit change lives, not gifted and godly teachers. God uses His people, without question, but the force behind all global movements building the Kingdom of God is His Word as used by His Spirit.

This leads to a controversial conclusion, but it's one that has played out time and again: the Discovery process can be done entirely by non-Christians; Christians do not even need to be present. It is the Father who draws people to Christ through His Word by the Spirit; He sometimes uses us in that process but we are, at best, secondary to the Spirit's work in the hearts and minds of the lost.

Encouraging unbelievers to discover God through the Word makes many Christians nervous. Some even argue that it is impossible, since "The person without the Spirit does not accept the things that come from the Spirit of God but considers them foolishness, and cannot understand them because they are discerned only through the Spirit." (1 Cor. 2:14). Roy Moran, an American Evangelical pastor who is active in Kingdom Movements, points out, however, that the alternative, that we need to connect people to someone before we connect them to God, has serious problems. He discusses the standard Global North model in this passage in his book, *Spent Matches*:

> Whether it is incarnational ministry, attractional meetings, or friendship evangelism, we still practice gospel outreach by connecting people to persons or a place in an effort then to connect them with God. We use terminology such as "earn the right to be heard" or "build bridges before you cross them" or "be credible in a relationship"—all in an attempt to connect to an individual before connecting them to God.
>
> Protestants accuse Catholics of heresy because they see the Virgin Mary, the clergy-led Mass, confession and the sacraments as humans mediating grace. Yet the Protestant orthopraxy of connecting people to people before connecting them to God is also mediation.
>
> It is hard for us to conceive of connecting people to God without an intermediary. But theologically that is exactly what we believe. There is one God and one mediator (1 Timothy 2:5), but somehow we feel the need to mediate the message to the uninitiated before Jesus can do His mediating work.
>
> Learning to use the discovery process to take spiritually interested people to a relationship with God allows us to put our energy into connecting people with God rather than with ourselves. Their first dependency in their spiritual lives is on God and not on us.[2]

---

[2] Roy Moran, *Spent Matches*, (Nashville: Thomas Nelson, 2015), 65.

> Our job is to facilitate Bible study; understanding, application, obedience, transformation—those are the job of the Holy Spirit.
>
> You know, when we come to the Bible, the church is used to having experts to teach and preach and tell people what to believe, what to do, what not to do. But in a Discovery Bible Study you don't teach, you don't preach in the traditional way of doing—you facilitate a process of discovery. People discover the truth and then they obey. Jesus said, "Go and make disciples . . . teach them to obey."
>
> —*Younoussa Djao Engage! Africa* video series

This is not to say that God's people should not deliberately get involved in this discipling process. But we do need to be prepared to change our ministry methods to fit the Kingdom rather than the other way around, as we've said many times—and this might require some creativity and flexibility on our part. Here are some examples that come to us from South Africa.

THE SOUL TRAIN

Namira (pseudonym), is an accountant who attends David Broodryk's church. She has a family and works thirteen to fifteen hours a day, but nonetheless wanted to get more involved in advancing the Kingdom. She approached David about this, and when he found out she had a ninety-minute commute to work each way, he suggested she start a Discovery Bible Study on the train. She soon had four people meeting regularly, and over time it expanded to take over the entire car. It then spread to a second car.

They spent the entire commute, in both directions, doing Discovery Bible Studies. They meet in groups of four, two and two facing each other. The groups are obviously not stable, with different people coming in and out of the cars. But they use this to their advantage: they have a natural connection with the people who participate, and they will follow them to their homes at the end of the day to build the relationship, find people of peace, and disciple them.

Namira and the others who participate in the studies consider their commute a church. When challenged on this by local pastors, Namira replied, "How much time do your church members spend 'churching' a week?" They answered, "Well, Sunday morning is from nine to eleven, so they spend two hours a week, then some do home studies." Namira responded, "Do you realize that these people are spending three hours a day, five days a week churching? How can you disqualify this as church?"

THE CHURCH IN THE FACTORY

A new Christ Follower wanted to start a prayer meeting in her workplace. Things started out well, with a small group meeting from seven forty-five to eight each morning—but the moment they extended a little past eight, management told them to stop. The group couldn't move the time to any earlier nor could they move it to after work because participants were dependent on public transportation, which had a fixed schedule. Tea and lunch breaks were too short.

After the group's leader prayed about alternatives, what emerged was very creative: Discovery Bible Groups were melded into their everyday work lives. Several people became involved as facilitators, and their responsibilities were to type up Scripture verses and paste them on the walls around the work place each day. Many of the people worked together in groups, so the facilitators began to prompt conversations with their workmates throughout the day about those Scripture verses—asking the same sort of questions that Jerry asked the woman on the airplane. "What do these verses mean?" "What implications do they have to your life, if they're true?"

Management didn't mind, because everyone was still doing their work—these conversations seemed to be happening at appropriate, non-disruptive times. It was just as effective as a Discovery Bible Group because they were essentially discipling one other in their conversations—while working. They were asking each other the basic questions: What needs do we have? What are we grateful for? How can we meet those needs? In tea breaks, they would pray for each other. So these people were having church eight hours a day, five days a week, instead of having a single fifteen-minute meeting each day. Many then started Discovery Bible Studies in their own homes, and also launched pioneer groups in new areas.

FINISHING THE TASK: THE ROLE OF CHURCHES

Peter Snyman pastors a church of about 1,500 people, and they began a transition to urban Disciple-Making Movements in South Africa in 2010. He had this to say about the power of discovery in a large urban area:

> The discovery process has advantages over traditional learning processes. Recovering drug addicts, for example, will tell us, "I've heard this preached all my life, but this time I've discovered it for myself. It became a truth that I owned, and I didn't hear someone preaching at me." We all have the tendency to reject what has been preached at us. A sinner knows he's a sinner, and you don't have to tell him that.

How do you discover God's truth without someone else's agenda getting in the way? That is important, because this is a journey that the Holy Spirit takes with an individual. And in a group-discovery learning experience, they hold each other accountable, and that makes it very much a Holy Spirit-prescribed experience. The Spirit of God sets the pace, He knows exactly what the person needs, and He convicts them of the right things in the right time for the right reasons—so it takes away all the human agendas that are often in programs.

We were one of the first churches in South Africa to adopt the cell-church model, but we found it to be just another way to control our own people and to manage our own structures. In reality, it was *our* cell churches, *our* cell leaders, *our* zones, *our* districts—and we were intimidated by anything different. Even one cell was intimidated by another and complained that they were "stealing our people." It was all about management of our resources and our people.

But in Discovery Bible Groups, if someone is willing to start one, the response is: "How can I help you do it?" We're not looking at growing our group or protecting our methods or expanding our ministry. We're looking at reproducing the process. It is a very different reality.

From the first day, people sensed that what was happening was not manipulated by church people because you can't control or manipulate it. The process cancels out our ability to control or manipulate for our own ends. And that is what makes it so accessible to the people who wouldn't darken the door of an institutional church.

A FINAL NOTE: USING DISCOVERY IN SERMONS

It is not uncommon for pastors to adjust their sermons to include Discovery Bible Study elements in places where Kingdom movements are springing up. For example, they might introduce a passage of Scripture to the church for a few minutes, and then transition the church to spend eight to ten minutes with three to four people doing the Scripture questions from the DBS, ending with:

"I will obey this passage by doing. . . ."

And

"I will share this passage with. . . ."

The pastor allows another ten or twelve minutes for people share their answers to those questions, and this is often a fun experience for the church. The pastors use good humor to gently correct answers that are too vague or off the point, thus helping maintain a good DNA for all the groups in the church. (Note that this is different from the approach used in Discovery Groups, as outlined above, since the pastor is the shepherd of the people; part of his job is such doctrinal teaching and correction. That approach is generally *not* healthy in Discovery Groups.)

The pastor wraps up the sermon with appropriate closing remarks based, in part, on what the members contributed to the exposition of the passage. This style of "discovery preaching" asks church members to be comfortable with sharing, but once it starts it tends to be very effective and popular.

Discovery Bible Studies have therefore proven to be effective at all stages of church life—at the beginning stages as churches form, and in the later stages as churches strive to become more Kingdom-minded. These concepts are so simple, so easy to implement, that the mere suggestion of trying them out could inspire you to turn to your seatmate on your next flight and ask an important question—one that could lead to making your very first disciple.

COURAGEOUS LEADERSHIP AND SACRIFICE

Matthew 10:16–39 NKJV excerpts:

Behold I send you out as sheep in the midst of wolves (v. 16a)

Do not fear those that can kill the body but cannot kill the soul (v. 28a)

And a man's foes will be those of his own household. (v. 36)

And he who does not take his cross and follow after Me is not worthy of Me. He who finds his life will lose it, and he who loses his life for My sake will find it. (vss. 38, 39)

THERE ARE NO DISCIPLE-MAKING MOVEMENTS WITHOUT COURAGEOUS LEADERS

In his first forty years of ministry, Jerry did not know of anyone in his circles being martyred. During that time he did observe that every success in ministry required someone to make courageous sacrifices, and that spiritual warfare often attended Kingdom advances.

Beginning in 2005, the launch of Disciple Making Movements in Africa had only moderate persecution and resistance in the first three years. Not surprisingly, some Christian organizations pushed back on movements simply because the concept was new and non-traditional.

Everything began to change in the third year. It was 2008 when opposition began to rise in Muslim regions as large numbers of Muslims exited Islam to become Christ Followers.

The following year brought the shock of the first Muslim background martyrs in two countries, and what would be the long imprisonments of several more. Within another two years, Disciple Making Movements in one African country had more than 200 martyrs, some just a few days into their journey with Jesus.

The response to these tragedies by our African colleagues and their ministries was a courageous one. They doubled down on disciple makers deployed to many more Muslim regions. The courage of those brothers and sisters meant that none of us could waver.

Around that time, all of the teams began to see bizarre family health issues and increased theological pushback on empowering ordinary people to be disciple makers and church planters.

About the same time, Jerry was with one Western colleague in a restricted area planning a covert DMM training. Jerry shared concern with his colleague that he was at serious risk. The response, with a smile, was, "Yes, I know. But I am doing what God told me to do a few weeks ago. My wife and I decided something way back when we were learning Arabic. You see, we died before we got here!" Those words and his gentle smile became the last memory Jerry would have of that brother, who was martyred a few days later.

Just before this chapter was written the New Generation Global team gathered for a week together. It was an extraordinary week of prayer and listening to the Lord. But early in the week news came of two senior Muslim background leaders of movements who were in dire straits.

One had been attacked by Islamic militants and his neck and head had been slashed with a machete. He was thought dead and thrown into a ditch. Some Christians had found him still alive and took him to a local clinic, but he was still in extreme danger.

At almost the same time, another former Muslim sheik, now a prominent Christian scholar, was arrested by militants and given a few days to publicly recant on television, or be executed. The man who had a mentoring relationship with both of the men was in our meeting and grieving the impending double tragedy.

And so the whole group took up the intercession for them. Every leader there knew that they were still alive only because of God's protection, and on the day of testing they knew what to say: they would all exalt Jesus, and speak a blessing on their executioners.

After one day of prayer, news came that a donor had wired an emergency gift that provided the seriously wounded brother with the logistics to get the medical care he needed to survive. And within another day of the praying for the former Sheik, the Muslim leader who captured him had a brain hemorrhage, and in the chaos, the Christian scholar was able to simply walk away from his captors.

THIS CHAPTER IS DIFFERENT

Reinhard Bonnke gave us the phrase: "*plundering hell to populate heaven.*" That is a good phrase to describe a core biblical value that resides in Kingdom Movements. Satan may tolerate Christian activities that don't produce multiple disciples, but hell will rise when it is seriously challenged by transformational disciple making. To participate in Kingdom Movements is to commit to a lifetime of bold, lion-like, Kingdom courage tempered with the demeanor of a sheep. Just like our King!

This chapter is different from all the others in this book. It is a reminder that reproductive disciple making never happens without courageous leadership in the face of all kinds of personal sacrifices. Every leader, every Kingdom catalyst without exception, has his or her own "sheep in the midst of wolves" seasons. This is because of the resistance of the world's systems to this disruptive movement, which threatens the reign of hell by bringing God's will, His glory, and His Kingdom from heaven to earth.

Over the last years of research for this book, we have collected interviews from twenty-eight senior leaders of movements from both the Global South and Global North. They have catalyzed hundreds of Kingdom movements around the world. We interviewed another 120 Global South Disciple Making Movement trainers, coaches, and mentors, as well as disciple makers and church planters. In almost every interview at some point it became obvious that what God had done in their lives had not happened without their courage being tested. They did not usually lead with that, but whenever we asked what courageous Kingdom leadership meant in their lives, the answers revolved around spiritual warfare, disapproval or rejection from

Christians, sometime heavy persecution, serious health issues, and family challenges.

But not one person we interviewed ever indicated that they would have done anything differently if given the chance. Instead, there was usually an expression of amazement and wonder and a sense that they felt privileged to have participated in Kingdom movements. The cost of participation was almost always made to seem irrelevant or taken as a sign that they were on the right track.

Every leader, every Kingdom catalyst without exception, has his or her own "sheep in the midst of wolves" seasons.

You could categorize almost all of the interviews as containing a sober sense of joy in having seen God at work through their lives. For them, the challenges were well worth the privilege of seeing with their own eyes Jesus' words writ large, "For I tell you that many prophets and kings wanted to see what you see but did not see it, and to hear what you hear but did not hear it." (Luke 10:23 NIV)

Later in this chapter, we will hear one contributor to this book reflect on the pain of watching eleven of his disciples in four different countries die in the same calendar year.

Another had a similar experience with the first six disciples he made—an experience that almost broke him, but that God redeemed for His glory.

These are not theological reflections! Nor is this just bad news endured. Great power and purpose are released when God's people are resolute in His service.

SECTION 1

KINGDOM ADVANCES CREATE OPPOSITION AND PERSECUTION

Our friend Hassan has a saying that he repeats often. Depending on the circumstances, it goes approximately like this, "When God's people make disciples and advance His Kingdom, the old devil is not happy. But he is not supposed to be happy! If we are doing the King's business, the devil will fight us. If we are doing the King's business we are going to be in a battle. So we pray— we have to pray and persevere to overcome!" We will always be in a fight, but when prayer is our weapon, we win.

When people who catalyze Kingdom movements gather for meetings, they often cover the waterfront of personality types, but they all epitomize courageous Kingdom leadership. James Nyman, in his book regarding cascading movements among Muslims, defines this characteristic as "Stubborn Perseverance."

JESUS PARTING WORDS WHEN THE TWELVE WERE SENT OUT

Have you ever noticed that when Jesus gave instructions to the Twelve as He commissioned them to go and replicate His own ministry, his parting words were longer than his commissioning?

Matthew was actually present when Jesus commissioned the Apostles to go on mission to advance the Kingdom. His account begins in Matthew 9:35 and ends at Matthew 10:39. That is 43 total verses. His account includes something not covered by other Gospel writer: Jesus' relatively long postscript.

The first nineteen verses (Mt. 9:35–10:15) relate to the instructions that Jesus gave to the Twelve about how to engage lostness. Those themes represent the core of this book's content to this point.

The next twenty-four verses (Mt. 10:16–39) relate to:

- Courage in the face of persecution, hardships, rejections, and even death.

- Innocence and humility (like a harmless sheep) to overcome these challenges.

- Preparation for certain opposition and persecution because even family members will seek to kill them, society will shun them, and what happens to Jesus will happen to them.

THE APOSTLE PAUL

This would also be Saul's lot in life. In his dramatic account of Saul's conversion, Luke recounts the stark words that Jesus spoke to Ananias about what would characterize the life of Saul, soon to be Paul:

> Go! This man is **my chosen instrument to carry my name before the Gentiles and their kings and before the people of Israel. I will show him how much he must suffer for my name.** (Acts 9:15, 16 NIV)

Then God sent him with some companions on missionary journeys to the Gentile world—the most unlikely place imaginable for a former Pharisee. And in the course of a little more than thirty years, Saul, the persecutor, became the Apostle Paul, the most important person in the first century's Kingdom Movements, which within a few decades spread across the trade routes of the Roman Empire.

In the economy of the Kingdom of God, every single Christ Follower has a life assignment that will give his or her life great meaning and purpose. It will require our very best efforts against seemingly impossible tasks. It will require dependence on God every day for resources, and the wisdom to do what He asks. The promise to Kingdom people is that their inadequacies will be mitigated by the unlimited power of the Holy Spirit and the promise of Jesus to be with us always. And there will be sacrifices—it is the nature of being a faithful servant of a King.

Paul is an ideal servant of the Kingdom of God. He traveled either by boat or by walking the Roman roads. God sent him to centers of trade and travel—major outposts of the Roman Empire. It is estimated that he may have walked as much as ten thousand miles and visited more than forty-five different places on his journeys.

His life was thus characterized by unflagging energy, but also hardships, sufferings, and persecution. He lists some of what he suffered:

> I am more: in labors more abundant, in stripes above measure, in prisons more frequently, in deaths often. From the Jews five times I received forty stripes minus one. Three times I was beaten with rods; once I was stoned; three times I was shipwrecked; a night and a day I have been in the deep; in journeys often, in perils of waters, in perils of robbers, in perils of my own countrymen, in perils of the Gentiles, in perils in the city, in perils in the wilderness, in perils in the sea, in perils among false brethren; in weariness and toil, in sleeplessness often, in hunger and thirst, in fastings often, in cold and nakedness— (2 Cor. 11:23b–27 NKJV)

In the midst of his suffering, sacrifice, and persecution, Paul maintained a remarkably positive attitude, which is attributed to his faith in Christ. He did not resent the persecution and difficulties but instead embraced them as coming with the territory as a Christian and an apostle. During one of his imprisonments, he wrote, "I now rejoice in my sufferings for you, and fill up in my flesh what is lacking in the afflictions of Christ, for the sake of His body, which is the church (Col. 1:24). NKJV

And after being chased out of several cities because of his preaching and being stoned and left for dead, he went back to some of the churches he had founded earlier and simply commented: "We must through many tribulations enter the kingdom of God." (Acts 14:22b NKJV), an extreme understatement in light of what he had just been through.

On top of all of that, after an absence from Jerusalem for several years, upon his return he was nearly beaten to death then arrested. After a dangerous transfer to Caesarea, he spent two years in prison awaiting trial. He appealed to Caesar, and on his way to Rome he was shipwrecked again. After finally arriving in Rome, he was put under house arrest for two more years. Christian tradition says Paul was beheaded in Rome.

CHANGED INTO THE IMAGE OF GOD

Growing in conformity to Christ will attract some people to the Gospel, but it will also attract persecution.

Jesus warned about this in the Upper Room Discourse:

"If the world hates you, keep in mind that it hated me first. If you belonged to the world, it would love you as its own. As it is, you do not belong to the world, but I have chosen you out of the world. That is why the world hates you. Remember what I told you: 'A servant is not greater than his master.' If they persecuted me, they will persecute you also. If they obeyed my teaching, they will obey yours also. They will treat you this way because of my name, for they do not know the One who sent me . . . .

"They will put you out of the synagogue; in fact, the time is coming when anyone who kills you will think they are offering a service to God. They will do such things because they have not known the Father or me. I have told you this, so that when their time comes you will remember that I warned you. (John 15:18–21, 16:2–4)

Paul tells us simply that, "everyone who wants to live a godly life in Christ Jesus will be persecuted." (2 Tim. 3:12)

Notice the "everyone."

Christians in the Global North, particularly in America, have had it remarkably easy due to the cultural influence of Christianity and the social acceptability—even desirability— of church membership for so many decades. As a result, many Christians have confused American cultural norms and political ideas with the Gospel.

Now that the culture is actively rejecting biblical norms and values, Christians are scrambling to understand why, and how to respond. Some push to adopt the ideas and values of the culture as a way of avoiding the judgment of the cultural elites and their followers, compromising millennia of biblical teaching in the process.

In other words, there is intense pressure to conform to the world rather than being transformed by the renewal of our minds (Rom. 12:2) to avoid the judgment of those who Jesus says do not know the Father or him.

Peter speaks about a similar situation, where there was social though not yet governmental persecution of believers:

Therefore, since Christ suffered in his body, arm yourselves also with the same attitude, because whoever suffers in the body is done with sin. As a result, they do not live the rest of their earthly lives for evil human desires, but rather for the will of God. For you have spent enough time in the past doing what pagans choose to do—living in debauchery, lust, drunkenness, orgies, carousing and detestable idolatry. They are surprised that you do not join them in their reckless, wild living, and they heap abuse on you . . . .

Dear friends, do not be surprised at the fiery ordeal that has come on you to test you, as though something strange were happening to you. But rejoice inasmuch as you participate in the sufferings of Christ, so that you may be overjoyed when his glory is revealed. If you are insulted because of the name of Christ, you are blessed, for the Spirit of glory and of God rests on you. If you suffer, it should not be as a murderer or thief or any other kind of criminal, or even as a meddler. However, if you suffer as a Christian, do not be ashamed, but praise God that you bear that name. For it is time for judgment to begin with God's household; and if it begins with us, what will the outcome be for those who do not obey the gospel of God? And, "If it is hard for the righteous to be saved, what will become of the ungodly and the sinner?"

So then, those who suffer according to God's will should commit themselves to their faithful Creator and continue to do good. (2 Peter 4:1–4, 12–19)[1]

Experience shows that the opposition to Disciple Making Movements often comes not only from the outside but from Christians who do not understand it or who reject its premises. DMM practitioners have been ostracized from their denominations, have lost friends, have been vilified and slandered, all from within the Christian community.

---

[1]   While it is true that people in the Global North are not [yet] being martyred, calling what is increasingly experienced there "persecution" is not an exaggeration. In Matt. 5:10-11, Jesus classifies insults and slander as persecution.

As Christians grow in their discipleship, opposition from both inside and outside the church is inevitable, and we need to be ready for it. Once again, the Global South provides us with examples and models of preparation.

SECTION 2

COURAGEOUS LEADERSHIP TO BE A "SHEEP AMONG WOLVES"

Spiritual warfare is real. Satan is not creative, but he is persistent and dogged to preserve his hellish work. The last Beatitude in the Sermon on the Mount is: "Blessed are those who are persecuted because of righteousness, for theirs is the kingdom of heaven. Blessed are you when people insult you, persecute you and falsely say all kinds of evil against you because of me. Rejoice and be glad, because great is your reward in heaven . . ." (Mt.5:10–12)

This was even true of Jesus Himself. Isaiah 52:13–53:13 prophetically describe Jesus as the Suffering Servant. These words show that He was much more than a religious leader asking his followers to expect persecution; rather, He joined them in suffering for righteousness' sake Himself.

COURAGEOUS KINGDOM LEADERSHIP REQUIRED

When Jesus Prayed "Thy Will Be Done"

When we pray, "Your will be done," what we are really saying is "Your will, not mine, be done."

And sometimes this can be very uncomfortable.

Jesus Himself faced this situation. In Gethsemane, knowing what was about to come, Jesus wrestled with God in prayer over whether there might be another way to accomplish God's purposes beside Jesus' torture and death: "Father, if it is Your will, take this cup away from Me; nevertheless not My will, but Yours, be done" (Luke 22:42).

When Jesus prayed for God's will to be done, it was in opposition to His own desires. For Jesus, it meant His own sacrifice, suffering, and death.

When we pray "Your will be done on earth as it is in Heaven," do we expect a more favorable outcome in line with our desires and will than the answer that Jesus got?

The rest of the New Testament warns us repeatedly of coming persecution. For example, the catalogue of the heroes of the faith in Hebrews 11 ends with people who were persecuted. As we have seen, Paul tells us that, "everyone who wants to live a godly life in Christ Jesus will be persecuted" (2 Tim. 3:12). But Paul also encourages us in the midst of our suffering, "Therefore we do not lose heart. Even though our outward man is perishing, yet the inward man is being renewed day by day. For our light affliction, which is but for a moment, is working for us a far more exceeding and eternal weight of glory" (2 Cor. 4:16–17 NKJV).

And Paul knew from his own experience how true this was in terms of physical, mental, emotional, and spiritual trials. "We are hard pressed on every side, but not crushed; perplexed, but not in despair; persecuted, but not abandoned; struck down, but not destroyed." (II Cor. 4:8, 9)

Persecution and the Early Church

Paul's sufferings, he tells us, are a reflection of the hardships that we all must go through to enter the Kingdom of God; on a larger level, though, his sufferings were for the sake of the church. One of the great mysteries of Christianity is the redemptive nature of suffering. Jesus redeemed us through suffering, and

Paul's sufferings served to advance the Gospel. We see the same thing in the early church. Opposition to Christianity started within Judaism, but by the mid-60s, Rome under Nero began extravagant persecutions of Christians. Christians were killed in the arenas, and Nero even rolled some in pitch and lit them on fire to provide light for public gardens at night. While Roman persecution was sporadic, when it came it could be vicious and deadly.

And yet it did not stop the growth of the church.

The martyrs went to their death with a degree of courage and fortitude that could not help but impress the Romans, who saw these characteristics as among the highest marks of virtue.

One of the great mysteries of Christianity is the redemptive nature of suffering.

The fortitude of the martyrs must have raised questions in the Romans' minds. Why did so many, young and old, go to their deaths for refusing to perform a simple civic ritual such as offering a sacrifice to a pagan god? With all of the tortures inflicted on them, where did they find the courage to remain firm in their faith? And perhaps more to the point, the Romans undoubtedly asked themselves if there was anything for which they would be willing to go through such abuse. There could be little doubt that the Christians had something the pagans lacked, and it began to attract more and more people to Christ's cause.

Tertullian (c. 155–240 A.D.) in his Apology was right: "the blood of the martyrs is the seed of the church."

In fact, right now we are in a new Age of Martyrs, with more Christians being killed for their faith than in any other period in history. Martyrdoms are occurring in the parts of the Global South where Disciple Making Movements are occurring, and people are making tremendous sacrifices and facing much suffering for the sake of the Gospel.

SECTION 3

NORMALIZING PERSECUTION ENDURED AS GOD'S SEVERE MERCY

Nik Ripkin has written a powerful book, *The Insanity of God*, which chronicles his family's experiences in Somalia where his disciples were martyred, and his journey around the world to interview people who experienced extreme persecution. One of the most compelling parts of the book is taken from interviews in Russia and Ukraine with Christians who suffered horrible persecution but experienced great strength in the process. After hearing their stories, he was astounded and urged them to write them down so that people would know about them. They did not understand why Nik was so insistent about this. Finally, he got an explanation:

> [O]ne of the older pastors stood and motioned for me to follow him. He led me over to a large window in the front room of the home. As we stood together in front of the window, the old gentleman speaking passable, but heavily accented, English said to me: "I understand that you have some sons, Nik. Is that true?"
>
> I told him that it was true. He nodded and then asked me, "Tell me, Nik. How many times have you awakened your sons before dawn and brought them to a window like this one, one that faces east, and said to them, 'Boys, watch

carefully. This morning you're going to see the sun coming up in the east?

"Well," I chuckled, "I've never done that. My boys would think I was crazy. The sun always comes up in the east. It happens every morning!"

The old man nodded and smiled. I didn't understand his point. "Nik, that's why we haven't made books and movies out of these stories that you have been hearing. For us, persecution is like the sun coming up in the east. It happens all the time. It's the way things are. There is nothing unusual or unexpected about it. Persecution for our faith has always been—and probably always will be—a normal part of life."[2]

MICHAEL HOPE ON TRANSFORMATIONAL PERSECUTION

You met Michael Hope (pseudonym) in chapter eight. Michael has spent twenty-five years as a leader in multiplying movements, some in very hard places. Incredibly, in one six-month period Michael could only watch as eleven of the leaders he mentored were martyred in five different countries.

He has been maligned because of his work in these movements. His family has endured many health issues, but he has managed to find ways to keep up an amazing pace, still training and coaching many movement catalysts. In our interview with Michael he shared some remarkable insights on persecution and suffering.

God has a purpose for persecution and suffering, and Satan has a purpose for it.

Satan's only purpose is to silence us! So, if we respond in fear and are silenced, we are helping Satan achieve his purposes.

---

2 Nik Ripken, *The Insanity of God* (Nashville: B&H Publishing Group, 2013), 161.

And even if we are just responding to the possibility of persecution, we are achieving Satan's purposes in that.

On the other hand, God has many purposes for persecution—a lot of purposes!

- Paul, James and Peter give lists of Godly character traits that are shaped in persecution.

- There is all that it does for our faith, for increasing our dependence on God, for refining, purifying, and proving faith.

- It also equips us for service, like Paul affirms that when we suffer, it equips us to minister to others who are suffering. (I Corinthians 1:3–7)

- It glorifies God. Peter talks about that in I Peter 4: 12–19.

When I'm doing trainings, I'll talk for a couple of hours about all the benefits that God intends through and by persecution and suffering. We do disciples a great disservice if we don't make very clear that suffering is normal and expected, and that there are many great results that can come from it.

Really, it's not just people that are catalyzing movements who need to be prepared for that. Anybody who's serious about living for God needs to be ready for whatever is thrown at them. They can really benefit from it. They can grow through it rather than becoming discouraged, embittered, confused, fearful, hopeless or depressed.

But the challenge is that it never lets up. I think that's why Paul says:

"Let us not become weary in doing good, for at the proper time we will reap a harvest if we do not give up." (Gal. 6:9)

The older I get, the more I appreciate perseverance or endurance. When I was young I assumed it's just doing the same thing again and again. But there is an added dimension of repeating the same things to continue being filled by the

Spirit, walking in His Power, day after day, because otherwise, you won't last.

Prior to his experience of seeing so many disciples die, Michael was extremely concerned about a team he had coached because he had lost all contact with them. At the time, he was at a new location with a new phone number. One day the phone rang and it was one of the leaders of the group calling to tell him that things were going well and that they were all safe. "How did you get this number?" Michael asked. The leader replied, "I don't know. God just told me to call this number."

In that experience, Michael sensed God speaking to him about suffering and sacrifice.

"Don't worry, they are mine! I've got this. You didn't call them, I called them.

If I want them to suffer, they will. If I want them to succeed, they will. You're wrong to be worrying about them."

That was very early in his ministry. God used that experience to prepare him for the many mentees who would later die, be tortured, have their children taken from them, be imprisoned, and so on. He was grateful for that experience, because if he had assumed the weight of all of those people, if the responsibility for them was on him, it would be a weight he could never bear.

That is a Kingdom mentality, and it shapes everything that happens to you, whether it's something the Lord shows you in His Word, something you hear in prayer, or something you experience in your church life. The point isn't to say, "Oh no! I'm suffering!" It's to respond, "Okay, what is God teaching me through this? Now, I need to make sure that I live that out, and that I'm sharing those lessons with others."

Breathe in; breathe out. Breathe in; breathe out.

Hear from God. Do it and share it. Hear from God. Do it and share it.

The whole mindset, the direction . . . the *whole point* is living in constant obedience and submission. God knows best. He is working through all of it for His glory and our good.

STEVE SMITH ON NORMALIZING PERSECTION

Steve Smith talked about "normalizing persecution" and shared insight into a phenomenon few Global North people get to see.

> There is a brilliant way for believers in a movement to deal with this issue of joy in the midst of persecution. There are some movements today where disciples come back each week in their churches, where they set aside time for accountability and encouragement. One of the questions they ask is basically, "did you get "oww-ees" following Jesus?" As they responded affirmatively ("Yeah, I got ridiculed," or "I got thrown out"), they began high-fiving each other and praising their Master. In this way they are internalizing God's promises and are normalizing persecution.
>
> They are consciously living out what the Beatitudes say:
>
>> "Blessed are you when people insult you, persecute you, and falsely say all kinds of evil against you because of me. Rejoice and be glad, because great is your reward in heaven, for in the same way they persecuted the prophets who were before you. Rejoice when men say all kinds of evil against you, for great is your reward in heaven." (Mt. 5:11,12)
>
> Though they don't prefer persecution, they give thanks to their King: "Thank you God, you give us strength to be faithful to you, and you increase our reward. We will continue to obey your will!"

One of the first things that we do in disciple making is to help people to understand the true value of Jesus as King, so that they know what they are getting. Early in the process of becoming a disciple, people discover who God is, and what His calling on us is about.

For some years we had three questions that we asked people to confess at the occasion of their baptisms. One day we were doing leadership training in one of the movements that was growing rapidly and were talking about the three questions I recommended asking people at their baptisms. An old man raised his hand and asked us to add a fourth question to our list. He said: "I want to ask this fourth question. When they come into your house, drag you away, throw you in prison, and threaten to kill you, will you still follow Jesus?"

And I began to weep! Because that's when I realized that these people truly understood Jesus' parable of the treasure in the field, and they were joyfully at baptism dying! That question confirms that you have died to Christ at your baptism, and it breaks the back of the paralysis that comes from fear of persecution. We have found that it is the *fear* of persecution that paralyzes, not persecution itself.

And time and time again, counting the cost on every continent, the same refrain will come from brothers and sisters. Though the thought of persecution gives them pause, once they go through it, and discover that God is with them and that they can get through this, then persecution is normalized. Nobody likes it, but in the process Jesus is with them, and they continue to press on.

One brother was thrown into prison, and he was being pressed to reveal where other Christians gathered. This particular day the policeman took this electric baton and hit him over the bare back and it shocked him. But the baton broke in half, and the brother who had been shocked said, "Wow, I think God is with me!" That made the policeman furious and he reared back and hit him in the face as hard as he could with his arm. But the blow did more damage to the policeman and he could not move his arm. And the brother who had just gotten hit in the face repeated: "Wow, God's with me!"

When these men and women share these testimonies with each other, it emboldens everyone else.

SIX BRAVE MARTYRS AND YOU

For thousands of DMM practitioners around the world, David Watson is the person that first introduced them to Church Planting Movements/Disciple Making Movements. The path the Lord invited David and Jan Watson to travel would eventually change the course of many hundreds of ministries and the destinies of millions of people. David's pioneering work did not happen without some pain and sacrifice for David, for his family, and for some of his closest colleagues.

The story started when David and Jan accepted their pastor's invitation for people to give their lives to serve the unreached peoples of the world.

Interestingly, David's family was about as unreached as the people he committed to engage. Jan had very strong personal goals to which she felt emotionally drawn, but she was willing to set those aside for a larger calling. That decision would be tested for a few extremely stressful decades.

In 1988 they arrived in Malaysia, where they would have some success planting churches among Muslims. The upshot of that success was David eventually being jailed and his family put under house arrest, until they were eventually deported.

Undaunted and ready for the next challenge, David asked his mission board to send his family of four to a place where no one else wanted to go. That request landed the Watson's in Northern India in the midst of the very birthplace of Hinduism.

David would often be gone for long periods, sometimes with limited communication, and Jan began to worry not only for David, but for her sons who intuitively knew that their father was often in challenging situations and that there was much spiritual warfare. In fact, he was once shot with an arrow at point blank range, but suffered no wound.

The family had to pay a price for David's commitment to DMM, however. Jan explains what it involved:

> Because of the nature of having to live remotely, it was painful for me to not be able to see the everyday joys of the things that went on. That's one of the things that I missed getting to share.
>
> But it was still a shared vision. I recall even sitting in church and feeling sad because David was not there beside me, and the tears would come. I recall very clearly God speaking to me, that this was my gift to him; that every tear, for David's being absent, was a gift to the Kingdom, for the Kingdom to be built. So that was what I believed, that is where I felt like my investment was valuable.
>
> The other sacrifice that came out of this, because we were doing something unusual, we became ostracized in many senses. We were ostracized from the religious community we grew up in. David was called a heretic, everything in the book, I think. It came in the form of comments like, "Yeah, you may call yourself one of us, but you're not!" "You may talk about being a Christian, but you aren't really!"
>
> A few years later the mission that they served terminated David. Ironically it was the same year that 10,000 churches had been birthed in the movement among Hindus. We just never dreamed that the people we loved, the people we had gone to school with, the ones we went to church with, would turn and say: "you're no longer welcome because of the way you are doing things." That was hard, but the joy God has given me is the chance to speak into the lives of

others and be on the receiving end of their encouragement. And I have never found us give up anything in the service of the Kingdom that God did not give back to us multiple times."

An uncomfortable truth comes out of this story: There is always a price to pay to advance the Kingdom, and sometimes that price is severe. Without the faithful sacrifice of six Hindu church planters, David would never have begun searching for answers; David's breakthrough to a new level of ministry led to a shocking amount of opposition from within the Christian world as well as external persecution; it also caused tremendous pain to his family. Yet God uses the suffering and martyrdom of His people to build His Kingdom—the great mystery of redemptive suffering seen most perfectly in Jesus' death.

Not long after these events, some of the other people interviewed for this book (e.g., Steve Smith and Michael Hope) were discovering the same things from God's Word. It was 1993 and suddenly things that were put in motion changed the global Christian enterprise.

We end with a final word from Jan:

When I meet people who have been touched by David's ministry, when I hear the kind comments that are made, when I hear him tell the stories, I feel like I have just been blessed beyond measure to just be part of it and see what a great God we have. He is far bigger than we ever imagined, and he has a plan that is far greater than we could ever imagine.

I used to pray regularly that He would come soon, but my heart continues to pray, "Not yet!" There are so many who do not know Him, I'm almost saying: "Please, not quite yet . . . in your time, but there are still so many."

THINKING AND ACTING LIKE JESUS DID

UNLEASHED! KINGDOM PARADIGMS THAT CAN MULTIPLY

I believe the traditionally conceived forms of ministry cannot move us beyond the current impasse because they have led to the structures that currently exist—and they continue to sustain them . . . . We cannot solve the problems of the church by using the same kind of thinking we used when we created those problems in the first place. We must thoroughly reconceive how we understand and practice ministry and leadership if we wish to truly be a movement.

—Alan Hirsch, *Serving a Movement*

UNDERSTANDING "PARADIGM PARALYSIS"

Jesus' descriptions of the Kingdom of God include images of abundance and fruitfulness, such as catches of fish that break nets and soils, seeds, and plants that bear fruitful harvests. Jesus spoke of yeast's power to be a medium of transformation and expansion. And He told his disciples that bringing a harvest from every people group into His Kingdom would be their Kingdom responsibility. He warned his disciples to never to bury the resources that they had been given, but multiply them according to their capacities.

When we look at the church in the Book of Acts, we see rapid expansion through families and social networks, extending into new, unevangelized areas—exactly the kind of expansion that we see in the Global South today. To recover that kind of growth, the church in the Global North will need to change its entire approach to ministry and even its vision of what the church is about.

In 1963, philosopher Thomas Kuhn proposed a theory to explain scientific advances in his book *The Structure of Scientific Revolutions*. His ideas may be helpful to us in understanding the necessary adjustments facing the church in the Global North. Kuhn argues that science operates on the basis of large-scale paradigms or models, rather than on a gradual, step-by-step increase in knowledge. Scientists develop a way of thinking which becomes the widely accepted paradigm. Over time, however, anomalies are discovered that do not easily fit that paradigm. When enough anomalies accumulate, a new paradigm emerges which accounts for both anomalies and the things that the old paradigm could explain. This paradigm shift leads to a new way of approaching science and paves the way for further discoveries.

Kuhn then points out that, when a paradigm shift occurs, the new paradigm may use such radically different standards of measurement and assessment that people schooled in the old paradigm cannot understand or evaluate it; they cannot break free of their old way of thinking. This leads to "paradigm paralysis," an inability or unwillingness to change from the old paradigm to the new—even when the new one solves obvious problems in the old. The old and new models are what Kuhn describes as *incommensurable*, or so different that they cannot even be compared to one another, like apples and oranges.

This analysis of scientific paradigms can be applied to the church, as well. The Reformation's rediscovery of justification by faith and the priesthood of all believers was a paradigm shift, as was the nineteenth century's renewed focus on bringing the Gospel to all nations. And the twentieth-century's understanding of "nations" as people groups, similarly, was a paradigm shift, one that led to the growth of movements.

The existing paradigm for the church, for missions, and for evangelism in the Global North has held up for quite a while and has had some great successes, but serious problems are beginning to accumulate. The slow decline of American and European cultures into humanistic worldviews, the inability to make obedient and replicating disciples, business-driven models of community and leadership—all these factors combine to make the task of completing the Great Commission unattainable.

We in the Global North church are at a point where we need to redefine our paradigms of ministry. This challenge to the church (and to any human structure) was famously summarized by Arthur Jones a few years ago: "All organizations are perfectly designed to get the results they get."[1]

Ironically, the way forward is to go back to the original model for growing the Kingdom as taught by Jesus. As we have seen, the Global North church has drifted away from this over a period of centuries. It is time to return to the way of disciple making laid out by Jesus Himself.

---

[1] This phrase appears to be the source phrase that has been adapted to phrases like: " Every system is perfectly designed to get the results it gets."

There are certainly some places in North America and Europe where you can find remarkable movement momentum, but with a handful of exceptions they generally tend to be more embryonic. On the other hand, movements are abundant in scores of countries in Africa, Asia, and to a lesser degree, Latin America. And every month, multiple new engagements with a movement DNA are launching somewhere.

These movements in the Global South were birthed in prayer thirty years ago, and now they are rapidly replicating and spreading. To get to this point, they had to build a model of ministry that was entirely different from ministries in the Global North to which they had often been connected. The early Disciple Making Movement pioneers did the most sensible thing they could: they turned to the New Testament and built their ministry model directly from the Lord's teachings.

There are certainly some places in North America and Europe where you can find remarkable movement momentum . . .

Not surprisingly, some of these ideas seem controversial; paradigm paralysis applies to the church just as much as it does to science, and in many ways the paradigms of the Global North and Disciple Making Movements are *incommensurable*. The two models look at the Gospel in different ways, have different visions for the church, and measure success differently. DMM does not make sense in the context of standard Global North models of the church, missions, and evangelism; it looks out of control, dangerous, or just wrong.

It is our contention, though, that from the perspective of biblical faithfulness and spiritual fruitfulness, the Disciple Making Movement ministry paradigm is more consistent with Jesus' instructions for His people, more aligned with the earliest church, and more empowering of ordinary people to change their world than the models of ministry that are currently in place in the Global North. If the Global North is going to join the Global South in advancing the Kingdom to unreached peoples in our midst, the church in the North must undergo a paradigm shift in how we re-engage Jesus' mandate for His church.

Some of the crucial elements of this paradigm shift are suggested in the following chart[2] of twelve mission-critical elements of Kingdom movements analyzed in terms of **the biblical assumptions** underlying the ministry model, **the paradigms that flow from those assumptions**, and **the outcomes expected from applying those paradigms**.

The chart is not exhaustive, but it provides a grid to begin to make comparisons between the ministry models with which you may be familiar, and Movement paradigms. Given the diversity of Christian traditions and practices, it is impossible to cover everything in a brief chart. We have offered suggestions for the traditional ministry column that may or may not fit your context to provide you with a starting point to think about your own ministry model. Please take your time with this: We all

---

[2] The table was created by the authors in part using material from David and Paul Watson, Critical Elements in Disciple Making Movements (see "Critical Elements" in contagiousdisciplemaking.com) and their book Contagious Disciple Making; Jerry Trousdale's "Seven Paradigm Shifts" chapter in Miraculous Movements; and Harry Brown, Strategic Shifts Coming in the Missionary Enterprise. All of these are referenced on the kingdomunleashed.org website. See also Ted Esler, "Coming to Terms: Two Church Planting Paradigms," International Journal of Frontier Missiology 30:2 (Summer, 2013).

have blind spots, and the trouble with blind spots is we usually can't see them without help.

The chart below is designed to help us focus on the relationship of our: 1st Assumptions and Values: our biblical/spiritual assumptions and Values.

2nd Ministry Paradigms: the applications or processes that we utilize to advance our values.

3rd Actual Outcomes: the empirical results that flow from the combination of the 1st and 2nd elements.

We encourage you to examine carefully not just your theology, but the hidden assumptions that are revealed in your practices to determine the principles that really underlie your ministry. You may find that they are not what you think they are.

12 MISSION-CRITICAL ELEMENTS OF KINGDOM MOVEMENTS	
1: THE KINGDOM AND THE CHURCH	
Traditional Ministry Assumptions	**Kingdom Movement Assumptions**
In some traditions, the Kingdom of God is primarily a future, eschatological event.	The Kingdom of God is the present and observable manifestation of Jesus' reign on earth.
The object of evangelism is to make converts who, over time, become faithful disciples.	The object of evangelism is to advance the Kingdom of God by making disciple-makers who establish churches.
In many traditions, discipleship is primarily defined in knowledge-based terms.	Disciple making from start to finish is a God-empowered journey into loving God and submitting to His Lordship.
Biblically sound leaders are responsible for facilitating most of the church's ministry.	Biblically-based leaders are responsible for equipping every Christian to do the work of ministry for which God has gifted them.

Traditional Ministry Paradigms	Kingdom Movement Paradigms
Goals are set by leaders and generally are in terms of what is possible.	God reveals His goals through fasting and prayer. Many, or most, may seem impossible when discerned.
People generally become a Christian by exposure to biblical teaching and lifestyles in a home, or exposure to professional pastors and leaders at a church.	God raises up ordinary people to become disciples of Christ primarily in relational contexts with a lifestyle of consistent obedience to God's Word as the key objective.
Church members invite unbelievers to church services or special events with a hope that their friends will feel welcome and become Christians.	Unbelievers are invited to a Discovery Group in which they will be discipled by discovering God's story in their natural social network, discerning His will for them, and choosing to obey His commands.
Grow the church centrally and incrementally through programs, winsome facilities, and a welcoming spirit.	Grow the overall community by strategic multiplication: making disciples who make disciples and planting churches that plant other churches as a normal progression of the Spirit filled life.
Random approach to identifying persons interested in the Gospel.	The first step in outreach is intense prayer focused on identifying persons of peace God has prepared and the network of lost people they will represent.
Church planting is strategic, programmatic, and often expensive.	Churches grow out of disciple making and reproduce naturally. Ordinary people typically launch new groups/churches.
Church planting is typically one-by-one.	Church planting is a natural progression of God's revelation of His nature and His power in a community of lostness, so everything is simple, replicable and scalable.
Churches celebrate milestones of growth, and decisions for Christ.	Churches celebrate spiritual and social transformations, which power multiplication in places of former spiritual poverty.

1: THE KINGDOM AND THE CHURCH (continued)	
Expected Outcomes	**Expected Outcomes**
Adding new members to our church. Maximize the natural appeal to the demographic profile of the local church.	The result of disciple making is multiplying disciples. The priority is planting new Discovery Groups that become churches among the social segments or places where the Gospel has never gone or thrived.
Make new believers who will join the church and invite their friends to do the same.	The fruit of disciple making is spiritual and social transformation happening in families and social networks.

2: ABUNDANT PRAYER	
Traditional Ministry Assumptions	**Kingdom Movement Assumptions**
Most traditions believe that God can and does perform miracles, but expectations tend to set limits on how we pray and what we anticipate is possible.	Prayer is both petition and proclamation which declares that Jesus' authority is more powerful than the gates of Hell. Prayer, by definition, is inviting the supernatural to earth.
Prayer styles and liturgies often represent the culture of the denomination and the traditions that are to be preserved. In many traditions, miraculous interventions that facilitate spiritual transformation and rapid replication are not expected.	Rapid reproduction based on prayer and discovering and obeying the Bible is common but does not typically replicate any single organization's traditions. Local churches are free to identify as the Holy Spirit leads them.

Traditional Ministry Paradigms	**Kingdom Movement Paradigms**
It is risky to pray for something that can only happen if God obviously intervenes.	Prayer for things that only God can do is the norm. There are no Kingdom movements today without abundant signs and wonders.

Strategic planning meetings and prayer meetings are separate events.	Prayer informs strategy, and strategy shapes prayer.
Corporate prayer is liturgical and general in character; specific requests are more common in small groups.	DMM practitioners model abundant prayer for specific, "impossible" Kingdom outcomes.
Calls for corporate fasting and prayer are rare.	Days of corporate prayer and fasting are common, often weekly, ending with celebrations of Kingdom advances, healings, and deliverances.
Churches may have prayer teams to pray for others.	All Christ Followers are involved in prayer. People who feel called to intercession are recognized, trained, and called upon for special seasons requiring much prayer.
For many churches, dedicated prayer meetings may be sporadic or attended by just a few people. Some churches may invite fasting and prayer for very important concerns.	Many DMM churches and organizations have high energy weekly days of fasting and prayer as a foundation of an annual calendar filled with abundant corporate, family, and personal prayer. Houses of prayer are common. Some DMM organizations can call upon hundreds to tens of thousands of dedicated intercessors who are always on standby for emergency prayer.
Expected Outcomes	**Expected Outcomes**
Ministry outcomes are created by great knowledge, great leadership, great funding, and great execution of programs.	Ministry outcomes are primarily created by abundant prayer that results in mobilizing Christians to fulfill all of the functions of the church.
Churches are unlikely to take risks that require divine intervention lest it discourage people if it does not happen.	There is a direct relationship between taking risks in prayer, and the process of growing in faith and experiencing the fullness of God's Spirit.

3. SCRIPTURE

Traditional Ministry Assumptions	Kingdom Movement Assumptions
Theologians and teachers interpret the Bible for the average Christian.	Teachers are an important part of the church, but biblical truth is better internalized when discovered personally and obeyed than when it is simply taught.
Lost people cannot understand the Bible because they do not have the Holy Spirit.	The Holy Spirit and the Word of God are enough to draw the lost to God, especially when they are systematically discovering God's Word, seeking to obey it, and sharing it with other lost people.

Traditional Ministry Paradigms	Kingdom Movement Paradigms
People learn the Bible best by teaching and preaching.	Teaching and preaching are important ways to communicate truth, but many DMM pastors now utilize quick Discovery Groups in the middle of sermons for greater impact and accountability.
Personal Bible study is encouraged among people who are already Christians.	Christians and non-Christians alike internalize the Bible best by a process of discovery and immediate accountability to obey and share what they learn.
Focus is orthodox teaching from Scripture.	In the presence of God's Spirit, Biblical truths, when discovered and obeyed, transform lives. Orthodoxy is maintained through group accountability to the Bible, along with training and coaching.
Christian leaders are literate and most have advanced secular and religious education.	In DMM movements today, God is raising up vast numbers of non-literate Christian leaders in oral cultures, utilizing oral recordings of Scripture, memorization, and appropriate coaching and mentoring by more mature leaders. This is an important shift that has transformed leadership training and created a new pool of sometimes brilliant leaders.

Expected Outcomes	Expected Outcomes
Maintaining denominational orthodoxy.	Proper disciple making leads to doctrinal orthodoxy coupled with lives and communities transformed through obedience.
Good growth from drawing people to a spiritual environment where they can encounter God.	The attractional power of changed lives and the presence of the Holy Spirit leads to rapid growth.
Knowledge-based approach to the Bible and traditional understanding of Scripture creates converts/believers.	Obeying self-discovered biblical truth is not legalistic: it is a direct, personal response to the Word rather than conformity to externally imposed standards. Jesus' promise is that it will be self-validating, transformational, and bear much fruit (John 15). An obedience-based relationship with the Bible creates disciples/followers.

4. DEPENDENCE ON THE HOLY SPIRIT

Traditional Ministry Assumptions	Kingdom Movement Assumptions
The Holy Spirit's primary work is internal to the individual believer, though some spiritual gifts may be acknowledged in the church.	The fruit of the Holy Spirit reproduces the character of Jesus among His disciples. The gifts of the Holy Spirit reproduce Jesus' authority and ministry among His disciples today.

Traditional Ministry Paradigms	Kingdom Movement Paradigms
Since miracles are rare, attractional programs are the primary ways that churches gain access to new communities.	In the presence of compassion for the lost, much prayer for the harvest, and the Word of God self-discovered and obeyed, the Holy Spirit releases abundant spiritual giftings in ordinary people, along with abundant signs and wonders.

4. DEPENDENCE ON THE HOLY SPIRIT (continued)

Expected Outcomes	Expected Outcomes
Bold prayers are affirmed as a good thing, but in many traditions rarely put to the test in a public gathering. Prayer is not commonly connected in public with engaging lostness, making disciples, and raising new generations of ordinary people to be great leaders.	Through the work of the Holy Spirit and the Word, we will see unprecedented harvests of disciples. Perhaps the most remarkable manifestation of the Holy Spirit in movements is the millions of ordinary people that God is empowering to be great leaders. Most will never draw a salary from a movement, however never-ending training, coaching, and mentoring of them is almost always the single largest expense for most movements.
Making converts to Jesus is the goal. For some traditions the "Sinner's Prayer" is the gateway to conversion, with the expectation that discipleship will follow. Discipleship is a value, but often attempted through classes without mentoring and coaching.	Making disciples of Jesus is the goal. Often whole families or communities will walk together a path of collective progress: repentance of sins, public confession of Jesus' Lordship, water baptism, a lifestyle of discovering and obeying all that Jesus taught, and progressive Holy Spirit transformations into Jesus' character and His ministry. Again the most expensive element of DMM is the never ending training of vast numbers of leaders who train, coach, and mentor.

5. MAKING DISCIPLES

Traditional Ministry Assumptions	Kingdom Movement Assumptions
Discipleship is knowledge-based.	Disciples discover God in His Word and choose to obey Him out of deep love of Christ.
People come to Jesus as individuals, not as part of larger social networks.	Disciples are intertwined within families and networks and are typically not extracted unless they are in danger. Even then, with prayer, God sometimes redeems the situation for the family to become disciples.

Traditional	Kingdom Movement
The Gospel is typically presented by one outsider to many strangers.	The Gospel flows relationally from one family member to friends, family, and networks. Everyone is expected to present the process of becoming a Follower of Christ.
Gospel presentations are driven by a range of informational and preaching models by an expert to a group of seekers.	Discovery of God's Word is achieved by interactive group processes with a group accountability for sharing what they learn (and experience) with lost people.
High control: Outsiders orchestrating things themselves.	Disciple making by a cultural insider results in high trust. Leaders allow others to be catalysts rather than trying to control the movement.
Goal: good church members.	Goal: transformation and fruitfulness.
Traditional Ministry Paradigms	**Kingdom Movement Paradigms**
Outsiders use personal evangelism or crusade evangelism leading to individual decisions.	Evangelism is a process whereby an unbeliever discovers God and shifts allegiance to Christ in the context of Discovery Groups that become self-replicating churches.
Convert, then disciple.	Disciple to conversion.
Churches make disciples through preaching, education, and training.	Disciples are made in spiritual relationships through Discovery Groups, mentoring, coaching, and making other disciples.
Expected Outcomes	**Expected Outcomes**
Orthodoxy and Christian character.	Obedience, transformation, and fruitfulness.
Start the way you want to finish. Bring people to church to convert them, then disciple them in church as well.	Start the way you want to finish. If seekers see themselves as disciple makers and church planters, they naturally replicate what was done with them.

6. DEPENDENCE ON GOD'S PHYSICAL RESOURCES

Traditional Ministry Assumptions	Kingdom Movement Assumptions
Do not outplan your budget.	Jesus' encouragement to first century disciple makers to depend on Him for needed resources in the harvest is still valid. DMM budgets that support movements of hundreds of new churches each year almost always suggest that God's winning strategies require many Christians to sacrifice something precious, but they are not primarily dependent on human resources.

Traditional Ministry Paradigms	Kingdom Movement Paradigms
Church planting and expansion are expensive and require careful planning, project management, and sufficient financial resources either committed or in hand.	Local disciple making and church planting projects are typically very inexpensive. Foreign, cross-cultural engagements cost more. But depending on the availability of veteran, indigenous DMM practitioners, it is typically much less expensive than traditional Western missionary models.
While some cooperation with other churches and ministries may be beneficial, leaders should not risk losing people to other ministries.	Developing strategic partnerships and sharing resources among Global North sending agencies as well as Global South CPM/DMM ministries and churches can be a very powerful force multiplier. Sharing strategic resources and people with other DMM ministries and churches tends to create more Kingdom outcomes for both organizations.

Expected Outcomes	Expected Outcomes
Available resources are predictable based on pledges and cash in hand.	Resources will become available as needed to accomplish God's purposes, leading to breakthrough engagements, holistic impact, spiritual transformation, and rapid replication.

Churches and ministries rely on fund raising and stewardship campaigns for financial provision.	DMM practitioners rely on God's supernatural provision through prayer, sacrificial giving, and divine intervention.
Costs per baptism in traditional ministries are very high, as are costs for traditional church plants.	In DMM organizations financial costs per baptism and churches planted are often shockingly low. Part of that is the result of catalytic partnerships, but it is primarily the result of organic momentum that can only be understood in spiritual terms.

7. DEPENDENCE ON GOD'S PERSONS OF PEACE FOR ACCESS INTO A COMMUNITY

Traditional Ministry Assumptions	Kingdom Movement Assumptions
Building bridges into new communities is a lengthy and difficult process.	Jesus' person of peace principle bypasses the need for traditional and lengthy cross-cultural strategies.

Traditional Ministry Paradigms	Kingdom Movement Paradigms
The Gospel comes to unreached peoples through cultural outsiders, typically over many years.	The Gospel comes to unreached peoples through a cultural insider, the person of peace whom God has pre-positioned as a bridge into the community or culture. If one is not found, disengage and move on.
The strategy must generate a large number of converts to find the few who will be disciple makers and leaders themselves.	Indigenous leaders keep ministry replicable, and therefore scalable, frequently traveling to new regions, finding new persons of peace, and starting new churches, or starting new movements in proximate people groups or social segments.

Expected Outcomes	Expected Outcomes
It takes many years for an outsider to successfully engage an unreached community.	Persons of peace may be found as early as the first week of engagement, quickly launching the disciple making process. Successful movements will find and engage hundreds and sometimes thousands of people of peace.

7. DEPENDENCE ON GOD'S PERSONS OF PEACE FOR ACCESS INTO A COMMUNITY (continued)

Mature movements will look like the parent church or organization.	DMM will result in disciples that replicate naturally in every village, community, or urban social segment. Over time, the Bible and prayer will guide their contextualization of the Word of God where they live.

8. EVANGELISM

Traditional Ministry Assumptions	Kingdom Movement Assumptions
Make knowledge-based converts one at a time.	In some cultures, baptism is grounds for being disowned by families or killed by authorities. DMM encourages giving time for whole families to respond. When making disciples (obedience-based) in a group context, baptism is a natural and often a family or group response to Jesus' commandment to be baptized in His name.
Develop programs to draw non-believers into church to start the conversion process.	The Gospel moves on the wings of relationships. Ordinary people can easily gather within social networks to discover God together.
Focusing on the Gospel of Salvation produces believers.	Focusing on the Gospel of the Kingdom produces true Christ Followers.
Wait until sent.	Disciple makers share what they know as they learn it.
Traditional Ministry Paradigms	**Kingdom Movement Paradigms**
Members are encouraged to share their faith and invite friends to church outreaches, including attractional events and services; ministries may rely on mass media as well.	Members of a Discovery Group commit in each group meeting to share what they have just learned about God with a specifically named, lost person whom they know. They will share how it went the next meeting and repeat the process.

Expected Outcomes	Expected Outcomes
People come to faith at church.	People come to faith in the context of their Discovery Group and natural social relationships.
Growth through conversion is slow.	Movements see rapid growth through networks of new churches emerging out of Discovery Groups.
Although personal evangelism is encouraged, it rarely happens.	Evangelism is decentralized, inexpensive, and happens rapidly.
Growth sometimes happens more from reshuffling people who are already believers between churches than from conversions, although some of those happen as well.	Growth is natural. Early on it may appear to be rapid because of addition, plus some multiplication. But more momentum happens in a few years as new leaders mature and become effective.
Having a large church with many programs and ministries encourages growth.	Having many generations of Discovery Groups/simple churches creates rapid growth.

9. HOLISTIC KINGDOM MINISTRY

Traditional Ministry Assumptions	Kingdom Movement Assumptions
Focus on evangelism OR compassion is common. Some churches or ministries attempt both, but few are great at both.	Holistic focus on both evangelism AND compassion is normal.
Church members are encouraged to be involved in approved church ministries.	Every local church and Christ Follower is responsible to serve both of Jesus' Kingdom mandates: (1) compassionate service and prayers for God's healing, and (2) being a transformed disciple and discipling others.

9. HOLISTIC KINGDOM MINISTRY (continued)

Traditional Ministry Paradigms	Kingdom Movement Paradigms
A relatively small percentage of compassion ministries consistently leverage the good will they create to make disciples and plant churches. A relatively small percentage of proclamation ministries lead with healing or compassion ministries.	Evangelism, disciple making, healing, and compassion are so deeply intertwined that they cannot be separated.
Expected Outcomes	**Expected Outcomes**
Compassion ministries will help alleviate some problems in the community. Proclamation ministries will result in some people coming to Christ.	Holistic transformation of individuals and communities is the natural result of disciple making.

10. COURAGE, SPIRITUAL WARFARE, AND PERSECUTION

Traditional Ministry Assumptions	Kingdom Movement Assumptions
For most Global North Christians, sacrifice for Christ is primarily related to time and money.	Serious sacrifices for the sake of the Kingdom are normal for all Christ Followers.
Spiritual warfare is real but rare and intangible.	Spiritual warfare is real and is a normal part of the Christian life.
If your approach to your faith isn't obnoxious, then it will not raise much opposition.	Jesus warned his disciples that bearers of the Gospel of the Kingdom will experience challenges, persecution, and even rejection from family members.

Traditional Ministry Paradigms	Kingdom Movement Paradigms
All Christ Followers are expected to grow in their faith, and some are called into Kingdom ministry.	All Christ Followers are called into Kingdom ministry, which by definition advances Jesus' reign into Satan's strongholds. They can pray with authority for people oppressed by Satan and for those who are simply ignorant of a different path for their lives.
Dealing with opposition is not discussed. Dealing with felt needs is more important.	In Disciple Making Movements in dangerous places, a common pre-baptismal commitment is a promise that in the face of death, they will never renounce Jesus as their Lord. In some places disciples prepare what they will say when they face death for Jesus' sake.
Expected Outcomes	**Expected Outcomes**
If we are good neighbors, we will not face opposition.	If we seek to live a godly life, we will be persecuted.
Most Christians will never encounter the demonic and so will not be involved in spiritual warfare.	Every Christian will need to use prayer as a weapon for spiritual warfare at multiple times in their lives.

11. A COMMUNITY OF DISCIPLES

Traditional Ministry Assumptions	Kingdom Movement Assumptions
Some tasks in the church require ordination.	Every Christian is a priest empowered to make disciples, proclaim the Gospel, baptize people into Christ, and minister communion.
Believers should be participants and stakeholders in the church.	Disciples are participants and stakeholders in the Kingdom of God.

11. A COMMUNITY OF DISCIPLES (continued)

Traditional Ministry Paradigms	Kingdom MovementParadigms
The church is a community of believers where the Gospel is preached, orthodoxy maintained, and baptism and the Lord's Supper are celebrated.	The church is a community of Christ Followers that worships God, discovers and obeys God's Word, experiences the biblical "one anothers," and whose members form new groups of obedient disciples that grow into new churches.
Ministry is typically branded, often by denomination, sometimes even by its non-denominational distinctions.	Disciple Making Movements may have an organization structure and name, but still tend to exhibit an unbranded mentality relative to partnering and serving with other churches and ministries.

Expected Outcomes	Expected Outcomes
Churches maintain denominational orthodoxy, grow in membership, and shape the worldview of the worshipping community.	DMM has an orthodoxy of Kingdom values, worldview, and best practices. Churches consistently strive to represent the glory of God's character, equip each member for ministry, and advance the reign of Jesus where it has not yet gone.

12. SPIRITUAL AUTHORITY/LEADERSHIP

Traditional Ministry Assumptions	Kingdom Movement Assumptions
Leadership is a function of calling and training.	Leadership is a function of gifting, faithfulness and fruitfulness. People become leaders by leading and replicating faithful disciple makers.
The offices of apostle, prophet, evangelist, pastor, and teacher are not all operative anymore, and those that are operative are the leaders of the church.	The offices of apostle, prophet, evangelist, pastor, and teacher all continue to operate in the church, at least in part to "equip the saints for the work of ministry."

Traditional Ministry Paradigms	Kingdom Movement Paradigms
If apostles still exist, they are cross-cultural missionaries often raised up in the church by short term mission trips.	Romans 1:4 defines the apostolic calling: "Through him and for his name's sake, we received grace and apostleship to call people from among all the Gentiles to the obedience that comes from faith." Apostles serve both the lost and the saved, the churched and the unchurched. It is not a title, but a life calling.
If prophets still exist, they illuminate God's Word on important themes and bring it to bear on current cultural events or circumstances.	Prophets tell the lost and the saved what will happen if they obey the Word of God in all circumstances, and what will happen if they disobey. The Bible is their authority, and the Holy Spirit is their power.
Evangelists are people gifted in sharing the Gospel or in creating programs to evangelize the community. Not all churches have evangelists.	Evangelists bring a community to obedience through engaging a segment of lost people, finding persons of peace, and coaching them in the Discovery Bible processes.
Pastors and Teachers are the only office(s) in Eph. 4 in place in all churches. They instruct in Bible and doctrine, preach, baptize, and celebrate the Lord's Supper.	Pastors and Teachers shepherd, coach and mentor other leaders, shape Discover Groups curricula, and engage in leadership training, coaching, and mentoring.
Clergy leads, laity follows.	Leaders equip; every member does the ministry.
A few people actually do the work.	All disciples share the work of ministry.
Traditional Ministry Paradigms	**Kingdom Movement Paradigms**
Church leaders emerge through personal calling, natural gifting, and proper education.	Leadership is a function of fruitfulness, making transformed disciples of Christ who replicate the process.
Recognized leaders are those who have formal ordination.	Leaders are those who model the character of Christ, make disciples, and create new leaders, and are considered by the body as leaders.

12. SPIRITUAL AUTHORITY/LEADERSHIP (continued)	
Leaders, especially pastors, receive formalized training via seminary or Bible college.	Leaders are trained initially through coaching and mentoring. As they rise in responsibility, many leaders will need to pursue more formalized higher education.
Pastors may or may not have made disciples.	Pastors typically have a track record of making generations of faithful disciple makers.
Nurturing and growing the local church is a core value for leaders.	Making disciples outside the church and equipping believers to do the same is a core value for leaders.
Expected Outcomes	**Expected Outcomes**
Churches are well organized, highly educated, and grow by incremental addition of converts.	Disciples make disciples who replicate the process through Discovery Groups in their social networks. Discovery Groups transition into churches. Churches repeat the process of making disciples and planting churches.
Ordinary Christians can fulfill services that do not require ordination.	Every Christian is empowered to make disciples, proclaim the Gospel, baptize people into Christ, and minister Communion.

Which model is more faithful to Scripture: the slow and steady growth of the church of the Global North or the explosive, accelerating growth of the church of the Global South? Consider Luke's account of the first decades of the world Christian enterprise:

- It began with prayer and patience on the part of the disciples (Acts 1:14). Then the Spirit came upon them at Pentecost, and from there the church began to grow. After the initial 3,000 at Pentecost, Luke tells us that people were added to the church daily (Acts 2:47), that many believed (Acts 4:4), and that the pace grew ("increasingly added," "multitudes of men and women," Acts 5:14).

- From there, the language changes to multiplication (Acts 6:1, 7; 9:31): a great many priests (Acts 6:7), Hellenists (Acts 11:21), and Gentiles (Acts 14:31) believed, and the Word spread (Acts 6:7, 13:49) and that churches (not disciples!) increased in number daily (Acts 16:5).

- This process of accelerating growth continued until entire regions reached the point of saturation (Acts 13:49; 19:8–10, cf. the witness of the pagan silversmiths, Acts 19:26–27).

We might write off this account as a "one-off" event unique to the Apostolic Age, yet we see precisely the same kind of trajectory occurring in Kingdom movements in the Global South today. These passages were given for our instruction.

Shouldn't we see in them what is possible for the church even in the Global North?

Shouldn't we let it stir our passion and lead us to recognize the limitations of current ministry models?

Shouldn't we let it challenge the distorted worldviews, truncated vision, and broken paradigms that keep us from seeing the Kingdom of God triumph over the Gates of Hell in the Global North today?

CHAPTER 18

FIRST STEPS

Earlier in the book, David Broodryk spoke about the pain that he experienced on leaving the pastorate of 200 people because he felt a burden for his city of twelve million people. But a decade later, he's had the privilege of seeing the people he coaches and mentors bring 100,000 people into the Kingdom in more than 15 countries. He ended his interview by explaining what he has learned about the Kingdom of God in this journey.

I went into ministry with a deep desire to see the kingdom come. I went through Bible college and seminary and eventually ended up in pastoral ministry. I got caught up in "doing church" the way that everyone else does church, all the American Western ways. It didn't take long before I was thoroughly disillusioned with the disconnection between that and the reason why I got into ministry in the first place.

I'm putting it in drastic terms, but to me, what I was doing was building a business, and I candidly said to God, "I can do the same things in the business world and make more money. If this isn't about the kingdom, then let me go and do business, because this does not seem to be a good investment."

For me, Jesus' words *your kingdom come* meant to actually see God at work through people. The kingdom of God is not a matter of talk but of power. And it is not a future kingdom, it's not a kingdom that is only spiritual, divorced from current reality. It is the kingdom that really comes and is at hand. We can rephrase that statement as "God is close, and He's closer than you think!" He's actually right here.

In Luke 10, Jesus' words were "heal the sick" and then say the kingdom is here; the kingdom of heaven has come to you. Which was always very profound to me, because He did not say "talk about the kingdom and heal people." They weren't even making a statement about the kingdom. They were healing the sick, and then they were saying: "Do you see what God has just done? This is the kingdom of heaven and it has come to you!" So you almost can't fulfill what Jesus says there without first healing the sick.

And what Jesus is saying to Nicodemus is essentially, "This requires a reboot." I think we've missed it when we make it only about salvation, and we make it about saying a simplistic little prayer of salvation.

SOME THINGS TO KNOW AND DO

A few chapters ago we introduced Dannemiller's version of the change formula, C=(D x V x FS) >R, which can be paraphrased:

Change happens when Dissatisfaction with the Status Quo (D), multiplied by a Vision of What is Possible (V), multiplied by First Specific Steps to Take (FS), must exceed the Resistance to Change (R).

As we noted earlier, Jesus ended his charge to Twelve Apostles and the seventy-two unnamed disciples with a warning that disciple making required **Courageous Kingdom Leadership.** We have seen that throughout this book. In all Kingdom Movements, courage in the face of opposition from both inside and outside the church is essential.

This book obviously makes a case for **Dissatisfaction** with the current condition of the church in the Global North, which has largely lost its Kingdom vision and discarded the supernatural worldview that Jesus promised would empower His people for His purposes. The resulting decline begs for the church to experience something like the radical "reboot" that David Broodryk finds in Jesus' words to Nicodemus, and to fulfill once again its role to make disciples, transform communities, and bring the Kingdom's shalom to the chaos that defines the Global North.

Connecting with these movements just might be the key to a God-sized vision in which you can gladly invest your life.

From the first chapter this book has sought to create among Global North readers a holy jealousy for a **Vision of What is Possible,** drawn from the life experiences of many highly successful Kingdom catalysts from both the Global North and Global South. There are hundreds of great movement successes to celebrate in the Global South and a few dozen in the Global North. Connecting with these movements just might be the key to a God-sized vision in which you can gladly invest your life.

That brings us to the last of the three elements required for change—**First Steps**. In the past, there was little concrete information on this for people living in the Global North because there were relatively few movements that were accessible or feasible to observe, and a limited number of veteran practitioners available to coach and mentor in the Global North. Today that is changing.

Disciple Making Movements are going to be more and more important for leaders of existing churches or ministries, and also for any Christian who is sensing a calling to partner with God and others in catalyzing Disciple Making Movements. Assuming you don't yet have a coach/mentor, we close this book with some very important action items that will point you in the right direction

FIRST STEPS

Prayer, Prayer, and More Prayer

Expect that your personal times of prayer and fasting, whether alone or with others, will be your most productive.

Develop weekly disciplines of consistent prayer and fasting. In most movements, you see a high percentage of Christ Followers praying with intent. But they did not all start this way, so as you begin to pray, you will need to develop a strategy for also mobilizing other people for prayer. As you commit yourself to fasting and prayer, invite others to join you. As they grow as intercessors, encourage them to invite others or to start their own groups and replicate the process. Over time, plan to multiply intercession in sync with new disciples and churches.

Pray for Clarity for God's Calling for You

What should you pray about? Ask for clarity for God's specific ministry calling for you, for Kingdom-minded partners in the harvest, for first steps, for the social segments to which God seems to be calling you, for needed resources, for people of peace, for opportunities to pray with people for Kingdom healing and deliverance, for God's spiritual protection, and for next steps.

Make a list of lost people you know and begin to pray for them. Prayer walk the community asking God to bless the people and reveal multiple persons of peace.

Experience the Impossible—Visit a Thriving Movement—And Start New When You Come Home. The best way to begin to understand the nature of Kingdom movements is to spend time among mature Kingdom Movements and the leaders and intercessors who are catalyzing and experiencing them. Most people have a hard time grasping the nature of movements without seeing them and meeting the people whom God is using.

Before you come back home, ask their intercessors to partner in praying for your efforts to use people in a church to catalyze a movement among lost people.

In Indonesia, Kingdom Movements have a "forty-eight-hour rule" that says that if you do not obey what you learn in a Discovery Group within forty-eight hours, you will forget the point of obedience or the commitment to share. So when you get back, take action and hit the ground running with some first steps. Movements depend on the power of the Holy Spirit, but the Spirit only seems to work when we do. Roll up your sleeves and get going!

The "big idea" of DMM is about lost people becoming faithful disciples and reproducing the process among other lost people. But many Global North Christians, when they hear about Kingdom Movements, tend to default to traditional goals of "making saved people better." The attempt to make what already is in motion into a movement may bear some fruit, but it is usually harder than launching something fresh with a strong movement DNA.

Start Doing Discovery Bible Studies Right Now. You can use Discovery Bible Studies in your own devotions, but you will need to put your focus on obeying Scripture yourself. Only as you personally mature as a disciple (learning to observe all that Jesus has commanded) will you be able to make disciple-makers.

Regardless of your education or life experiences, you can't coach or mentor what you have not experienced. As Discovery Groups mature and are mentored, they transition seamlessly into churches that can replicate the process.

Use the template of a Discovery Group in chapter fifteen as your model. When you start you may not realize why each element is important, but they are. If you are consistent, you will see the results soon enough.

Find a Mentor, and Commit to Become a Mentor to People Who Will Repeat the Process.
As soon as you can, find a Kingdom Movement Mentor who has actually catalyzed multiplying disciples who have replicated the process. If you have to connect with them virtually then do that. Everyone needs someone who is at least a couple of steps beyond themselves. So when you begin to see some Kingdom momentum, then invest time in the leaders that are emerging.

Movements require a new leader at every link of growth in the chain. You must invest more heavily in coaching and mentoring than in teaching if you want the leaders you are working with to do the same with the leaders they raise up. Be more focused on developing skills and capacities that produce obedient disciple-makers than on transferring knowledge.

Today there are a wide range of DMM resources on-line covering dozens of categories and regions of the world. See the Appendix for a list of DMM resources. The book website, www.kingdomunleashed.org, contains a more extensive resource guide.

- **Launch the Way You Want to Finish.** Disciple makers are sometimes tempted to take "temporary" shortcuts and start with a methodology or practice that is not sustainable or replicable. For example, it is tempting to start by funding everything oneself, or making all the decisions, or letting Discovery Groups bring in commentaries and new books. Shortcuts set up a system that may work, but only for a short time before it inevitably fails.

- **Developing Partners in the Harvest.** Ask your church to bless your vision of ministry and pray for you. Do not limit yourself to your own church, however. Envision and equip other leaders and ministries.

  Many large DMM Movements have launched with one or two small churches and ministries working together for a common goal. As movements grow, sometime more partners are needed for things like Scriptures resources, urban access, etc.

  One warning: Do not compromise any Kingdom values for the sake of partnering with another organization. Bless them, but avoid the challenges that conflicting visions will bring.

- **Access Ministry.** Pray for God to show you how ordinary things that you can do may provide access into the homes of persons of peace. Praying for someone's need may be your easiest access. If you provide a service, then also let people know that you would like to pray for needs in their lives or families.

- **Find People of Peace Who Are Ready for a Discovery Bible Group.** If you know an experienced DMM catalyst, ask them to coach you through a person of peace search so you can learn how they find people of peace. Develop a list of potential people of peace and pray over it. When you find a person of peace, offer to help him or her launch a Discovery Bible Group with his or her family or friends. After one DBS you become an Outside DBS Coach and Mentor while the person of peace remains the Inside DBS facilitator.

  Note: if you look for only one person of peace you may miss ten. If we are spiritually conspicuous and are looking for every person of peace, we may find many.

- **Be Intentional, and Focus Praises on the Lord!** Highly successful leaders of movements are typically very intentional people, but are not self-promoters. They are sought out by others because of the fruitfulness seen in their lives. They tend to lean into biblical theology, but have little interest in creedal distinctions that don't advance the Kingdom of God or empower ordinary people to bear much fruit in Jesus' name.

  If they are outsiders to a movement's culture, they are essentially mentors and coaches of the key leaders. That is why you will hear stories of a movement catalyst observing training events where there are thousands of new churches represented, but only a handful will ever know about the catalyst's role in launching the movement.

◗ **Take Risks to Nurture a Supernatural Worldview.** Look for a coach who can help you to step into a spiritual world many have never experienced. Most of us don't just ease into a comfort zone of praying for the sick without some encouragement, modeling, or coaching. The main thing is to be willing to pray for people with needs and be faithful in doing what Jesus invited us to do in His name. Most people learn to pray effectively for the sick, which starts out by being vulnerable enough to ask God how to pray for people and follow the trail of His nudgings. You can go from praying a general prayer with someone to asking him or her questions that the Lord might prompt. You then go back to listening to the Lord and again follow His leading until He tells you the prayer session is complete. Sometimes you might pray Scriptures over people. Simply let God lead you. As you get comfortable with that, it becomes a non-threatening experience for you and the person for whom you are praying. Expect to be challenged and stretched, but never forget that all transformational movements bear God's fingerprints.

◗ **Expect Opposition.** This can come from within a traditional Christian organization, a government, or hostile religious entities. Spiritual forces will strongly oppose your work. It will come from places you did not imagine. The hurt may be tremendously painful, and it will be easier to give up than to go on. Once you have set your hand to the plow you must not turn back. Satan does not want to see God's Kingdom advance in righteousness, peace, and joy in the Holy Spirit, and he will fight you every step of the way. He may allow you to win small battles, but he will work hard to make you lose the war. Regardless, we have the victory through Christ, though like Him, we may end up wounded.

- **Expect Discovery Groups among Lost People to Become Embryonic Churches that will Grow where the Holy Spirit Leads.** A recent New Generation research analysis of 4,381 churches planted in one region of Africa (among many unreached peoples) over the last six years showed that on average, when 1.7 Discovery Bible Groups were launched in the region, one church was eventually birthed. If those sorts of outcomes can be replicated in the Global North, then church leaders may decide that Discovery Bible Groups launched outside the church among unchurched segments of society are a higher value proposition than just another inside-the-church group—but only if they are more concerned about building the Kingdom than building "their" church or brand.

- **Discovery Bible Groups in an Existing Church Can Also Be a Powerful Tool.** As a footnote to the previous discussion about the "Big Idea" of Movements not being primarily for serving saved people, it is also true that in many movements, churches use Discovery Groups for spiritual formation for all of their segmented groups (women's groups, youth, and even children's ministries, etc.). But the celebration comes in taking the Discovery process outside the walls of the church to lost people.

- **Don't Be Surprised If God Does More Than You Envisioned, but Never Touch His Glory.** Understand that God's calling for any of us is very often one that we would have never chosen. Trust the discernment that comes from fasting and prayer. Pay attention to your heart when you read the Bible, when God repeatedly arrests your eyes on key Kingdom values in Jesus' teachings. Set your life goals accordingly.

One common experience among people who are participating with God in birthing Kingdom movements is that the challenging goals they first sensed from God turned out (a decade or so later) to be much less than what God actually did. When you ask God for His vision for your life, don't prejudge your boundaries or His boundaries. Our obedience is important, imperfect though we are, and He calls us to be ambassadors of His reign. And eventually we realize that we are being propelled along, not by our power, but by a cascade of God's glory being manifested, establishing His Kingdom where it must be.

With all your heart, resist the urge to take personal credit for what God is doing. The words we use to describe what is happening need to point to God and to His Everlasting Reign advancing where it has to go.

WHAT HAVE WE DISCOVERED?

1. You know that **Disciple Making Movements are real,** and they are possible where you live. Today America, Europe, and Oceania are once again "new frontiers."

2. **The King has a role for you to play in these movements** if you are willing to pay the price. Jesus' Kingdom values and lifestyles, summarized in His instructions on making disciples, are the difference between churches closing every week, and movements advancing the Kingdom today where it has to go.

3. Today, **ordinary Christians, churches, and ministries have a roadmap to see the Kingdom come where they live!** These are not theoretical ideas. The Kingdom is closer than we have imagined. And the experience that Jesus said kings

and prophets longed to experience but missed . . . is near, right here for courageous Kingdom men and women.

"But you are a chosen people, a royal priesthood, a holy nation, God's special possession, that you may declare the praises of him who called you out of darkness into his wonderful light. Once you were not a people, but now you are the people of God; once you had not received mercy, but now you have received mercy." (I Peter 2:9–11)

"Now to him who is able to do immeasurably more than all we ask or imagine, according to his power that is at work within us, to him be glory in the church and in Christ Jesus throughout all generations, for ever and ever! Amen." (Ephesians 3:20, 21)

APPENDIX: KINGDOM MOVEMENT RESOURCES

Visit www.kingdomunleashed.org for a more complete list of available resources on Kingdom Movements, resources from the contributors to this book, links to the websites of DMM ministries and practitioners, and other relevant materials.

Here, we want to leave you with some of our favorite resources that have been helpful to us, whether cited in the text of this book or not. Most of them have been published in the last five or six years, but some of them have been formative in our thinking about the Kingdom of God and the church since seminary years.

Others are new resources for finding great Scripture sets for Discovery Bible Groups, or useful resources to advance your practical applications that we shared in chapter seventeen.

We cite some ministries that have practical daily activities to help you get started making disciples tomorrow and throughout the next weeks. Note that due to security concerns, some ministries prefer to remain anonymous.

FOR FURTHER READING

On the Kingdom

Jones, E. Stanley. *The Unshakable Kingdom and the Unchanging Person*. New York, Abington Press, 1972

Ladd, George Eldon. *The Gospel of the Kingdom: Scriptural Studies in the Kingdom of God*. Grand, Rapids: Eerdmans, 1990.

_____. *The Presence of the Future: The Eschatology of Biblical Realism*. Grand Rapids, Eerdmans, 1996.

McKnight, Scot. *The King Jesus Gospel: The Original Good News Revisited*. Grand Rapids: Zondervan, 2011.

Willard, Dallas. *The Divine Conspiracy: Rediscovering our Hidden Life in God*. New York: HarperOne, 1997.

Wright, N. T. *How God Became King: The Forgotten Story of the Gospels*. New York: HarperOne, 2012.

On Movements

Garrison, David. *A Wind in the House of Islam*. Monument, Colorado: WIGTake Resources, 2014.

Jenkins, Philip. *The New Faces of Christianity: Believing the Bible in the Global South*. Oxford and New York, Oxford University Press, 2008.

_____. *The Next Christendom: The Coming of Global Christianity*. Oxford and New York: Oxford University Press, 2011.

Keller, Timothy, et. al. *Serving a Movement: Doing Balanced, Gospel-Centered Ministry in Your City*. Grand Rapids: Zondervan, 2016.

Robertson, Patrick and Watson, David, with Benoit, Gregory C. *The Father Glorified*. Nashville: Thomas Nelson, 2013.

Trousdale, Jerry. *Miraculous Movements*. Nashville: Thomas Nelson, 2012.

Watson, David and Watson, Paul. *Contagious Disciple Making: Leading Others on a Journey of Discovery*. Nashville: Thomas Nelson, 2014.

On Related Themes

Billheimer, Paul. *Destined for the Throne: How Spiritual Warfare Prepares the Bride of Christ for Her Eternal Destiny*. Minneapolis: Bethany House, 1975, 1996.

Fielding, Charles. *Preach and Heal: A Biblical Model for Missions*. Richmond, The International Mission Board, 2008.

Hayford, Jack W. *Prayer is Invading the Impossible*. Alachua: Bridge-Logos, 1977.

Moran, Roy. *Spent Matches: Igniting the Signal Fire for the Spiritually Dissatisfied*. Nashville: Thomas Nelson, 2015.

Ripken, Nik. *The Insanity of God: The True Story of Faith Resurrected*. Nashville: B&H Publishing Group, 2013.

DMM Video Series

Engage!Africa: Through Disciple Making Movements. Available through Final Command, http://www.finalcommand.com/store/engage-africa-dvd